ST BARTHOLOMEW'S NIGHT

St Bartholomew's Night

THE MASSACRE OF SAINT BARTHOLOMEW

by

PHILIPPE ERLANGER

Translated from the French by
PATRICK O'BRIAN

WEIDENFELD AND NICOLSON
20 NEW BOND STREET LONDON W1

PRINTED AND BOUND IN ENGLAND BY
HAZELL WATSON AND VINEY LTD
AYLESBURY AND SLOUGH

17/6985

CONTENTS

Introduction   xi

PART 1
THE ORIGINS

I	The Cross-roads	3
II	The Pawns on the Chessboard	11
III	The Protestants in 1559	21
IV	Catherine de' Medici, Ruler of France	27
V	The Blaze of Fury	38
VI	The Diplomatic Prologue	46
VII	The Characters	55

PART 2
THE WEB OF CIRCUMSTANCE

I	'We are too old to deceive one another'	69
II	'The rope is being pulled to the breaking-point'	77
III	'You hide yourself from your own mother!'	84
IV	'So long as they keep on their mask . . .'	94
V	'Genlis was to wait'	102
VI	'It is necessary that you should leave my kingdom'	110
VII	'Slaughter all the Frenchmen?'	116
VIII	The 'Blood-Red Wedding'	125

PART 3
THE 'GREAT MADNESS'

I	'See how honest men are treated'	137
II	'Kill them all!'	144
III	'He is a boor!'	156
IV	'Death and blood are running in the streets'	162
V	'If only he were the last of the Huguenots!'	174
VI	'I beg that I may continue to be obeyed'	182

PART 4
THE UNFORESEEN CONSEQUENCES

I	'Madame la Serpente'	197
II	'Some do not think it pretty'	207
III	'The wretched Huguenot party is still in existence'	216
IV	Twenty-five Years On	221
	Epilogue	225
	Appendix A. Paris in 1572	229
	Appendix B. The Massacre of Saint Bartholomew as seen by Contemporaries	238
	Chronological Table	256
	Genealogical Tables	267
	Bibliography	271
	Index	279

LIST OF ILLUSTRATIONS

1 A concert given by Diane de Poitiers. *An enamel from The Louvre*   *opposite page* 18

2 Charles IX. *Painting by François Clouet from the Musée de Chantilly*   19

3 Members of the court of Charles IX. *Bibliothèque Nationale*   50

4 Charles IX on the balcony of the Louvre. *Bibliothèque Nationale*   51

5 Catherine de' Medici. *Mansell Collection*   82

6 The children of Catherine de' Medici: Henri d'Anjou, Marguerite de Valois, François d'Alençon   83

7 Four royal couples: Philip II of Spain and Elisabeth de Valois; Francis II of France and Mary Stuart; Henry, King of Navarre and Marguerite de Valois; Charles IX of France and Elizabeth of Austria. *Miniatures from Catherine de Medici's Book of Hours, Louvre*   114

8 Gaspard de Coligny. *Bibliothèque Nationale*   115

9 The massacre begins. *Bibliothèque Nationale*   162

10 St Bartholomew's Night depicted by Dubois. *Musée Arlaud, Lausanne*   162

11 The murder of Coligny. *Bibliothèque Nationale*   163

12–14 Panoramic view of the massacre. *Bibliothèque Nationale*   226

INTRODUCTION

LOUIS XI, in accomplishing the first of the royal revolutions [1] (a revolution which was to be sealed and confirmed by his daughter Madame la Grande—Anne de Beaujeu) brought the French nation into being and made it conscious of its unity. The towns emerged from the isolation in which they had lived for centuries, behind their walls. Paris recovered the importance that it had lost during the Hundred Years' War and its standing as the capital. From one end of the realm to the other, the classes, and particularly the bourgeoisie, became aware of their community of interest. The fairs multiplied, and they gave rise to an immensely increased commercial interchange.

The guilds, it is true, had turned the masters into something not unlike a hereditary feudal class; but the associations of journeymen, together with the religious brotherhoods, had created an exceedingly important network of mutual help and support among the wage-earners.

In the Sorbonne a workshop already harboured the first of those printing-presses that were to be the liberators of thought and its disseminators.

The Frenchman felt himself less solitary. A hundred years of war and anarchy had persuaded him to place his 'will and his liberties' entirely at the king's discretion; but he was surrounded by a national feeling, a warmth of national feeling, that he had never known before.

Now, with her people rallied once more about their ruler, France was a great country. No other had this degree of centralisation, this military power, this wealth and solidarity: and in no other country had the nobles been reduced to obedience at last. The Treaty of Troyes in 1422 had seemed to be the death-knell of France: but by 1494 she was the dominant power in Christendom. It was then for

[1] The second was that of Richelieu, carried on and increased by Louis XIV. The third, belatedly undertaken by Louis XV in 1771, came to nothing at his death, three years later.

the first time, apart from the Crusades, that France launched her armies abroad and intervened in the life of other nations. The wars in Italy were to cost terribly dear in men and treasure, without any tangible profit: yet they were not the foolish escapade that they are so often said to be. The Spaniards, the Germans and the Turks were all lying in wait for Italy, an easy prey. Her conquest could give the victor supremacy in Europe. An eager, strong, yet very vulnerable France had a right to shut her rivals out of Italy and to install herself as ruler upon the shores of the Mediterranean, still the centre of the western world.

After many successes and defeats, the victory of Marignano in 1515 brought a fleeting triumph for this policy; and Francis I, who at twenty had just assumed the crown, found himself the arbiter of Europe.

But this was no longer the Europe of Louis XI. New powers had arisen: England, recovering from the Wars of the Roses and, like France, rallying to the dynasty—the Tudors, in this case—and above all Spain, freed from Islam and united, the explorer of the seas and the conqueror of unknown worlds.

The young Charles of Austria, already master of Flanders and the Franche-Comté, heir of the Spanish kingdoms, of Naples, of the Habsburg lands, and soon to be a candidate for the Empire, 'in his sole person formed a coalition' that was inevitably directed against France. He was going to try to become Caesar, the idol of the century as Alexander had been that of the Middle Ages; the same hero who was the object of Francis I's ambition—Francis, who was indeed called Caesar by his mother. The victor of Marignano could not prevent the rise of the Habsburgs. But on the other hand he did sign an important treaty with the Pope, the Concordat of Bologna. By this the Papacy gained the withdrawal of Charles VII's Pragmatic Sanction, which, while it allowed the cathedral chapters the right of choosing their own bishops, forbade annates, the papal tax upon churches, and subjected all bulls and conciliar canons to the king's approval.

The king gained still more. The agreement delivered all the bishoprics, all the livings, all the possessions of the Church in the realm up to him, by giving him the right to appoint to them any man he saw fit, subject only to formal approbation by the Pope. Thus the Valois and his successors acquired an exceedingly powerful tool of government, and, thanks to the sale of benefices, an inexhaustible source of supply for their treasury. The scope of the Concordat was by no means limited to this: for just at the moment when an enormous upheaval was to threaten the very foundations of the Roman Church, His Most Christian Majesty found himself closely bound to it, both on the worldly and on the spiritual plane. This was one of the chief reasons that made him oppose the Reformation in his own country; although abroad, in order to counteract Charles V, the Catholic champion, he allied himself with Protestants.

The Concordat was ratified in February, 1517. On 31st October in the same year Luther nailed his theses upon indulgences to the door of the castle church at Wittenberg.

At this moment the Renaissance, in one of Nature's great compensatory movements, had already shattered the old boundaries and altered the framework of life: ideas, principles, morals and customs were changing; the proportions of the universe were no longer the same. All at once man had become aware of his personal destiny, and his horizon was widening as fast as that of the adventurers by sea.

The Catholic Church had had to deal with heresies ever since its first foundation. This time Luther, stirring up a flame that no repression had been able to stifle, set in motion one of the greatest spiritual and political revolutions in history.

Those Frenchmen who were intoxicated by his teaching had no suspicion of the peril that it was about to bring to the unity of their country.

P. E.

PART 1

The Origins

CHAPTER I

THE CROSS-ROADS

MARTIN LUTHER, declared a heretic at Cologne and Louvain and condemned by Pope Leo X, agreed to submit his doctrines to the Faculty of Theology at Paris. The Elector Frederick of Saxony, his protector, wrote to learn the University's opinion of this monk, whose ideas were causing so great a ferment in Europe.[1]

On 2nd May, 1520, Noël Bédier, more usually known as Béda, the syndic of the faculty, read the letter to his colleagues and appointed what we might now call a committee of investigation. In the event, it was he and Jacques Barthélemy who were to be the most active members of it.

Although it was in decline, the University of Paris was then still the highest spiritual authority in Christendom after the Holy See itself. It constituted a real federative republic with its own territory and its own justice; and it possessed immense privileges. In its colleges, of which the Sorbonne was the chief, scholasticism, the method of authority, reigned supreme: the object of study was not things in themselves, but the pronouncements that had been made about them and handed down by the masters.

The university, fiercely independent, ultramontane and conservative, hated innovators. It had condemned Joan of Arc. It had encouraged the six thousand manuscript-writers and illuminators of Paris to charge the printers with sorcery. Without any serious discussion of the nascent Reformation it declared it to be criminal in the highest degree and deserving of the ultimate punishment.

On 15th April, 1521, the Faculty of Theology, having pronounced

---

[1] Some historians, such as Doumergue and Pannier, hold that the Reformation in France was an independent movement, which was capable of developing by its own power and which owed nothing essential to Luther. The Rev. J. Viénot believed this to be mistaken. Our intention is not to take sides in the argument but to show the evolution of the struggle between the innovators and the defenders of the traditional faith.

Luther's theses impious, heretical, schismatic, blasphemous, pernicious and abominable, laid down that their author should be compelled to a public renunciation and that their supporters should be exterminated. The avenging fire should destroy the men and the books that were infected by such monstrous errors. This condemnation was sent to the Elector of Saxony, the Emperor and the King of France.

The parliament,[2] that supreme court of law whose competence included religious matters, shared the university's orthodox rage. From 1521 onwards, a man suspected of Lutheranism in France was in danger of death—and of what a death! But even so formidable a dam as this could no longer contain the thrust of the new ideas.

In spite of the anger of the doctors, the world was changing at a bewildering pace. The old order was giving way. Men had once placed all their hopes in heaven: now they were beginning to look for their happiness here on earth again. The individual found that he could himself be his own end; and the state worked out a moral system very far removed from holy laws. The voyages of a few caravels had destroyed ideas that had been as firmly and as devoutly held as articles of faith. The general increase of wealth and well-being and the discovery of antiquity profoundly modified the social system, altered life's accustomed setting and broadened the perspectives of the mind.

A society which for a great while had been preoccupied with local quarrels suddenly beheld the horizon torn wide open before it; and at the same time it became conscious of curiosities, doubts and wild irrational beliefs. From the south there came the glories of the Renaissance; from the west the treasures of America; from the east the first burning pangs of the Reformation—all the memories, the youth, the restlessness of the whole world itself.

The Bible, suddenly printed, translated, spread abroad and made known, provided a great spur to this restlessness. The France of Francis I was widely anti-clerical. The subversive teachings spread fast, first among the regular clergy and then among the scholars. The parliament and the Sorbonne were already shocked and horrified, in this year of 1521, by 'the pernicious and seditious' books that were sold in their own precincts.

The year 1521: the decisive moment when the unending struggle between Francis I and Charles V began; when a ferocious invasion

---

[2] This refers to the *Parlement de Paris*: there were also *parlements* in many of the provinces. (Translator's note.)

brought misery into the north of France; when the common people cried out against a Church that was indifferent to their sufferings; when the king decided to summon the Gallican Councils, intended to 'reform and do away with many abuses'; and when, at the council of the archdiocese of Sens, held at Paris,[3] there was thus prepared the great trial of modern times between the letter and the spirit, liberty of conscience and the supremacy of tradition.

The young monarch who was responsible for this terrible debate was, according to Cavalli, the Venetian ambassador, 'of excellent good sense and a great deal of knowledge'. He did not limit himself to honouring and protecting writers and artists: he loved them. He despised the stupid, cruel intolerance of the men of the Sorbonne. His mother, Louise of Savoy, and still more his sister Marguerite, 'the Pearl of Pearls', had always favoured the mystics and the philosophers, and delighted in their daring.

For many years this humanistic court counterbalanced Church, university and parliament in their furious repression of any kind of free enquiry. Louis de Berquin, 'the most learned of the nobles', translated certain writings of Erasmus and Luther: he was arrested and his work was burnt. The king set him free by force. He was often obliged to act like a despot in order to protect a thinker from the legal authorities. He had farces played before him in which Luther and the Pope belaboured one another; and his mother wrote, 'In the year 1522, by the grace of the Holy Spirit, my son and I began to have a knowledge of white, black, grey and smoke-coloured hypocrites, hypocrites of every shade; from whom may God, in His infinite mercy and goodness, protect and preserve us.'

Charles V, however, was beginning serious persecutions in the Low Countries, and Louise of Savoy, troubled by this, asked the advice of the Sorbonne: the Sorbonne advised the Inquisition. The time had come for the first French martyr of the Reformation. On 8th August, 1523, the Augustinian friar Jean Vallières, accused of blasphemy, had his tongue cut out in the pig-market by the Butte des Moulins, just outside the city. He was then burnt alive, without being mercifully strangled first.

The reaction was therefore already under way when the disaster of Pavia occurred and with it the captivity of Francis I. Louise of Savoy, now regent of a kingdom unprotected and exposed to invasion, yielded to the pressure of Rome and the parliament. Officials were charged with seeking out Lutherans: the stakes were set up

[3] The diocese of Paris was then under the archbishopric of Sens.

and the faggots blazed. The first to go to the stake were monks and men of the people, such as the hideously-tortured cloth worker Leclerc. Berquin went back to prison.

Francis I returned in time to save him, and also called back those who had fled, most of them to Strasbourg. He was solemnly presented with Zwingli's book, *True or False Religion*.

This proved to be but a brief period of enlightenment. Marguerite, widow of the Duke of Alençon, had now married the King of Navarre and reigned with him at the court of Nérac. Although the court became a place of refuge, it was too far away for Marguerite's influence to continue to be effective. The foreign policy of Francis I drew him nearer to the Holy See. Then a few fanatics broke the head of a statue of the Virgin near the Porte Saint-Antoine, holding it to be an idol, and the city was at once ablaze with fury. The subtle king saw it was essential to canalise this dangerous activity and ordered an expiatory procession. The 'burners' had the upper hand once more, and taking advantage of the absence of the king, seized Berquin again and put him to death. More desecrations and breaking of images were followed by more martyrdoms.

Intolerance bred intolerance. Fanaticism increased in the same measure as the struggle for the liberation of the minds of men.

In the 1530's, policy began to exercise a powerful effect on the development of the struggle. First, foreign policy: Francis I, allied both to the Pope and to the Protestant [4] princes of Germany, put into operation a balancing system intended to satisfy now one, now the other. Then home policy: the German princes, upholders of the Reformation, had made use of it for economic ends and in so doing identified the state with the new religion. In England, Henry VIII was about to proclaim himself the Pope's equal in order to obtain his divorce and to seize the wealth of the Church. In France the situation was entirely different: the king may have shown himself indulgent to the reformers, but he had no intention of changing his religion, nor of losing the great benefits that the Concordat had given him.[5] The line that we now draw between temporal and spiritual matters was at that time unimaginable, and opposition to the Church

---

[4] The word was used after the princes had delivered their protestation at Spires in 1529.

[5] As it has been already observed, the Concordat allowed the king to appoint the bishops and to name the members of Church benefices: this enabled him to control the clergy and the nobility, and at the same time it provided him with an important source of revenue.

must of necessity degenerate into opposition to the government. This, at all events, was what Anne de Montmorency, grand master of the household and, since the death of Louise of Savoy, virtually prime minister, tried to persuade the king, uneasy at the growth of the 'sect' in number, solidarity and intransigence.

However, the idea of sending these particular subjects of his to the stake merely to please the theologians could not but offend the man who had founded the Collège de France. The king knew how urgently the Church needed to be reformed; to persuade the Pope of this and to bring the Lutherans back to the fold would preserve both the unity of France and intellectual freedom: it would also rob Charles V of his Catholic champion's halo. 'At no time', writes Louis Madelin, 'was the traditional French policy of prudent balance so much in agreement with the personal inclinations of the ruler.' But until times should prove more favourable, the see-saw policy had to be pursued: while on the one hand the king commanded the parliament to take energetic measures against the Protestants, on the other he threw the raging Noël Bédier into prison and obliged him to make a public apology before Notre Dame.

In October, 1533, Francis I met Pope Clement VII at Marseilles. There Henry, Duke of Orleans, the king's second son, was married to Catherine de' Medici, both being fourteen years old. There a secret treaty was prepared, which was intended to bring the House of Valois back into Italy, but which in fact resulted in bringing Italy into the House of Valois. And there, to allow him to treat with the Protestants, Francis obtained a statement of approval from the Medicean Pope—an approval far less important in the papal eye than the most trifling territorial readjustment. But, to be prepared for all eventualities, he also obtained two bulls that would permit him to root heresy out of his dominions.

At the court, Guillaume du Bellay and his brother were the supporters of reconciliation; and Guillaume met the wise Melancthon, that 'temperate mind, Christian to the core, who did not merely wait for offers of reconciliation but who demanded them' at Augsburg. The death of the obscure, confused Pope Clement VII and the election of Cardinal Farnese, the advocate of the Counter-Reformation, as Pope Paul III, helped their understanding greatly. Melancthon was to be invited to Paris. Would moderation, mutual comprehension and the true spirit of religion triumph? In that autumn of 1534 there was a chance that the world might escape one of the worst crises in its history: two hundred years of war, of massacre and of proscriptions could perhaps be averted.

Alas, the prospect of this peace which so much horrified Charles V was equally repugnant to the extremists of both sides. Marcourt, the pastor of Neuchâtel, took it upon himself to make agreement impossible.[6] The tool with which he accomplished this was 'a sheet of paper in the form of a small poster (about fifteen inches by ten) . . . the type was close-set, but well arranged; the title in large, easily-read black-letter . . . the sections quite distinct . . . a short prologue and four exactly balanced paragraphs . . . A little sheet to plunge one into a brown study'.[7]

There was indeed a great deal to think about: for this sheet, this *placard*, as it was called, was printed, and in such numbers that the walls of Paris and the chief towns were plastered with it on 8th October, 1534. The king found it on his bedroom door and 'in the cup where he put his handkerchief'. And what this paper contained was enough to make schism inevitable; for in it there was no question of 'more of this, less of that'. It read, 'I call upon heaven and earth in witness of the truth against this proud and vainglorious papistical mass, by which the world is and shall be utterly ruined, destroyed, lost and made desolate . . . By means of this mass they have grasped all, broken all, engulfed all . . . Let them have the truth: truth threatens them, truth pursues them, truth hunts them down.'

There was a tremendous outcry. Sensible people tried to prevent irreparable acts. But in vain. The fanatics were overjoyed and took instant advantage of this godsend: before the king had given any order, the parliament placed two hundred persons under arrest.

Francis, personally affronted, could not contend with public opinion. He publicly condemned the heretics' presumption, but he advised prudent measures. This did not prevent the parliament from setting up six stakes that very evening. And others followed.

'There is no parleying with Antichrist,' instantly cried the French Protestant refugees in Germany, and their leader, the passionate Farel.

Melancthon no longer dared to go to Paris: the Sorbonne refused to read the statement that he had written. The Pope asked that those who had been convicted should be pardoned, but in vain; in vain

---

[6] We are here concerned only with the results of his action, not with deciding whether it was 'the attack of a madman' or the inspiration of one who could not refrain from proclaiming a truth of which he was possessed.

[7] Lucien Febvre, *Au cœur religieux du XVIe siècle*.

he gave a cardinal's hat to the chief of the moderate party, Jean du Bellay; in vain did he announce the summoning of a council, charged at last with the purification of the Church. Vainly, in a final effort, did the king renew his invitation to Melancthon and grant an amnesty 'desiring that the suspects should be disturbed no more and, if they were prisoners, that they should be freed'. The splendid opportunity was lost, and the nation was condemned to fratricidal strife for generations.

The idea of tolerance that some bold minds entertained could not withstand this. The Protestants, gathering in their turn into *churches* —ecclesiae—showed themselves to be as hard, self-willed and foul-mouthed as their opponents. They had no intention of asking for the mere right of worshipping as they thought fit. Was it possible to compromise with truth? Was it conceivable that truth might border upon error? To a truly religious mind of the sixteenth century such a thought was impossible. Naturally this led the innovators to wish to impose their beliefs upon others, a triumph that would not be possible unless they first seized power. The possibility of a revolution undertaken in the name of the Gospels became a real danger.

In 1536 Calvin published the Latin edition of his *Institutes of the Christian Religion*; and this, translated into French in 1541, was to cause a surprising number of men of all conditions to accept his doctrines. In his letter to the king, which was the real preface to the book, the new apostle explained how he had come to undertake the work of a political theorist. From that time onwards the divorce between the Renaissance and the Reformation was complete.

Francis I was no longer able to maintain a liberal attitude. He had always meant that the schism should be done away with by one means or another and that his kingdom should present a united front to the dangers from abroad. Conciliation having failed, he felt himself obliged to resort to force.

At the same time, the French gold that had been employed in Germany to raise enemies against Charles V now helped to bring about a positive explosion of Protestantism that soon reached as far as Denmark and Scandinavia. For the empirical, realistic Valois never thought himself called upon in any way to match his home and his foreign policies.

It was at this time, in 1535 to be exact, that he was confronted with an extremely serious decision. Charles V, having taken Tunis, wished all the Christian rulers, reconciled and under his leadership, to join him in a crusade against the Turk. The Pope exhorted the faithful to take part in this pious undertaking, and begged them to liberate Constantinople and Jerusalem.

France stood at the cross-roads. As at other grave moments in her history, she had to choose between Christendom, that is Europe, and her national interests. Francis I had once loved to play the paladin, and had he reasoned like his former model, he would have been obliged to join the standard of the Emperor and fight against the Turk, even if it had meant the hegemony of the House of Habsburg for centuries. This was the way Montmorency thought, and all those whose minds were still rooted in the Middle Ages.

Francis, on the contrary, was in the forefront of his time, and so that France should not become a vassal of the Habsburgs and of Spain, he determined to maintain the balance in the west—to hinder his rival's progress towards universal monarchy. In his opinion this political necessity was of greater importance than the spiritual aspects.

It was from political considerations that he set his face against the rise of the Reformation. It was from political considerations that he wrecked the imperial crusade. In doing so he established the pattern of behaviour of the modern head of state.

CHAPTER II

THE PAWNS ON THE CHESSBOARD

DURING THE LAST PART of the reign, French policy towards the Emperor frequently altered, but it remained unremittingly opposed to heresy. Yet heresy was gaining ground in all the provinces and in all classes of society. Preachers attacked confession and the invocation of the Virgin and the saints, and asserted that 'the ceremonies and the traditions of the Church were as nothing'. The king, uneasy about the danger of secession implicit in such an upheaval, and later, when his health deteriorated, uneasy about his own salvation, stood out less and less against the excesses of the repression.

The edict of 1st June, 1540, which gave the order 'to join together against the Lutherans' held up the informer as a dutiful subject. And the exceedingly important edict of 1st July, 1542, ordered forbidden books, particularly the *Institutes of the Christian Religion* to be delivered up to the parliament on pain of hanging. The same penalty applied to those who attempted to print anything without the sanction of the Church; and it was forbidden to publish anything without the printer's or bookseller's mark. The censorship of books and the searching of bookshops was carefully organised. The Sorbonne drew up a scrupulous Index and the works of Calvin, Erasmus, Lefebrve of Etaples and of many others were burned. Five officials were sent into the provinces to purge them. They were shockingly successful. Libraries and private houses were searched and the confiscation of books was followed immediately by arrests, trials and savage punishments and on occasion by massacres. In 1545 the parliament of Aix-en-Provence ordered the destruction of thirty villages. It is said that at that time twenty thousand Protestants were put to the sword. In Orleans the councillor Pierre Hotman distinguished himself by his ferocity (he was the father of François Hotman, who was later to put his formidable pen at the service of the Huguenots).

From one end of the kingdom to the other the defenders of the faith broke limbs, tore out tongues and burned bodies. At Meaux in 1546 sixty people who had gathered together to devote themselves to pious exercises were set upon with the utmost barbarity.

'Monsieur,' cried a girl to the officer who was maltreating her, 'if you had found me in a brothel instead of in this honest and godly company, you would not have bound me like this.'

Barefoot and in her shift, she was obliged to watch the burning of fourteen of her companions in the market-place.

As always happens in such cases, the persecution, instead of stifling subversive ideas, caused them to spread and multiply. The Protestants went to their death in a kind of ecstasy: but almost as surprising as their passionate heroism was the relentlessness of their persecutors; though indeed it must be said that there was no public opinion to restrain the ferocity of their judges. Dogma was then so absolute that it allowed not the least compromise, not the slightest variation. The insults of the good Catholics pursued the Protestant martyrs into the very heart of the flames.

A list of all the victims would be interminable: they ranged from Etienne Dolet, who published the *Summary of the Christian Faith*, to the Waldensian inhabitants of Cabrières and Mérindol, who were exterminated in spite of the wishes of the king. On his death-bed he 'charged his son not to delay the punishment of those who, using his name and authority, had committed this outrage . . . otherwise God . . . would avenge it'.

This was the humanistic ruler's final attempt at holding back the murderous fury of the fanatics. On 31st March, 1547, Francis I died, murmuring, 'Lord God, how heavy is this crown which I thought you had granted me as a gift.'

His successor, Henry II, read nothing whatever but tales of chivalry, and his religious faith was of the simplest, most unreflecting kind. Since his birth, this man of twenty-eight, apart from his idolatrous love for Diane de Poitiers, had known none of the pleasant things of life. He had spent four years of his childhood in a cruel Spanish prison.[1] After this he had been completely overshadowed by his brothers;[2] his father thought nothing of him; he

---

[1] As hostage for his father, who had been taken prisoner at Pavia, and who was released a year later.

[2] The Dauphin, François, who died in 1536, and Charles, Duke of Orleans, who died in 1545.

was married to an unattractive wife and then he was continually kept at a distance, treated with wounding indifference and even threatened. His best friend, the Constable de Montmorency, was exiled and disgraced; his mistress was perpetually attacked; rage and ill-will filled his mind.

But these bitter feelings gave way to an unconcealed joy when he found himself master of the most splendid kingdom under the sun. His shy and feeling heart took an instant delight in sharing his power and his happiness with those whom he loved so blindly. The new queen, Catherine de' Medici, counted for nothing. Ever since she had come to France she had been living from day to day, terrified of the future, discreet, retiring, trembling in case she should infuriate even by her willingness to oblige and her anxiety to please. For a long time she had feared that she would be repudiated and sent to a nunnery; and even when a long-delayed fruitfulness freed her from this dread she nevertheless put up with the position of a harem wife, humbly loving her lord and submitting to her successful rival. 'I loved him so much that I was always afraid,' she wrote later, speaking of Henry II. 'She continually visits the duchess [Diane de Poitiers],' noted the Venetian ambassador. 'On her side the duchess does her the greatest services in the king's opinion, and it is often she who persuades him to go and sleep with the queen.'

Nevertheless the 'Florentine banking-woman', small and plump, gentle and cultured, had both an extraordinary majesty and an extraordinary gift for running a court: she was allowed one, and presently this court of hers became outstandingly brilliant. But that was all. The real sovereign, universally recognised, was the forty-eight-year-old favourite, always dressed in black, and adorned with the crown jewels.

Henry promised Montmorency that he would treat him as 'a father and as his chief counsellor'. But the prudent Diane quickly provided this over-powerful minister with a double counterweight in the form of the famous soldier François de Guise and that crafty prelate his brother Charles, Cardinal of Lorraine and, since the age of nine, Archbishop of Rheims. She added to their number a personal friend of the king, Saint-André. 'These five', wrote L'Aubespine, 'were chosen to conduct and to direct the affairs of state . . . This was the field, this was the tilth in which the seed of our revolts and our factions was sown.'

Forty-eight hours after the death of Francis I, the state might have been likened to scales whose beam was a weak king supported by the strength of his mistress's will, and the two pans two ravenous families, kept carefully in balance by the favourite, who played Montmorency's most-favoured position against the formidable standing of the Guises. By the time the king and his Egeria had vanished, they had recreated a feudal system. Montmorency, confirmed as Constable of France and Grand Master, was also made governor of the Languedoc and given important sums of money. His oldest nephew, Odet de Châtillon, Cardinal-Archbishop of Toulouse since he was twenty-five, became Count-Bishop of Beauvais as well; and the second, Gaspard de Coligny, was made colonel-general of the infantry at the age of twenty-eight.

In spite of the Constable's greed and his relatives' ambitions, the clan was still less dangerous than the encroaching tribe of the Guises, whose dreams stretched to crowns and empires. These minor princes of Lorraine had been working to make themselves greater for twenty years, with the patience and the foresight of a monastic community: placing no reliance upon the shifting favour of Francis I, they had set themselves to winning popularity and at the same time making an enormous fortune out of Church livings. At his death the Cardinal of Lorraine had become almost the only bishop of France. From 1550 onwards he held eight bishoprics, of which three were archbishoprics, and countless abbeys. These were sources of wealth that were presently to hold the royal power itself in check.

The family consolidated the rising edifice by marriage. First the marriage of the third Guise, Claude, with the daughter of Diane de Poitiers; then that of the eldest, François, with Anne d'Este, granddaughter of Louis XII;[3] and finally the betrothal of their niece Mary Stuart, Queen of Scots, then still a child, to the Dauphin, François. Thus this junior branch, a family that was barely naturalised, drew nearer to the throne, not without proclaiming their Angevin and Carolingian ancestry. No year of the reign went by without their fortune being seen to grow—'headlong, violent, inescapable, through fire and water', a fortune that in one generation was 'to carry France away with it'.[4]

How insignificant in comparison seemed the Bourbon princes, of whom the eldest, Antoine, had married Jeanne d'Albret, heiress of the kingdom of Navarre, and the younger, Louis, Prince of Condé,

---

[3] By her mother, Renée de France, Duchess of Ferrara.
[4] Michelet, *Histoire de France*, ed. Chamerot, vol. IX, p. 49.

a niece of the Constable. The Guises and the Bourbons were already rivals: moreover, they were also first cousins.[5]

Montmorency and the Guises had the same zeal for the Church, the same hatred of Protestants. Their attitudes towards the House of Austria, however, were completely different. The Constable loved peace and revered Charles V. He would have liked to lead France back into a Christendom united by a Caesar against the heretics and the enemies of the faith. The Guises, on the other hand, thirsted for military glory and longed for an Italian principality; and they were entirely in favour of the resumption of Francis I's Italian policy— even of a stronger version of it.

Some recent historians admire Henry II, and they have asserted that it is to him that we owe the concept of natural frontiers, the end of wars of adventure, the recasting of the administration, and the triumph of the French Renaissance. Now neither the letters of this prince nor his deeds show any degree of intelligence above the commonplace. All his contemporaries blame the weakness of his character. Yet it would be an injustice to describe him as a puppet, without any authority of his own, lacking ideas and wholly wanting in grandeur. 'He wishes for the common good and he works for it,' wrote Contarini, the Venetian ambassador. Montmorency's policy was admirably adapted to Henry's slow earnest mind, his fear of quick decisions and his respect for old rules 'one king, one law, one faith'. But the son of Francis I also had a chivalrous heart and he yearned to emulate the heroes of mediaeval romance: it was here that the Guises had a hold over him.

Those who stood for activity, youth and the pursuit of conquest won the day against the Constable's immobility, and after concealed hostilities the fifth war against the Emperor broke out in 1551. In this war the German Lutherans were on the side of France; and in the course of it France conquered the district known as the Trois-Evêchés. Other incidents were the defence of Metz, which turned François de Guise into a national hero, and the battle of Renty, which Guise and Coligny each claimed to have won and after which they were for ever enemies. The Truce of Vaucelles, in 1556, con-firmed the victory of France—a victory that was to prove ephemeral —and maintained her conquests in Lorraine, Savoy, Piedmont and Tuscany: this was the moment of the supremacy of the House of Valois in Europe. Charles V, his dream destroyed, resigned not only

---

[5] Antoinette de Bourbon, Duchess of Guise and mother of François and Charles, was aunt to Antoine and Louis de Bourbon.

his crowns but also his ideal of the union of Christendom: by dividing his dominions he relieved his heir, Philip II, of the weight of the Empire and made a truly Spanish king of him, one capable of bringing his country's power to its highest point and of making it the secular arm of Catholicism.

And yet it was Pope Paul IV, a personal enemy of the Habsburgs, who began the war again. The Cardinal of Lorraine and Diane de Poitiers, now enemies of the Constable, also yielded to personal motives and with the utmost rashness dragged Henry II into it, thus justifying L'Aubespine's remark, 'these two alone were the sparks that kindled the blaze of our misfortunes'.

Francis I had often dealt tactfully with the Protestants out of respect for his Lutheran allies. No such idea ever occurred to Henry II. Diane always urged severity: the elderly favourite delighted in playing the Mother of the Church, and besides that she had an intense personal dislike for the Reformation, particularly after the well-known harangue to which she had been treated by one of the court tailors—'Madame, be satisfied with having polluted France with your infamy and your filth, without meddling in God's affairs.'

Charles of Lorraine, Archbishop of Rheims, had said, as he crowned the king, 'Conduct yourself so that posterity will say "If Henry II had not reigned, the Roman Church would have been destroyed root and branch." ' And the young king had replied, 'I consent to all that which you have said.'

He was outraged by freedom of thought, and he was utterly incapable of understanding it: he looked upon the heretics as so many rebels. At the time he was wrong. The Protestants were loyal subjects and their claims were still of a purely religious nature. But nobody could conceive the separation of the church and the state; and neither side could easily tolerate the idea of coexistence. The king and his councillors were therefore not mistaken in foreseeing that the dispute would presently reach the political plane: their error lay in believing in the efficacy of persecution.

A commission of the parliament was brought into being; it began its work in the autumn of 1547, and it was soon known as the Burning Chamber. Prosecutions became more frequent, and 'every day French men, women, children, old men of every condition, priests or laymen, died at the stake'.[6]

⁶ Dulaure, *Histoire de Paris*, 1837 ed., vol. III, p. 343.

On 4th July, 1549, the king went in person to watch the *autos-da-fé* that were made ready in front of Notre Dame, at the cemetery of Saint-Jean, in the Place Maubert and by the Halles. This was the day the tailor died, the poor man who had told the favourite of his contempt for her. 'Motionless, and as if he did not feel the flames around him, he fixed the king with a heavy eye, a steady gaze that weighed like the judgment of God.' [7] Henry was appalled: it made him ill: but his heart remained unchanged. 'The King of France continues in his madness,' wrote Calvin to Farel.

However, the 'dissidents' did not give way. They were ready for anything; they suffered; they died. And by suffering and death they multiplied. When one was killed ten more sprang up. The flames were prolific. [8]

Losing all patience, the king asked the Pope to set up the Inquisition in France. This extraordinary proceeding, so utterly against the Gallican tradition of the House of Capet, attained its end on 13th February, 1557. At almost exactly the same time the Colloquy of Worms brought about the definitive separation of Calvinists and Lutherans; and the Council of Trent was preparing the Counter-Reformation, the rebirth of Catholicism.

The time had come when each man was to take up his place upon the chessboard of fate for the match between countries and between religions, that was to lead, fifteen years later, to the 'Parisian matins'.

The Duke of Savoy, general of the Spanish forces, had persuaded Philip II to relinquish the old battlefields in Italy and to strike at the heart of France. The invasion broke all along the roads of the north. Coligny, now Admiral of France, heroically threw himself into Saint-Quentin with seven hundred men, and for a short while held back the enemy's formations. A great army was sent to his relief, but it was unluckily entrusted to Montmorency, who was completely defeated at the battle of Saint Lawrence (10th August, 1557) and made prisoner. Shortly afterwards Coligny was obliged to surrender. In these few days 'the glory of a reign' was ruined and the fate of Europe determined for the next hundred years.

And yet as early as 11th August the worst was averted. The Spanish armies were only three days' march from Paris—an entirely unprotected Paris. But in spite of the Duke of Savoy's entreaties Philip would not seize the opportunity: chief among his obscure and com-

---

[7] Michelet, *op. cit.*, vol. IX, p. 91.
[8] Dargaud, *Histoire de la liberté religieuse.*

plicated motives was the fear of seeing a too successful captain diminish his own royal glory.

Paris, the court and the whole of the Ile de France knew nothing of this remarkable genius for letting the fruits of victory rot, and a wild panic ensued. Streams of fugitives hurried off 'to the far end of the kingdom'. The king was 'completely stunned and cast down by this disgrace'. It was a woman who showed a manly heart and who saved the situation, at least in Paris. Nobody expected it, and the proof of her courage was more than a surprise when on 13th August Catherine de' Medici walked into the Hôtel de Ville—making, at the same time, her entrance into history. Dressed in deep mourning, the queen asked the miserly and stubborn townsmen for the money to raise a new army. She got a considerable sum from them, and she thanked them for it with tears. They all wept with her, and the admiration that she aroused restored both calm and confidence. 'She is wise and prudent,' wrote Contarini. 'There is no doubt that she is capable of ruling.'

Her whole life long, Catherine was to be haunted by the recollection of those tragic hours when the Spaniard could have marched into Paris without so much as striking a blow. The memory was to be of vital importance during the drama of the summer of 1572.

Another portent appeared on 4th September of the same year. On that night there was discovered 'a meeting in the rue Saint-Jacques, where were gathered an extraordinary number of nobles, both men and women, as well as others of the same persuasion, in the act of worshipping after the manner of Geneva'. A furious mob besieged the house. The gentlemen were able to get out, sword in hand. The others, particularly the women and children, were arrested and taken to the Châtelet under the insults of the Parisians, who hit at them and tore their hair and clothes. The hatred of the mob had never, before that time, shown so dreadful an aspect.

In October François de Guise, recalled from Italy, returned like a saviour. In January, 1558, he took Calais from the English, the allies of Spain, and gave the French back their honour and their happiness. In April he became the dauphin's uncle; for in spite of Catherine's desperate resistance the dauphin was then married to Mary Stuart. 'He rose, borne on the back of that fiery charger public opinion. His fortune had two wings: the one, the people's infatuation; the other, the calculated passion of an endangered party.' [9]

Yet, absurd as it may seem, the Catholic party did not owe its

[9] Michelet, *op. cit.*, p. 149.

1 An open-air concert given by Diane de Poitiers

2 Charles IX

triumph to Guise, but to a new alliance between Diane de Poitiers and the Constable, whose nephew, Coligny, had just become a Calvinist.

In a France undermined by anarchy in the highest places, by economic distress and by internal disunity, the Reformation had become too powerful a movement not to have its say in the nation's future. Calvin wrote to the minister Macar, 'The fire is lit in every corner of the realm and all the water in the sea would not be enough to put it out.' The Most Christian King was no longer to concern himself with wondering how far he ought to go in his defence of orthodoxy: a question of quite other magnitude was before him— the choice between internal unity and hegemony in Europe; the choice between France's religious fate and her territorial destiny.

If Henry were to turn about and adopt the Reformation as Henry VIII of England had done, if he were to put himself at the head of this vast revolution which step by step was making such progress, he would transform the war into a reversed crusade against Rome and the House of Austria. On the other hand, if he wished to master heresy in his own kingdom, he would have to stop the war and thus leave the Continent to the Habsburgs.

Henry II had neither the constitution of mind nor the mettle that were called for if he were to launch himself into the hazardous adventure of conversion, he therefore favoured peace, but a peace far removed from surrender, for was not Philip II in financial difficulties quite as grave as his own?

At this juncture there occurred the affair of the Pré-aux-Clercs (13th May, 1558). In this great open space, which belonged to the university, thousands of Protestants marched past singing psalms, led by Antoine de Bourbon, King of Navarre and first prince of the blood. The authorities of the town were powerless to reduce them to silence, and the police were obliged to give way. Henry supposed that the Protestants had risen and that they controlled the streets. He was terribly shocked. 'I swear,' he cried, 'that if once I can settle my foreign concerns I shall make the heads and the blood of this Lutheran rabble run in the streets.'

This would not be possible so long as the war went on—this war that the Guises did not wish to end. So, urged by his old mistress, from then on the king put his trust solely in his friends, Montmorency and Saint-André. Both were entirely devoted to the Spaniards, who at once proposed extravagantly harsh conditions. To the profound indignation of the queen, the Guises, the nobility and the army, the king accepted them. He gave up the conquests and gains made since the time of Charles VIII: Savoy, Corsica, the *comté* of Nice, Piedmont, Bresse, Bugey, the Milanese and many fortresses in the east and in the Alps. Only the Trois-Evêchés remained to him, and Calais, which in any case was to become English again eight years later.

Such was the Treaty of Cateau-Cambrésis: such was the nature of the agreement that they concluded against the Reformation, and about which the specialists of the sixteenth century are still arguing to this day. We, with Lucien Romier and Jean Héritier, look upon it as a disastrous renunciation on the part of France, a renunciation that allowed Spain to maintain her hegemony until the Treaty of the Pyrenees. It must nevertheless be conceded to the historians on the other side that during the reigns of the last three Valois 'the frontier of the realm was not disputed, the civil war was never made worse by one of these great threats from outside that compel the reunion of all the forces of a nation into a single body' [10]—a misfortune that Catherine de' Medici was to strive to prevent for thirty years on end.

[10] A. du Ruble, *Le Traité de Cateau-Cambrésis*, Paris, 1889, p. 111.

CHAPTER III

THE PROTESTANTS IN 1559

WHAT STAGE in its revolutionary progress had the Reformation reached at the moment when the King of France declared a pitiless war upon it? It had won a great part of Central Europe, the Baltic shores and Scandinavia. The death of Mary Tudor and the accession of Elizabeth in 1558 had delivered England into its hands. But on the other hand it was rapidly losing ground in the Mediterranean countries: Italy, momentarily threatened by the Reformation, had bowed to the pontifical authority again; and at that moment, with the death of Paul IV in 1559, there vanished those Popes who were more concerned with their own passions and their worldly interests than with the fulfilment of their spiritual mission. Phillip II was making Spain into the impregnable stronghold of Catholicism.

Between these two extremes lay the divided countries, brought by their division into a state of political decline. Germany, which had been the first battlefield of the fratricidal war, was enjoying a lasting peace, which she owed to the Treaty of Augsburg and which she was to continue to enjoy for half a century, before being ravaged and depopulated in the name of the Lord. The voice of Calvin resounded from Switzerland; but the cantons were as ready to supply soldiers to the Catholic as to the Protestant armies. In the Netherlands, one of the King of Spain's possessions, the Reformation had made considerable progress, particularly since 1550. In France perhaps a third of the people counted themselves among its adherents.

The great majority of these Huguenots had adopted the Calvinist doctrines, for since the Colloquy of Worms Lutheranism was scarcely the same living influence that it had been. Calvin, unlike the German churches, placed the state under spiritual authority, and in doing so he won considerable prestige: though not, it must be admitted, without shocking the susceptibilities of the Gallicans. His dogma of predestination caused a pious excitement in many

French minds. 'The provisional elect of God endeavours to keep himself in a state of grace, whatever the cost.' [1]

The geographical distribution of Protestantism was diverse in origin. As it began in Germany, it is not surprising to find that it had spread widely in the region of the frontier and across the eastern plains, still suffering from the Peasant Wars. The Trois-Evêchés were very much affected; the movement had reached Château-Thierry, Epernay, Chalons, Vitry-le-François and Wassy; it was stirring up Burgundy, the Bourbonnais and the Nivernais.

Other factors had come into play in the north. Trade and economic exchanges between countries had brought the teachings of the Reformation to the commercial cities and ports: there were many Protestants in Dieppe, Caen, Le Havre, Rouen, Saint-Malo, Nantes and Vitré.

If they were solidly established on the banks of the Marne, the Seine and the Loire, they owed it primarily to the scholars; and sometimes, as in the case of Orleans, to the men of the university. But their principal domain lay elsewhere. It was the south that saw the triumph of Calvinism: Béarn, converted by Jeanne d'Albret, Queen of Navarre, who had the churches pulled down; the Languedoc, once the centre of the Albigensian heresy; and the whole length of the Rhône valley below Lyons, a city exceedingly busy with its trade and overflowing with ideas. From the south the wave flowed up to the west, spreading strongly in Guyenne, Aunis, Saintonge and Poitou; and at La Rochelle it rejoined that wave which had crossed Brittany.

The country districts were much less affected than the towns. But the hardships that had been brought about by the wars and the excessive taxation bred discontent, and this manifested itself in conversions—the more a province suffered under taxation, the more rural converts it provided for Calvinism. This was so even in prosperous Normandy, for there was much poverty in the countryside about Rouen, as well as in the Auvergne, the Vivarais, Rouergue and the wretched Gévaudan.

As it has already been observed, the originators of the Reformation were scholars, learned men; and the monks and the parish priests continued to supply the Reformation with many of its new members. A very sharp line divided the lower clergy, quick to condemn the

[1] Devèze, *Les Guerres de Religion en France, Angleterre, Pays-Bas* (Centre de Documentation universitaire).

Church's faults, from the higher clergy, who persecuted the innovators with unrelenting fury. Very few of the prelates abandoned
Rome; and of those few, the most important, Odet de Châtillon,
wanted to keep his cardinal's hat, married or not.

The university was no longer all of a piece: although the masters
may still have been aggressively Catholic, the foreign students from
Germany and Switzerland had already cast doubt in the minds of
their fellow students. The revolutionary vortex was drawing in part
of the country's youth.

Far from the realm of the mind, it was also attracting the humble
people, most of them illiterate, but turning towards the hope
that seemed to shine before the everlasting victims of the social
order. Since Henry II came to the throne, the position of the
craftsmen had worsened, because of the rise in prices and taxation.
Remote in their evil-smelling mazes, almost out of hearing of the
world, the working-men of the towns came in a body to join those
who set themselves to interpreting the will of God.

Protestantism attracted the poor in search of a religion that would
be more compassionate towards their misfortunes. Its magnetic
power for the rich was equally great, especially for the middle
classes; this state of affairs has been very well analysed by Lucien
Febvre:

'At that time, because of certain political, economic and social
circumstances which have often been listed, a whole class of men
attained both wealth and at the same time a considerable degree of
privilege and dignity . . . Not all of these people were unscrupulous
adventurers, upstarts sprung overnight from the void . . . Among
these men of the middle class, these bourgeois . . . there was to be
found a fundamental earnestness and a need for moral rectitude
which was unaccompanied by any social hypocrisy, any Pharisaical
prudery or any outward show or parade of austerity, all things which
most of them instinctively detested; yet their unambiguous realism
was by no means without a deep sense of duty, nor . . . without a
burning need for religious certainty. This mercantile bourgeoisie
which . . . like Ulysses, knew the ways of many men, and drew from
its varying experience the invaluable sense of the relative; this legal
and official middle class, firmly established with its graduated
ranks . . .; all these people, in short, in whom the practice of exact
professions and meticulously careful techniques had developed a
strong practical common sense given to simple, clear solutions, had

a corresponding need for a clear, reasonably humane religion which would be an inspiration to them and at the same time a support.' [2]

There was another factor: as they were aware that they owed their positions to themselves alone, 'everything that had to do with mediation or intercession vexed them; it wounded them both in their pride and their sense of responsibility . . . the pride of a merchant who deals directly with another, as man to man . . . The Reformation, in announcing justification by faith alone, gave these deep trends a new and profound satisfaction.' [3]

Furthermore Calvin denied the proposition of the Fathers of the Church that 'it was a great virtue to long for voluntary poverty'. He allowed the taking of interest, which had hitherto been considered a defilement reserved for the Jews: he attested that 'it is a special grace of God when it comes into our understanding to choose that which is profitable for us'.

The upper middle class of businessmen, the bankers (among whom were many Italians), remained attached to Catholicism. The Reformation gained its first footing in the lower ranks of the bourgeoisie, the tradesmen, the apothecaries, the physicians, the barristers, the solicitors, the attorneys. The condemnations of 1559 were to mingle the lower bourgeoisie with the craftsmen: merchants, goldsmiths and haberdashers with metal-workers, carpenters and shoemakers. A pedlar was to burn next to a scholar.

Towards 1555 an important event occurred. The higher level, that at which justice was pronounced, was no longer in safe keeping. The parliament which had so eagerly pursued heresy for thirty-five years now allowed it to make its way into its own body. The causes of this remarkable development were many and complex. Let us merely cite the humanism that was so widely spread in this most cultivated body of men and the haughty independence that the judges assumed in relation to the crown. The parliament had been pitiless under Francis I, that friend of the innovators, but under Henry II it showed an understanding attitude whose sympathy was in inverse proportion to the king's fanaticism.

At about the same time other symptoms showed themselves, symptoms quite as alarming for the Church, and even for the monarchy. The employment of numbers of Swiss and German mer-

---

[2] Lucien Febvre, *Une Question mal posée. Les origines de la Reforme française et le problème général des causes de la Réforme (Revue Historique,* 1929.)   [3] Lucien Febvre, *op. cit.*

cenaries had spread Protestantism among the soldiers. And suddenly, in its turn, the nobility came under its contagious influence.

To his horror Henry II learnt that Coligny, in prison, no longer went to hear mass, and that his brother Dandelot was also 'infected'. After a furious scene he had the brilliant commander arrested, but then pardoned him when he showed some signs of repentance. This angered the Pope, who wrote, 'It is an error to suppose that a heretic ever returns: it is mere dissimulation, and only fire will cure the malady.'

The king tried in vain to turn a blind eye: among the women who had been caught in the rue Saint-Jacques were Madame de Rantigny, Madame de Longjumeau, Madame de La Ferrière, Madame de La Rivière, Madame de Saint-Yon and Madame de Villiers. Heresy had made its way into the families of Roy, of Rohan, Crussol, Soubise-Parthenay and so many others.

The Peace of Cateau-Cambrésis was to bring matters to a head. Many gentlemen, leaving the army, found that they were ruined. The empty treasury could not produce their arrears of pay. The cost of wheat, which was used as the basis for the valuation of their property, had not risen as much as prices. Feudal rights, which were more or less fixed, had also declined in value. In order to keep up a suitable standard of living they would be obliged to go to the hateful extremity of selling estates and country houses to bourgeois purchasers. The nobles 'felt the ground slipping away from under their feet . . . They found themselves excluded from economic life at a time when the increased volume of trade was so profoundly changing the distribution of wealth.' [4]

An abrupt military unemployment, coming after sixty years of fighting, caused a no less intense frustration. Boyvin de Villars explained this to the king. 'France, being of a martial and a stirring nature, and having lost this admirable school and nursery-plot of war, will never contain herself in time of peace unless she has some goal towards which she can direct her courage and valour. Your Majesty knows better than anyone that the Frenchman has no greater enemy than peace and prosperity, which make him restive, wanton, bold in wrong-doing, eager for disturbance, contemptuous of his own tranquillity and welfare and apt to run after anything new.'

The nobles who joined the Protestant cause brought it that which it lacked, a secular arm—a political and above all a military pro-

[4] Duc de Lévis-Mirepoix, *Les Guerres de Religion*, p. 20.

tection. But unfortunately they also brought with them their vices, their ferocity, their violence, their rapacity and their private quarrels.

Nothing more remained to be won by the Reformation except the palladium, the fetish, which at that time could legitimise even rebellion itself—the royal blood of France. This difficulty no longer existed after the conversion of the Bourbons, Navarre and Condé, who were furious at seeing themselves powerless, discredited and poor beside the overflowing fortune of the Guises and the Montmorencys.

From that time onwards there were cells of Calvinists (in the sense that one now says 'cells of Communists') throughout French society, from top to bottom. The 'sect' had become a firmly established party. According to the report that Coligny was to submit to Catherine de' Medici in 1561, it numbered 2,150 churches, 'sharing all the provinces among them'.

On 25th May, 1559, the first Protestant synod was held in Paris, under the presidency of the pastor François Morel. Soon the Calvinists were to have, besides spiritual leaders, their political chiefs, their generals, their troops, their treasury and their diplomatic service.

The abuses of the Church of Rome, the mechanical teaching of theologians living in a vacuum, the invention of printing, the liberation of ideas, a mutual intolerance, the ravages caused by the wars and innumerable invasions, an over-hasty peace, an economic crisis and a ruinous financial system, the errors and weaknesses of a ruler who entrusted his power to a few favourites and set up new feudalities one against another: all these were necessary in order that this situation should be arrived at—a situation that, not long before, would have been unthinkable in the most highly centralised kingdom of the West.

Never, since the days of Joan of Arc, had the unity of France been so gravely imperilled.

CHAPTER IV

CATHERINE DE' MEDICI, RULER OF FRANCE

DURING ADVENT AND LENT in 1559 the preachers made the churches tremble with their din. They worked the faithful into an extraordinary state of emotion—a state which shows how violent a turmoil the king would have aroused had he made an attempt at a liberal policy.

'Death to Lutherans' was the cry; and the populace 'sought their vengeance blindly, seeking to kill—to kill anybody at all. At Saint-Eustache a schoolboy unhappily laughed during a sermon. An old woman saw him and pointed him out. He was killed on the spot.' [1] In March, there were appalling scenes in the Church of the Holy Innocents—a senseless, mad killing in which there were two outstanding victims, a Catholic gentleman and a canon.

The Edict of Ecouen appeared on 2nd June. This was a declaration of war, and after it the Protestants no longer had any choice except that between flight and revolt. The application of such a law called for judges whose zeal could not be doubted. But the parliament now no longer concealed its sympathy for the new ideas. The president, Antoine Fumée, very strongly criticised the Church, and he was generally applauded: he declared that it was the duty of a synod, of a council of the Church, to correct the errors of the heretics.

Henry II was profoundly disturbed, and he ordered the court to apply to itself the form of reprimand or censure known as the *mercuriale* (because of the opening of the session on a Wednesday, and the parliament's custom of delivering rebukes at the time of this meeting). After heated debates among the lawyers, moderation seemed to be gaining the day, so the king went in person to the parliament, accompanied by the Constable and the Guises. The Keeper of the Seals called up the judges for their opinion: but the

---

[1] Michelet, *Histoire de France*, vol. IX, p. 164.

simple-minded monarch did not receive the submission that he had hoped for. Some unimpeachable Catholics, such as Séguier and Harlay, boldly defended the liberty of the judicature, while Claude Viole and Louis du Faur called for a Church council. Then Anne du Bourg, who had just pardoned four heretics condemned at Toulouse, made a daring speech in which he stigmatised the corruption of certain prelates (the Cardinal of Lorraine found this unbearable) and undertook the defence of the Protestants—'These men who pray for the king are not guilty of high treason . . . they are trying to sustain a Church that is falling to pieces . . . Can it be supposed that it is a small thing to sentence men who call upon Jesus Christ in the midst of the flames? I have searched into this, and I find that the doctrine of the Lutherans agrees with the Scriptures, whereas that of the Pope is founded upon no more than outward show.'

Du Bourg called for the convocation of a 'good, holy and free council', and said that until it met the execution of believers should be stayed, except for the Anabaptists, Servetists [2] and other heretics. This qualification, on the part of a potential martyr, shows how narrow were then the limits of toleration.

The king, beside himself, seized the register in which these declarations were to be preserved and tore out the leaves. Then he ordered the Constable himself to arrest Du Bourg and Du Faur. The next day Fumée, Du Ferrier and some others were also locked up in the Bastille.

One month later the Protestants praised and glorified the justice of God. The king lay dead, having been struck in the eye by the lance of Montgomery, the captain of the Scotch guards, in a joust. Before dying he had committed the crowning error of calling upon Philip II to protect his son and his people: the King of Spain thus had a perfect excuse for interfering in French affairs.

The new ruler, Francis II, was a youth of limited intelligence, violent, sick and completely under the spell of Mary Stuart's beauty. It needed no more to ensure the decline of the monarchy to the level that is usual when the king is a minor. In accordance with tradition, the great nobles returned to their feudal ways and did their best to ruin the dynasty's work of centralisation. By giving up the whole of his power to his wife's uncles, the Guises, the king could not but prompt them to adopt this traditional plan, the more so as they

[2] Followers of Michael Servetus, who was burnt at the instigation of Calvin.

were helped by the troubled conscience of the time, the economic distress and the discontent that was everywhere apparent.

And other countries were filled with hope and covetousness. 'I think the time auspicious for all those who wish to revenge themselves on France,' wrote Throckmorton, the English ambassador: he, like his Spanish colleague Chantonnay, was going to do all in his power to foment discord.

The Guises were by no means devoid of political and military talent. But as their first concern was their family's welfare they acted as heads of a party from the very beginning, and wantonly angered the princes of the blood, the great nobles and an important section of the people. As the Duc de Lévis-Mirepoix puts it so happily, the government became an unacknowledged republic, having neither the advantages of an avowed republic nor those of a determined monarchy.

However, one last bulwark remained against partisan rage, the threatening civil war, the magnates' greed and foreign enterprise— the queen-mother, that Italian so long kept at a distance from business, that dull woman who for the last twenty-five years had looked like a Cinderella at her own fireside, and who from now onwards never appeared but in mourning. Although inconsolable at the death of her husband, Catherine de' Medici now threw off all disguise and displayed to an astonished court her real spirit. Her son revered her. He caused public documents to begin 'This being the pleasure of my lady mother the queen, and I approving that of which she approves, I order...'

Vain words. Although she was loaded with honours, Catherine still felt the disadvantage of her 'mercantile' birth and her weakness with regard to the princes of Lorraine, whom she sensibly took care not to offend. Although her ideas were very different, she therefore left the new government to carry on with the persecution of the Protestants for some months.

Anne du Bourg died at the stake. The Calvinists acclaimed his sacrifice with a kind of delight. Certain pastors openly rejoiced, for now the 'new Christians' had a martyr 'who was not a pedlar, a workman, an unfrocked monk or a schoolboy'.

Yet the opposition had found its leader. A role of such importance naturally fell to the first prince of the blood, Antoine de Bourbon, King of Navarre, an odd, changeable creature, with no standing at all: but his brother, Louis, Prince of Condé, took his place. This younger son was infuriated at his lack of influence, command and fortune. He possessed courage, ambition and dash, as well as a high degree of levity and a deplorable propensity for amorous extravagances. When he was converted, one may be quite sure that religion was not his only guide. What he was looking for was a means of revenging himself for the injustice of his fate and of standing on an equal footing with his cousins the Guises, whose insolent good fortune outraged him.

Setting himself up against the Catholic champions, he invoked the old law of the monarchy by which the princes of the blood might look upon foreign regents as usurpers. 'The Lorrainers had the *de facto* situation for them; the Bourbons tradition. The leading theme of the Wars of Religion was already to be heard.' [3]

Condé was almost alone among the great nobles in wishing for a trial of strength. The Guises were afraid of it. Towards the end of the winter of 1560 they made up their minds to follow the advice of the queen-mother and Coligny, who were at that time closely allied, and reversing their policy they promulgated the Edict of Amboise, which did away with that of Ecouen.

'If a drop of blood were to fall,' declared Calvin, 'it would cause whole rivers to flow. Better that we should all perish a hundred times over than that the names of Christianity and the Gospels should be exposed to such infamy.' But in his own town of Geneva, where Hotman was writing *Le Tigre* against the Cardinal of Lorraine, the refugees were stirring dangerously.

In France there were many officers who had been discharged without pay after the Treaty of Cateau-Cambrésis, and they were looking for some employment for their swords. Both to these men and to the refugees of Geneva, England poured out subsidies. Queen Elizabeth was extremely uneasy at the marriage of Francis II and Mary Stuart and the union of France and Scotland: she also longed to take possession of Calais again. We now know that her ambassador, Throckmorton, was the prime mover in the conspiracy of Amboise.

Monsieur le Prince (Condé) did not wish to show his hand too soon, so an adventurer named La Renaudie brought together the troops charged with kidnapping Francis II in Blois. The venture should have succeeded and one may dream of the incalculable consequences if Avenelles, the lawyer in whom La Renaudie had so unwisely confided, had not warned the Cardinal of Lorraine. The result was the capture of the attacking force before Amboise, where

[3] Jean Héritier, *Catherine de Médicis*.

the court had taken refuge, and the execution of its members. Agrippa d'Aubigné was then aged eight, and his father made the little boy look at the bodies hanging from the battlements.

'My child,' he said to him, 'you must spare nothing, not even your life, to avenge those leaders, who are men of honour. If you spare yourself, my curse be upon you.'

'The incident deserves profound attention,' writes Louis Madelin, 'for it holds within it France's future for the next terrible, threatening half century.'

Olivier, the chancellor, died of grief. Catherine de' Medici managed to have him succeeded by Michel de L'Hospital, a declared enemy of fanaticism and an uncompromising defender of the rights of the state. For some months the balance inclined towards liberalism once more. The Edict of Romorantin, which was the work of the queen-mother, abused the Protestants verbally, but in fact allowed them to escape the Inquisition for which the Guises and their supporters were clamouring. The States General were called. But throughout the kingdom scenes of violence grew more and more frequent. In the Lyonnais, in Dauphiné and Provence, Catholics and Protestants were already killing one another under the leadership of men as resolute as they were bloody. And though Coligny supported Catherine's policy, Condé was hatching new plots.

The Guises were thus able to resort to repression once again and to prepare the ruin of the Calvinist princes of the blood. Navarre and Condé, summoned to Orleans, were there arrested. The intention was to assassinate the one and send the other to the scaffold. At the last moment Francis II hesitated and the life of Navarre was saved. Monsieur le Prince was brought before a judicial commission and condemned to death.

Yet death chose not Condé but the unhappy child crushed under the weight of the crown. On 5th December, 1560, Francis II died; and Catherine de' Medici, having cajoled, terrified or deceived all the princes and all the parties, became the mistress of the realm, the chief of the government. 'She had raised herself to the highest place by such well-calculated steps and so gently that during her advance she had not appeared to move.' [4] Regent? The queen did not have even this title—she was merely governor [5] of France. When the great nobles came to pay their duty to the new king, Charles IX,

[4] Mariéjol, *Catherine de Médicis*, p. 87.
[5] *Gouvernante*, a woman governor, but not in the modern sense of governess. (Translator's note.)

who was then aged ten, they found his mother beside him; and she answered in his name. That was enough.

The next day, the Constable returned in glory and dismissed the corps of guards recruited by the Guises. He thought he was going to take the helm again: but in the event he was only the eighth member of the secret council appointed by the Florentine whom he had formerly insulted.

Presently the foreign ambassadors were reporting that the queen did everything. And in fact we find her conducting business, negotiating, making speeches, sending instructions to her ambassadors, watching over the smallest affairs, taking care of her son, hurrying from one end of the kingdom to the other, going into shops almost unaccompanied in order to learn the opinion of the townspeople, conferring offices, livings and pardons, overseeing the private life of her maids of honour, ordering revels, building palaces and, if we are to believe Montmorency, on occasion displaying the talents of a military leader.

When one reads her vast correspondence,[6] it is impossible not to admire her optimism, her spirit, and so much good sense, opposed, as she said, to the madness of 'motley minds'. The queen-mother was to do her best to act as the sick country's physician: and later she was to excuse herself for having 'laid every kind of simple to its wounds'.

As early as the first session of the States General, the chancellor exclaimed, 'Let us do away with these devilish words Huguenot and Papist! Let us keep the name Christians!'

Soon the queen made Coligny a member of the council. She made use of the still bitter dislike between the Montmorency-Châtillon clan and that of the Guises. But a threat on the part of the States against the rapacious favourites of Henry II became more definite, and this drew the Constable and his old enemies together. On Easter Day, 1561, 'a day that history will underline with a sombre red',[7] Montmorency, Guise and Saint-André formed the Catholic Triumvirate and at once called upon the queen 'to declare for one side or the other'.

It appeared that the Florentine, forced to come to the point, would choose the Reformation.

Theodore Beza, writing to Calvin, called her 'our queen'. Catholic preachers held forth about the nullity of oaths made to apostate rulers. After the coronation, the Cardinal of Lorraine said to Charles

[6] We have about *seven thousand* of her letters.   [7] Michelet, *op. cit.,* p. 245.

IX, 'Whoever advises you to change your religion is at the same time wrenching the crown from your head.'

A royal conversion therefore seemed possible: and in fact the little king openly made game of the bishops, and his brother Henry played at Huguenots, throwing their sister Marguerite's prayer-book into the fire.

The Colloquy of Poissy brought about the meeting of the bishops and the pastors, and much ability and knowledge was exercised upon this occasion. In vain. It was an extremely serious set-back and made recourse to arms inevitable.

But still Catherine, with a noble steadiness of purpose, refused to give up the idea of conciliation, in spite of the threats of Philip II and the triumvirate. Her Edict of January (1562), which allowed the practice of the Reformed religion in places other than certain prohibited towns and which foreshadowed the Edict of Nantes, was entirely revolutionary. By permitting the coexistence of the two religions, this niece of popes committed sacrilege and destroyed the unity of the realm: this was the judgment of public opinion and of the Guises.

Catherine asked Coligny how much help against the Spaniards and the Lorrainers she could count upon.

'Two thousand five hundred churches would give their fortunes and their lives,' replied the Admiral.

The queen sometimes hid near a Protestant church in order to make sure of the size of the congregation for herself. She deliberately encouraged the Protestants to become a warlike and military party. 'If the Protestants' political sense had been as acute as their religious sense there would have been a massive response. But . . . their response was not unanimous, and this brought on the very war that it was desired to avoid.' [8]

In spite of the rising danger, the Florentine kept up an unshakeable appearance of calmness. She asked a delegation from Paris, that had expressed indignation at the sight of a building devoted to Protestant worship, 'Do you want them to stay out in the rain?'

'Madame,' was the reply, 'unless the rain falls on them, it will fall upon you and your children.'

The King of Navarre, afraid of losing his little kingdom, turned his coat and allied himself to the triumvirate—a disastrous reverse. And then, on 1st March, 1562, the storm broke over Wassy.

[8] J. Viénot, *Histoire de la Réforme française des origines à l'édit de Nantes*, Paris, 1926, p. 356.

François de Guise, riding towards Paris, there fell in with about a thousand Protestants, who were listening to a sermon in a barn and who overflowed on to the road. A scuffle took place between the Protestants and the escort. The duke, having had a hail of stones thrown at him, gave his people the order to charge. Sixty Huguenots were killed, two hundred and fifty wounded.

Was the massacre intended beforehand? The Protestants always maintained that it was, and the truth is still in dispute. It may be remarked that in his last moments Guise asserted that it was not; and it is difficult to believe that he was lying at such a moment.

However that may be, this 'nuisance', as Guise called it, spread terrorism abroad, and both sides sought to outdo one another in atrocity.

The queen fled to Fontainebleau. Her horror of the Guises was so great that she was determined to entrust the monarchy to the Protestants. She wrote no less than four letters to Condé begging him to hurry to her and conjuring him to 'preserve the children and the mother and the kingdom'.

It was a solemn moment. A few hundred horsemen round Fontainebleau would have been enough to make the Bourbon the protector of the crown and to put the law on the side of the Protestants. But Monsieur le Prince had no head for politics. He was suspicious; he hesitated and shuffled; he let fortune slip from his grasp. His enemies knew how to seize it. It was the triumvirate who took control of the court. Catherine, their prisoner and hopelessly compromised by the letters that Condé had insanely published, was reduced to powerlessness.

The provinces then became the scene of what Michelet calls the first Saint Bartholomew. The tocsin rang, and the country priests led their parishioners in hunting down the heretics.

The whole Huguenot population was in danger of extermination. And yet still the Protestant gentlemen hesitated in face of the irreparable. It was the women, the Princess of Condé and above all Madame de Coligny (Jeanne de Laval), who urged them on. The Admiral held out no longer when his wife said, 'I call upon you in the name of God to cheat us no longer, or I shall bear witness against you upon His judgment day.'

And yet Catherine had written to him, 'You have always claimed to be a good patriot: at this critical time you will prove that you and your brothers do not wish to be the cause of your country's ruin.'

So the Protestants took up arms. That is to say, they performed as rebels the act that would, a few months earlier, have made them the upholders of the law. From the very beginning the war was particularly cruel. The 'Florentine shopkeeper' was the only person to invoke the country's good: the triumvirate turned to Spain and the Protestant leaders to England, without giving it a thought.

The Vidame de Chartres, Robert de La Haye and Briquemaut were sent across the Channel, and negotiated the Treaty of Hampton Court, by which Elizabeth promised her fellow-Protestants ten thousand men and a hundred thousand crowns. In exchange Calais was to be given up to her and Le Havre put into her hands as a pledge. A secret clause spoke of Rouen and Dieppe.

This caused a great burst of indignation, even among the Huguenot nobles, many of whom left the army. Condé and the Admiral accused their emissaries of having misused their power, but the English nevertheless occupied Le Havre, which was handed over to them by the governor, Coligny himself. The queen never forgave her former friends for this. For the first time she spoke of 'seizing the authors of sedition . . . and of having them fully and deliberately punished'.

She tirelessly hurried from place to place, negotiating, fighting, trying to intervene, wretched at the least weakness on the part of either faction. Fortunately, fate was working for her.

Navarre was killed at the siege of Rouen, Saint-André at the battle of Dreux; Montmorency became the prisoner of the Protestants, Condé of the Catholics. It seemed that François de Guise, the victor of Dreux, was to be left alone, the master of the field. He invested Orleans, the Protestants' chief fortress. Just as it was about to fall he was shot down by a fanatic, Poltrot de Méré.

'This death,' cried the Admiral, when he heard of it, 'is the best thing that could have happened for the kingdom, for the Church of God and especially for me and all my people.'

He very strongly denied having instigated the murder, but he nevertheless admitted that he had made use of Poltrot as a spy, and he scornfully added, 'I did not deter him from it.'

His contemporaries had no doubt whatever about his guilt, and they suspected the queen, who gained more than anyone else from the crime, of complicity in it, as Sir Thomas Smith, the English ambassador, told his sovereign.

Had Machiavelli's pupil incited Coligny to kill François de Guise as she was to incite Henri de Guise to kill Coligny, ten years later? People were surprised to see that as she sprinkled the holy water at the duke's funeral she was almost fainting. And later she made two strangely compromising remarks. To Tavannes she said, 'The Guises wanted to make themselves kings: before Orleans I prevented them.' And to the ambassador of Savoy, 'Behold the work of God! Those who wished to destroy me are dead.' [9]

In 1872, T. W. Ebeling, the German historian, purchased a curious document, an account of an interview between Poltrot de Méré and one Albanus, an agent of the queen-mother. According to this letter, which was written in Latin by Albanus to another man in Catherine's confidence, Poltrot was bitterly wounded at not having been encouraged enough by Coligny; but the incentives offered on the queen's behalf had, on the contrary, been quite sufficient. It would seem that the Medici had urged him not only to assassinate Guise but also to lay the blame for it on Coligny.[10]

Who was Albanus? Some think he was Arnaud de Sorbin de Saint-Foy, the king's preacher: Pierre de Vaissière holds that he was Pierre d'Elbene, later a royal chaplain. There is indeed a disturbing similarity between the plan here ascribed to Catherine and the plan that she did in fact conceive on the eve of Saint Bartholomew's day.

Whatever the truth may be, from that moment on the Lorrainers brooded their revenge against the Châtillons; and now to all the country's unhappiness was added that of a vendetta.

However, the chiefs of the two factions had vanished, and Catherine, busy and enterprising, alone remained. Condé was a prisoner, and he was bound even more firmly by the charms of his mistress, Mademoiselle de Limeuil, one of the members of the Flying Squadron, that troop of beauties, of Delilahs, who formed part of the queen-mother's political armoury. In spite of Coligny, he signed the Peace of Amboise.

The contending forces, gorged with booty, worn out with massacres, disbanded their troops. But on her side, Catherine kept her mercenaries, under the command of Charry, a soldier as ruthless and as faithful as a mastiff. With this power at her bidding she was able to postpone for three years the action that the Guises brought against Coligny, to pacify most of the local centres of unrest and

---

[9] Letter of 12th April, 1562, from Chantonnay to Philip II, *Archives Nationales*, K. 1493, no. 51.

[10] Part of the letter was published in the *Bulletin de l'Histoire du Protestantisme*, pp. 147–152. Ebeling disposed of it afterwards, and what became of it is unknown.

to oblige the judges to make their decisions without regard to the religion of the parties concerned.

The English refused to leave Le Havre, and she aroused an extraordinary wave of national solidarity against them. 'From here to Bayonne everyone is shouting *Vive la France*,' wrote the Constable, leading towards Le Havre an army in which Catholics and Protestants marched side by side on the best of terms. In the meantime the queen declared that Calais formed part of the realm once more, England having broken the Treaty of Cateau-Cambrésis.

Le Havre surrendered, and Elizabeth, her heart burning with fury, had to sign the Treaty of Troyes, which gave up Calais to France for good. The clergy paid the cost of the war (1564).

Catherine's victory was complete, and only one thing cast a shadow on her happiness—the assassination of Charry, killed in broad daylight on the Pont Saint-Michel by Monsieur du Chastelier-Portaut, the Admiral's standard-bearer. The queen had been much attached to this valuable servant, but fearful of jarring the structure that she had so laboriously built up, she hushed up the affair: yet her score against Coligny grew that much longer.

The Florentine might well be proud of her accomplishment: peace restored, the great nobles brought to heel, a show of tolerance insisted upon, the English beaten, the rights of the monarchy protected, Calais restored to France: and all this in thirteen months.

A little later, Catherine had a serious fall from her horse, and she was obliged to be trepanned. If she had died then, history would no doubt place her upon the same level as such women as Blanche of Castille and Anne de Beaujeu.

CHAPTER V

THE BLAZE OF FURY

CATHERINE DE' MEDICI once wrote that she intended to show her gratitude to the Great King (Francis I) for having admitted her into his family. To this end, she had appointed herself two tasks—to protect the domain and the rights of the crown, and to ensure her children a royal future—and she worked at them her whole life long.

She had been an amorous woman, very much in love with her husband; but since her widowhood a passion for politics and an all-consuming desire for power seemed to have absorbed her femininity, the maternal instinct alone excepted. Although she was much harder on her daughters than on her sons, Madame Catherine loved them all, and one of them she idolised: this was Henry, Duke of Orleans and later Duke of Anjou, the heir to the throne. He was her darling, the apple of her eye, her 'eaglet'.

As soon as the 'blaze of fury', as Jeanne d'Albret called it, had been put out, the queen, in pursuit of her double aim, wished to gather the nation round the young sovereign and to betroth Henry to a princess who would bring him a kingdom as a wedding-present. A journey was decided upon: it was to last for twenty-six months and it would take the king, that sacred fetish, from province to province, his appearance bringing back at least a semblance of harmony to them. 'Everybody is dancing,' wrote the queen, 'Huguenots and Papists together! '

But unhappily the second project caused the failure of the first. Philip II's sister, Dona Juana, Queen of Portugal, had just lost her husband. Catherine thought of this strict, devout woman as a match for her second son, who was then aged thirteen; and she supposed that her dowry would be one of the many Habsburg principalities. This fanciful idea led her to ask that there should be an interview between her son-in-law [1] and herself at the time when she would be near the Pyrenees.

[1] Philip II had married her eldest daughter, Elizabeth de Valois, after the signature of the Treaty of Cateau-Cambrésis.

Machiavelli's pupil sometimes had an exaggerated notion of her diplomatic genius—a genius much dreaded, however, by other sovereigns. She thought that she would be able not only to make the King of Spain agree to her plan for the marriage, together with certain other ideas, but also to induce him to stop thwarting her policy of tolerance.

Philip II replied to her approach by calling for the extermination of the French heretics. The betrothal would crown this happy event. Moreover, the enmity between France and Spain was breaking out everywhere—in America, where the colonists of Florida were at grips with those whom Coligny had sent to Louisiana; in Corsica; and in Rome itself. Catherine would have understood these omens if her maternal persistence had not blinded her. By way of a threat she suggested Charles IX as a husband for Elizabeth of England and spoke of granting an audience to an envoy of the Sultan who followed the court at her bidding—that is to say, of forming a Mediterranean league against Spain.

Philip II gave way. Not that he agreed to come face to face with his crafty mother-in-law, however. He only allowed his wife, Queen Elizabeth, to meet the French court at Bayonne: as mentor and as plenipotentiary he gave her his most immovable, most fanatical minister, the Duke of Alba.

The meetings at Bayonne were to bring about one of the worst misunderstandings in history. The queen and the duke could agree on nothing. The one was trying to establish her children in exchange for nothing more than some imprecise assurances calculated to please the Catholic King: the other desired only the destruction of the Reformation in France. Catherine pretended to ask his advice, and Alba told her that she should surprise the Calvinist leaders and have them executed and then banish the whole of the 'evil sect'. He also called for the dismissal of the chancellor, de L'Hospital.

Catherine had no intention of doing any of these things. She was now at last aware of the emptiness of her hopes, but she had become a prisoner of the situation. She was too much afraid of the power of Spain to let the failure of the talks be known or to make the break complete. A friendly parting, at the very least, was quite essential. She promised, in short, 'to restore good order in the matters of religion', and the Constable announced that the king 'was prepared to chastise the Huguenots'. These were merely formal engagements, and Philip was so little pleased with them that he at once dissuaded the Emperor from giving Charles IX his daughter, by way of revenge.

Moreover, it is clear from the dispatches of Fourquevaux, the French ambassador in Spain, that His Most Christian Majesty and the Catholic King never came to any sort of agreement or pact against the Reformation.

Unfortunately this essential disagreement between the Medici and the Habsburg remained generally unknown for several centuries. The requirements of her foreign policy and of her dangerous balancing between London and Madrid prevented Catherine from letting it become known. What is more, her long apprenticeship as a Cinderella queen had so accustomed her to dissimulation that it had become natural—a part of herself. 'It had grown almost impossible for her to appear straightforward, even when she was perfectly sincere. She had striven to hide her real feelings for so long that now she was unable to make them understood.' [2]

The Calvinists suspected a plot: they did not believe in her good faith. A rumour spread that their throats were to be cut. And this was just at the moment when the Pope was vehemently denouncing the queen's indulgence towards them! In these circumstances the admirable Enactments of Moulins and the spectacular reconciliation that Coligny and the Guises were obliged to make were ineffectual.

At this juncture the Spanish Netherlands rose in revolt. The Duke of Alba, who was given the task of reducing them to order at the head of a powerful army, asked permission to march through France. The queen refused, laughing at the ferocious grandee's protestations of friendship, 'seeing that when we made so much of him at Bayonne', she wrote, 'he behaved so coldly that it never seemed to me that he could possibly ever wish to be friends'.

The tension between the two countries increased; the threat of war became apparent, and Condé asked for the command of an army. Catherine, who wanted to preserve the peace, gave this request a most unfavourable reception. Monsieur le Prince, bitterly resentful, dreamed from that moment on of taking up arms again. The Admiral was by no means in agreement with this, and violent arguments took place between the supporters of the two different lines of conduct. Condé was overruled at first, and he called a meeting at his house, taking care to invite all the idle swashbucklers, all the extremists of the party. At this point Alba arrested Count Horn and Count Egmont at Brussels. Condé's friends regarded or feigned to regard this as the first part of a plot worked out at Bayonne by Philip and his mother-in-law: unless they were to be

[2] Duc de Lévis-Mirepoix, *Les Guerres de Religion.*

exterminated, the Calvinists must follow the example of their Dutch comrades. Terrifying rumours were cleverly spread abroad, and the masses rushed blindly into the net that the ambition of their leaders had spread before them.

The unsuspecting court was at the château of Monceau, enjoying itself. In this month of September, 1567, Catherine somewhat naïvely congratulated herself for having averted the war and for being able to contemplate a pacified kingdom. She was still shaken by her recent brush with Philip II, and she took particular pains to be tactful with the Protestants. On 24th September she wrote again to insist upon the strict observance of the Edict of Amboise. The next day she was told that Monsieur le Prince's men were making ready to seize the person of the king.

The undertaking seemed so hare-brained and the error so monstrous that at first neither the queen nor the chancellor believed in it. However, the court thought it wise to retire behind the walls of Meaux.

On 26th September Catherine, who was always sanguine, felt reassured: the Admiral was busy gathering his grapes at Châtillon-sur-Loing. On the 28th the Huguenots seized fifty positions and Monsieur le Prince concentrated a large body of cavalry around Meaux.

Six thousand Swiss mercenaries reached the place before him. Surrounded by their pikes, the court at once set out for Paris, and on the road between Lagny and Chelles appeared Condé's horsemen. They turned vainly round and round the steel square, while the enraged Charles IX longed to charge them himself. When the party came near to the capital the Swiss troops formed an impregnable barrier the whole length of the road, and under this protection the royal family was able to gallop into Paris. The Protestant coup had failed.

The consequences were incalculable. Neither the still dumbfounded queen nor the young king ever forgave the Huguenots for having 'made them go faster than a walk'. The chancellor de L'Hospital could no longer exercise his beneficent influence. 'It is you,' cried the queen, 'you, with your fine words about tolerance and justice, who have brought us to this.'

On 29th September, Michaelmas day, the Protestants of Nîmes threw a hundred and fifty Catholics down a well. Massacres took place in many other towns. This is what was called the *Michelade*.

The frightful war began again. The Protestants daringly attacked

Paris. Montmorency, having repulsed them at Saint-Denis, was murdered on the battlefield.

'I have two reasons for thanking Providence,' said Catherine, when she heard of it, 'the one that the Constable should have revenged the king upon his enemies, and the other that the king's enemies should have disembarrassed him of his Constable.'

A 'patched-up and lopsided' peace was signed at Longjumeau in March, 1568; but it was scarcely even a truce. The Catholics went on hunting the Huguenots and the Protestants refused to give up their fortified towns, especially La Rochelle. This great port sheltered a fleet of privateers which supplied the party at the expense of Philip II's galleons. Thanks to their fellow Protestants, William of Orange and his brother, Count Louis of Nassau, acquired bases for their operations and volunteers in abundance. The queen, always haunted by the idea of foreign intervention, threatened those who were thus responsible for the risk of a war with Spain with the direst penalties.

The year 1568 was a turning-point. Catholicism was making its extraordinary recovery under the leadership of Pope Pius V, aided by the Jesuits, and at the same time Catherine de' Medici became the declared opponent of the Protestants. For eight years she had tried to treat them with consideration and to rely on them as supporters against the party of Guise and Spain, but now she decided, judging everything upon the political plane, that they were weak and that they had no feeling for the country. Therefore, she thought, it was better to go back to Henry II's policy and to give back to the Church's eldest son his position of protector of the faith. L'Hospital, who stood for the now abandoned past, was no longer of any importance. After the Cardinal of Lorraine, the Italians Birague, Gondi and Gonzague-Nevers became members of the council: they were the queen's devoted servants, but they were unfortunately steeped in the treacherous and tortuous methods so usual among the rulers of their native land.

At a memorable session of the council on 1st May, 1568, the defeat of the last supporters of moderation was finally accomplished. From that time onwards, religion was to incite men to a struggle like that between the Guelphs and the Ghibellines, and the monarchy was to identify itself with one faction.

An odious action soon made the new state of affairs quite clear. Catherine, committing the same crime with which she had reproached the Protestants, tried to have Coligny and Condé kidnapped, they being at that time both at the castle of Noyers. But Tavannes, to whom the operation was entrusted, was an honourable man who respected the knightly code. He gave the Protestant chiefs time to escape and then, with his mind at peace, he sacked the empty castle.

The 'blaze of fury' flared up again at once. Everywhere the Huguenots rose: they called in the veterans of the Italian wars and allied themselves to William of Orange and the German princes. An English fleet threatened the coasts. Once more the followers of war appeared—lawlessness, crime and horrors.

A new edict forbade Protestant worship and ordered the pastors to leave the kingdom. This had no effect other than bringing about L'Hospital's resignation and making the queen's complete reversal of policy evident to all.

However, the Florentine had no intention of leaving all the advantages of this situation to the Guises and their leader, the young Duke Henry. His innumerable followers claimed the command of an army for this young man, hoping to win for him his father's renown and the glory of the Catholic hero. But Catherine did not wish anyone to have this particular halo except her favourite son.

Henry, Duke of Anjou, known as Monsieur, was appointed lieutenant-general of the realm at the age of seventeen, and commander-in-chief. His mother was almost frenziedly devoted to his success, and in daily letters she told him how to act: in times of difficulty she hurried to his headquarters in person. The best service she did him was to place him under the guidance of Tavannes.

The armies of the two parties, swollen by a great many mercenaries, were roughly equal. They began a long series of marches and counter-marches, not without pillaging and torturing the innocent people who happened to lie in their path. The first serious encounter took place on 13th March, 1569, at Jarnac, where Tavannes beat the Protestants. It would have had little importance if Condé, thrown from his horse, had not been assassinated, and if the Duke of Anjou had not made himself conspicuous by his courage.

The soldiers attached a great deal of importance to the myth of royal blood, and because of this Jeanne d'Albret, Queen of Navarre, and the Princess of Condé brought their young sons into the Huguenot camp. In fact, the Admiral became the only leader of the Protestants.

On the other side, an intensive propaganda held up Monsieur as the champion and hope of Catholicism. Furthermore, the young prince was able to acquire enough military experience in the next few months to allow him to reap the honour of his victory at Moncontour.

This terrible battle, 'swift, fierce, and skilful', was fought on 3rd October, 1569. The fortune of the day wavered at first, but when the Admiral was wounded in the mouth and obliged to retire, it turned completely against the Protestants. The Swiss mercenaries cut the throats of their competitors, the German lansquenets, to the last man. Many thousand French prisoners would have shared the same fate, but for the intervention of Monsieur.

Henry had shown the courage of a knight, the intelligence of a general. All Europe rang with his praise, and Ronsard joined in the chorus.[3] He was compared to Alexander, to Caesar. Philip II sent him a sword of honour. Elizabeth of England herself was moved: she sent to see the demi-god's portrait, and she felt a stirring in her heart.

This triumph infuriated Charles IX. The king loathed his brother, who was the favourite not only of Catherine but also of their younger sister Marguerite (Margot), for whom both Charles and Henry entertained a very curious emotion. Defying his mother, he hurried to take over command, and in his thirst for trophies he insisted upon besieging Saint-Jean-d'Angély. The royal army melted away in front of this impregnable fortress, losing the fruits of their victory and allowing Coligny time to build up his forces again.

The Catholics still believed that the Admiral was weakened, demoralised and dug-in behind his positions when suddenly they saw him pass to the offensive, cross the south of the country and conquer the Languedoc. He was already coming up the valley of the Rhône, and he did not hide his intention of advancing as far as Paris. A poisoner and two assassins were sent out, but they were unable to stop him.

The queen then reverted to the system that she preferred, and sent Biron and Malassis to negotiate. Coligny agreed to meet them at Montréal, near Carcassonne. Biron did not conceal his admiration for this repeatedly vanquished man who 'had the air of a victor'.

---

[3] Ronsard, *L'Hydresfaict, ou la louange de Monseigneur le duc d'Anjou, frère du Roy.* A poem published in 1569 after the victory of Moncontour in *Paeanes sive Hymni in triplicem victoriam*, Paris, Jean Charron, and reproduced in Ronsard, *Œuvres complètes*, Paris, Bibliothèque de la Pléiade, 1938, vol. II, p. 624.

'If he were to die,' he told the Protestants, 'we would not offer you so much as a glass of water.'

As the conference could reach no conclusion, the Admiral sent his son-in-law Téligny to the court. The Huguenots claimed Calais and Bordeaux as fortified places—that is to say, the ability to open the kingdom to the English. Each side broke into expostulation. Charles IX, in a fit of rage, wished to stab Téligny.

The Admiral, however, continued his advance, leaving a trail of ruins behind him. He reached the Loire. Catherine, overcoming the Guises and their party, who were speaking of a Catholic uprising, then signed the truce that became the Treaty of Saint-Germain, or the Queen's Peace.

'We won by fighting, and they win by these damned documents,' cried the savage Monluc.

In fact, the position of 1563 was restored: freedom of conscience, freedom of worship according to the provisions of the Edict of Amboise, four fortified towns of the first importance for the Calvinists' security—La Rochelle, Montauban, La Charité and Cognac (8th August, 1570).

A good peace had to be guaranteed by a good marriage. As a proof of her good faith Catherine did not hesitate to offer the Protestants her daughter Marguerite, the pearl of the Valois, to be married to Henri de Bourbon, Prince of Béarn, heir of Navarre, the son of Jeanne d'Albret and Antoine de Bourbon. But that was not enough to restore confidence.

Exhaustion, lack of money and even a certain regard for the common good did, however, incline the two parties to lay down their arms. The king asked the members of his council to swear that they would respect the agreement. When his turn came, the Duke of Anjou swore 'to exert himself no less in maintaining the peace than he had exerted himself during the war'. The same day the Admiral wrote to the queen, 'I beg you, Madame, to believe that you have no more loving servant than I have been and have wished to be.'

CHAPTER VI

THE DIPLOMATIC PROLOGUE

DURING THE YEAR 1570–1571 international politics assumed a greater importance than home affairs. As this immense chess match, in which the stake was supremacy in Europe, was to have a direct influence upon the drama of Saint Bartholomew's day, we must take a view of the positions of the chief powers at this particular juncture.

Ideologies in those days, as in ours, were possessed of such strength that territorial interests were entirely subordinated to them: Islam was in arms against Christianity; the Catholic Church against the Reformation. All other problems existed in relation to these.

In the course of the century the Turks had overrun a large part of the West. They had been held before Vienna in 1529 and they had been stopped at Malta in 1565: since then they had made their presence felt by piracy and terrible slave-raiding and plundering all along the coasts of the Mediterranean. Then suddenly the Ottoman Empire set out upon its conquests again, and in 1570 seized Cyprus, the eastward bastion of Venice.

The chessboard was in complete disorder. Venice was the only power that had tried to preserve its political independence and its economy by remaining outside the religious struggles. Until that moment she had continued to trade with the Porte and had encouraged the queen-mother's liberal policy in France. The conquest of Cyprus forced her to join the ranks of the ultra-Catholics, chief of whom, of course, was the Holy See, whose interests in Italy were opposed to those of Venice.

The Pope was horrified: he called for a crusade and did his utmost to reconcile the House of Austria with that of France. Pius V was, as the Inquisition understood it, a saint. Like Pius IV, his predecessor, he pursued an ambitious, passionate policy against the infidels and the heretics, deliberately ignoring local necessities. With regard to

France in particular he retained an archaic notion in which the consequences of the terrible religious argument that had been going on for fifty years counted for nothing. In his eyes, the obvious duty of His Most Christian Majesty was to follow Philip II's example and maintain orthodoxy by the slaughter of the rotten sheep.

This somewhat over-simplifying rigidity defeated its own end. Later on it was to bring about the most dreadful misfortunes. Far from helping reunion, it strengthened Protestant fanaticism, antagonised the moderate Catholics and incited the others to rebellion. Both Coligny and the Guises felt an equal hatred for the Turk, and both had thought, from a purely personal point of view, of attacking him. But instead of taking advantage of this state of mind, the Sovereign Pontiff insisted upon the annihilation of the followers of Luther and Calvin in order that Christianity might present a united face to the Turk.

But Catherine, the niece of two Renaissance popes (Pius V was a pope of the Counter-Reformation), belonged to a school with quite a different sense of realism. She had no intention of tearing up the Treaty of Saint-Germain nor of breaking the old alliance that Francis I had made with the Sublime Porte. Furthermore, she had just obtained new capitulations from the Sultan, and they were remarkably favourable to French trade and to the port of Marseilles. For her no mere doctrine was more important than the interests of the kingdom and the balance of power in Europe.

To the great scandal of the godly, therefore, Charles IX remained the friend of the infidels and refused to join the Christian League which the Holy See, Spain and Venice combined to create. The Sultan even suggested bestowing half Cyprus upon the Duke of Anjou.

Philip II was the leader of the Christian League, and this added further brilliance to his splendour: ever since the Treaty of Cateau-Cambrésis there had been no possible doubt of the Spanish king's dominant position in Europe. His flag waved over Madrid and Lima, Brussels and Naples, Milan and Mexico. The gold of the Americas flowed into his coffers. His cousin the Emperor—a sensible man, capable of keeping the German world at peace—respected him as the head of his house. The Catholic King, the true secular arm of the Church, also had a great many men in each of his countries who were devoted to his cause—powerful, resolute men, whose beliefs he embodied. To his three and twenty crowns he added the immense prestige that surrounds the chief of an *Internationale*.

Philip wielded this enormous power himself; and unlike Catherine he did so with his ideals for his guide. Many historians have misrepresented Philip's ambitions concerning universal monarchy. For this slow, mystical, suspicious, narrow mind there was no great difficulty: the son of Charles V wished, when he died, to be welcomed to Heaven by the Trinity as his father had been—and no doubt ever crossed his mind that this had been the case. Like his father, therefore, he was to be the 'director of Christendom' and he was to maintain the integrity of the faith everywhere, whatever the cost. His mind was much more turned towards preservation than conquest; and if at times he was brought to claim or even to seize certain territories, his true intention was limited to preserving the traditional order. He was convinced that his mission was to destroy infidels and heretics [1] and above all that Protestant revolution which, having won the day in England, was tearing France apart and even infecting his own possessions. Very naturally, the only valid remedy for the leprosy that was spreading over these countries appeared to him to be that he personally should rule them.

In Spain itself the Catholic King had, at the cost of cruel torments, put down subversive ideas and the threat of civil war. The Inquisition could pride itself upon an equal success in Italy, the whole of which, with the exception of Venice and, to a certain extent, Tuscany, was obedient to the Habsburg. But the people of the Low Countries would not stand tyranny, and they boldly gave the lie to the system's worth.

In 1570 the revolt in the Netherlands had acquired new force. The Beggars [2] replied to Alba's executions by a formidable sea-borne guerrilla war carried on with the help of the English. 'The privateering began by single ships at first, then by fleets. The Mexican mines found that they were working for London. Galleons that were awaited at Cadiz dropped anchor in La Rochelle. To the din of the shattering of Brussels and the sacking of Rotterdam, Elizabeth replied with the sound of the opening doors of the London 'Change'. [3]

The Queen of England, in spite of her continual procrastination and the remarkable wavering within that tenacity which was to serve her better than courage or high ability, now resigned herself to open war with Spain. During the first years of her reign she had dealt tact-

---

[1] The only regret that he expressed before his death was that he had not burnt enough of them.

[2] They had adopted as their name the insult which had been hurled at them not long before by the Regent of the Netherlands.

[3] Michelet, *op. cit.*, p. 372.

fully with the King of Spain, both from policy and from gratitude, for Philip had saved her from having her head cut off when he was married to her sister, Bloody Mary. These ties had been broken after the treacherous capture of Mary Stuart, who, fleeing for safety to England, had found only a prison.

Mary Stuart nevertheless remained heiress to her rival's throne and the hope of the English Catholics, as well as being, after all, the Habsburg's natural ally.

Philip II urged the Pope to declare Elizabeth an apostate and a bastard, and, as such, deposed. In this way, and always under the cover of religion, there began that long struggle between Spain and England which was eventually to transfer the common of the sea from the one to the other.

Neither of the adversaries was in any violent haste to begin. Elizabeth's first need was to gain time in which to bring about unity within her kingdom. Philip hoped that some knightly champion of the lovely prisoner would arise, dispatch the bastard and hand over Great Britain to Mary Stuart, in fact to Philip himself. The Catholic Duke of Norfolk, in love with the Scottish Rose, undertook the task; but he was discovered and seized. Elizabeth at once offered Charles IX a pact that would counterbalance the Christian League.

Yet in truth England and Spain both looked upon France with the same uneasiness. It was in the interest of each to keep that country in a state of disorder and to profit by it. Each feared that a victory of the opposing side would cause the balance to lean in an unfavourable direction. Thus the Spanish ambassador harried the queen-mother with his complaints and tirelessly urged her to 'get rid of' the heretics. And Elizabeth more and more persistently tried to win over her 'gossip' with fair words and promises.

Catherine de' Medici's foreign policy never had the great scope of that of a Henry IV or a Richelieu; but it is nevertheless absurd to impute limited, niggardly schemes to her and to contrast these with the ideas of a Coligny, all impatient to renew the traditions of Francis I.

The Florentine had been brought up on these traditions. Her tears and her fury at the signing of the Treaty of Cateau-Cambrésis were not forgotten. But alas, this kingdom, torn by fratricidal strife, and with its treasure exhausted, was no longer that of her father-in-law. The queen-mother, haunted by the memory of Saint-Quentin and by the power and evil intentions of Spain, wished to avoid all trials of strength. She hated her former son-in-law, above all since the somewhat suspicious death of her daughter, Elizabeth de Valois. She was perfectly aware of the Queen of England's underhand dealing and of her real feelings towards France. But she considered herself big enough to confront these formidable opponents and to accomplish at least some of the dynasty's historic ambitions, and that without a war.

At that time a large family was an uncommonly successful means of expansion. The House of Austria had founded its greatness on marriages, not on victories. Madame Catherine, combining her maternal hopes with her duties towards the state, dreamed of seeing her sons and daughters sitting on thrones geographically so well disposed that the House of Valois would hold, as she said, 'both ends of the strap'—a strap that would almost without effort be able to break the supremacy of the House of Austria, already threatened by the Turks, the Beggars, the English and many serious economic difficulties; and threatened, too, by the methods of Philip II who, having created the worst bureaucracy that can be imagined, delighted in drowning business 'in a flow of sticky mud'.

For fighting men like the Admiral ideas of this sort were disagreeably reminiscent of 'the shop-woman'.

Two Protestant leaders, Cardinal Odet de Châtillon, Coligny's brother, and the Vidame de Chartres, were in London, exiled. Being eager to return, and knowing the queen-mother's weakness, they worked out an extravagant plan—the marriage of the Queen of England and the Duke of Anjou.

Today the unlikeliness and the extravagance of this union between the Anglican ruler, the symbol of the Protestant revolution, and the idol of the French Catholics, between the thirty-seven-year-old Vestal virgin, the subject of so many scandalous tales, and the Prince Charming of not quite twenty-one, is obvious enough. Yet it is true that Catherine greedily took the hook, and that the arduous negotiations which were opened, broken off, taken up again and finally abandoned, between the winter of 1570 and the autumn of 1571, troubled and disturbed all the courts and all the parties.

The Cardinal de Châtillon was the victim of his own scheme: he died suddenly. Philip II thundered. Prompted by the Guises, the clergy of France offered the immense sum of four hundred thousand crowns [4] for the match to be broken off. Coligny, no less uneasy, thought of putting up a rival to Monsieur, and proposed the young

---

[4] Something in the nature of £3,500,000 of today. (Translator's note.)

3 Members of the court of Charles IX

4 Charles IX on the balcony of the Louvre

Henri de Bourbon. In the end, despite the inevitable failure of the main plan, the two 'gossips' did attain one of the goals common to both, which was to worry Spain and to hold Philip II in check at the time when the Christian League was bringing him so formidable an increase in power. Yet after all this was but a negative success. To shake this colossus it was necessary to concentrate upon his weakest point, the Low Countries.

The explosive idea of persuading the King of France to intervene in the Netherlands was a thought born not in the mind of a Protestant, but in that of a Medici, Cosimo, the Grand Duke of Tuscany.

The Grand Duke had reason to fear the House of Austria and the dangerous pressure that it exerted upon his dominions. He trembled lest Philip II should occupy Florence on the pretext of winning support for the Christian League. Cosimo was an ardent Catholic, at least outwardly, but that made him no less of a banker and, anxious to preserve the balance, he lent money impartially to the heretics and to the Church's defenders. Through his agents Petrucci and Frégose he kept in close contact with the Protestants, and he was thus able to persuade Louis of Nassau to ask Charles IX for help. If Philip II had the French as well as the Flemings on his hands he would have no time to think about Italian enterprises.

Louis of Nassau found the advice to his liking. For a time he thought of offering the crown of the Netherlands to Monsieur, so as to conciliate the queen-mother. (Philip II was told of this.) Then, reflecting upon Catherine's rooted love of peace, he thought it better to enter into direct communication with the young king. They met secretly and in disguise—wearing a smith's apron, the heir of Saint Louis wielded a hammer in the darkness of a forge—and Nassau, who was a brilliant talker, showed the young man the splendid road by which he might leave mediocrity and cause his younger brother's triumphs to be forgotten; holding up his ancestor as an example, Louis persuaded Charles IX that he might take the first place among the Christian monarchs.

Charles was beginning to grow a little weary of his mother's authority: he was also a young man with a vivid imagination—he took fire, and promised money and a fleet, with better to come.

The queen-mother had to be told, however. An interview took place between the sovereigns and Louis, who spoke as if he were now opening the question for the first time: he was not rejected. At that time Catherine was still hoping to succeed with the English marriage. She thought she had found a way of charming Elizabeth without going so far that she would endanger her position with Philip. And she thought that she might at the same time gain the good will of Coligny, who was so worried at the prospect of the Duke of Anjou reigning in London. Cossé-Brissac, who was conducting the negotiations for the marriage of Marguerite de Valois with the Bourbon, gave the Admiral to understand that a French intervention in Flanders was possible.

But when the queen learned of the private meetings between the king and Nassau and of Charles's nascent urge for independence, another aspect presented itself. Louis had to leave the court having obtained nothing; but he was convinced that he had won over the king. Like the ambassadors of the foreign powers, he had carefully noted the divisions in the royal family, those forerunners of unhappiness. Charles had detested Henri de Guise from the moment he knew that he was the lover of his sister Marguerite. Even more he hated Monsieur, who now possessed the title of Intendant-General of the Realm and who was looked upon as their chief by the Catholic party, now that the Lorrainers were in disgrace.

The enmity between the two brothers had reached a high pitch of intensity, and the Duke of Alba did not scruple to prophesy, 'Either the king must lose his crown or the Duke of Anjou his head.'

All this had erased from the king's mind the unfortunate memories of Meaux, and drew him towards the Protestants. Catherine knew that if she could succeed in making the Huguenots an integral part of the national community, it would be a fresh reason for her son to admire her and so to obey her. And in any case, had she not always pursued this aim of unification?

Yet so long as Jeanne d'Albret and Coligny remained in their fortress of La Rochelle, the representatives of a state within the state, unity would remain a myth. The queen-mother therefore grew very active in trying to bring them to court: surely the symbolic marriage of the Bourbon and the Valois called for a return to the fold? The Protestant leaders were very stubborn, however. The Admiral lived in the midst of his 'brothers' like a mediaeval suzerain: he feared the corruption, the traps and the assassins of the royal palaces. The Queen of Navarre was equally candid. 'You are so kind as to assure me, Madame,' she wrote to Catherine, 'that my son and I would be honoured, well treated and received with favour in your house . . . but I have the vanity to wish to be received there with the honour and the favour that I believe I deserve more than others who are more honoured and more favoured than myself.'

And, as Biron and Quincey, the queen-mother's envoys, redoubled their efforts, 'I do not know why it is, Madame, that you send to tell me that you would like to see my children and me, with no intention of doing us any harm. Forgive me if, in reading these letters, I have been near laughter; for you seek to calm a fear in me that never existed—I never thought that you really were an eater of little children, as they say.'

Another kind of fear—the fear of seeing France truly at peace—was born in London. Louis of Nassau had come to La Rochelle: an English agent, Robert Beel, asked him to offer Jeanne d'Albret Elizabeth's hand for Henri de Bourbon, her junior by twenty years.

The extraordinary thing is that Coligny and Nassau allowed themselves to be dazzled by this mirage, dazzled even to the point of forgetting the Netherlands, where there would be no question of a French expedition if a break with the king's sister were to cause another breach between Catholics and Protestants. But Jeanne d'Albret, an intelligent woman, did not fall into the trap.

Shortly afterwards, Philip II learned that Coligny was drawing up plans for an invasion of Flanders. His ambassador complained and threatened, and once more relations between France and Spain grew strained.

While the Queen of Navarre continued to procrastinate, the Admiral listened more and more willingly to the queen-mother's overtures. He did not give in without conditions, however: the man who was but the other day a rebel asked for a considerable share of his brother the Cardinal's former benefices, a hundred and fifty thousand *livres* in cash (over four hundred thousand pounds sterling today) to 'refurnish the château of Châtillon', and a seat on the council, as his price for taking up his place at court again. Catherine agreed to everything.

It was settled that His Majesty would go to Blois at the beginning of September and that there the Admiral would present himself, escorted, according to the old feudal custom, by a large company of gentlemen. The Duke of Montmorency and the Duke of Bouillon would precede him and would act as sureties for him. At the request of the Huguenots, ten companies of guards would be gathered in the town on the day of their chief's arrival.

The Guises left the court and retired to Joinville.

On 1st September, 1571, the king came to Blois, and immediately made many gestures of appeasement. On the 8th, in his mother's company, he received the brothers Contarini, the one the ordinary, the other the extraordinary, Venetian ambassador, who requested him most earnestly to ensure his glory and his salvation by joining the Christian League. With all the phrases and circumlocutions required by the long-established friendship between France and Venice, the king refused.

The next day, having had the exceptional honour of being invited to their Majesties' own table, Contarini reported the arrival of the Admiral to the Republic: the court awaited his arrival to make plans for the marriage of the Prince of Béarn (Bourbon); and it was widely rumoured that Coligny was also 'to confer with the king about a war with Spain by land and sea'.

Everything was in place. The curtain could now rise upon one of the most passionate tragedies that fate, unknown to all, had ever had the pleasure of making ready.

CHAPTER VII

THE CHARACTERS

AT FIFTY-TWO, a considerable age for a woman at that period, Catherine de' Medici still had all her remarkable bodily and mental strength. She was short, very stout and round: her eyes protruded from her pale, colourless face with its strong, carnivorous jaw: her hands and her feet were admirably delicate. Her look could terrify: her smile could be wonderfully seductive. Her voice still retained those Italian echoes that so delighted Francis I.

Before the court, the queen always affected good humour and serenity, but her nerves would often betray her when she received bad news. 'I know', wrote Correro, the Venetian ambassador, 'that more than once she has been found weeping in her closet; but she wipes her eyes directly and hides her sorrow, and in order to deceive those who judge of the state of affairs by the expression of her face, she shows herself in public with a calm and cheerful air.'

She had learned the value of a black dress from her old rival, Diane de Poitiers; and the world and posterity saw her in perpetual mourning. Yet this funereal aspect in no way corresponded to her real nature. The 'Florentine shopkeeper' was cheerful, talkative and even jolly; she loved ribald stories and broad jokes, amusements, hunting and good food. There was nothing studied or pompous about her. 'She walks so briskly', wrote Correro again, 'that nobody in the court can keep up with her. All this exercise keeps her in very good appetite. She eats a great deal and without discrimination; and the doctors say that this is the cause of the illnesses that sometimes bring her to the edge of death.'

She was a commanding figure, however, without any doubt—so commanding that her children never spoke to her first and were never able to throw off a kind of reverential awe in her presence. Commanding, like a matron sure of her power, her authority and her strength: not, said her detractors, like a 'great princess'. For

the arrogant nobility of France the Medici was always to have something of the middle class about her.

And indeed it is the middle class, the bourgeoisie, that her conduct calls to mind. Madame Catherine was the head of a family,
filled with a sense of her responsibilities as the guardian of the family
property; she did her utmost to keep the estate together and to protect it from unfaithful servants, from the cupidity of foreigners and
from all those people who were so eager to carve out a part of it for
themselves. She embraced her children with a possessive, commanding, jealous love: one of her great ambitions was to see them well
established. No one was a better housekeeper; and no one could
arrange such wonderful entertainments and feasts, in spite of the
unpromising times. No one was more careful of detail: she was continually to be seen 'leaving her room to go into an antechamber, a
corridor or her chapel, always talking, always moving, conversing
with some, greeting others'.

She had a most surprising capacity for work. 'Her industry', wrote
Correro, 'is a subject for astonishment; for nothing is done without
her knowledge, not even the merest trifle. She cannot eat or drink,
nor scarcely even sleep, without its being discussed.'

Her realism was bourgeois, too; and her practical common sense
and her occasionally cynical contempt for those ideologies that set
the world ablaze.

Neither the nobles nor the common people esteem these virtues in
their rulers. So Catherine was continually reproached with her birth,
her foreign way of thinking (foreign, the daughter of a Frenchwoman
from Auvergne, and brought up in France from the age of fourteen),
whereas they would never have done so had she been an Infanta of
Spain. The nation never forgave her for being 'born a private person,
quite unequal to the splendour of the realm'.

After an eleven years' reign filled with toil, the queen-mother
still remained incomprehensible to her subjects: she was therefore
still suspect. Her great ability in dissimulation, that sad fruit of her
married life, served her politically, but it prevented her from being
popular. The people were ignorant of both the anxieties and the true
nature of this princess who was 'good and kind to everybody and
who set herself to satisfy all those who appealed to her.' [1]

Of course, by this time the queen would no longer expose herself
to mockery as she had once done by begging the Constable to pardon

---

[1] Correro. (His dispatches, which have not yet been published, are in the
archives of Venice. They are quoted by Pierre Champion and Jean Héritier.)

a poacher. Many trials and the shocking example of the fierce men who surrounded her had hardened her. Her daughters, her maids of honour and her servants trembled before her. In the sixteenth century no ruler could afford to be sparing with punishments and executions. Catherine was very far from being as cruel as Philip II or Elizabeth, but she was capable of an unrestrained delight at hearing of an enemy's death. She could also look upon a still-quivering corpse without betraying any emotion. This had been observed at Amboise.

Yet rather than killing she still preferred the results of intrigue and stratagem, and of even less avowable proceedings. This inconsolable widow, unimpeachably virtuous, nevertheless prostituted the beauties of her Flying Squadron in order to hold dangerous characters in check. And her closet was the centre of an immense system of espionage.

Those she caught in her net cursed her and called her Madame Satan and Madame la Serpente. But as she could not control the ferocity of those between whom she had to act as arbiter, she could not possibly discard the weapons of weakness. She was 'a foreign, friendless woman . . . unable even to tell her friends from her enemies . . . crushed by the general terror, never hearing the truth'.[2]

Because she came from a country where the princes freely used poison, she had at that time a firm reputation as a poisoner—a reputation that has lasted. Did she in fact commit any secret crimes of this kind? History records no proof of a single one.

Her real poison was the one that had infected Catherine herself— the need to rule. This passion, which was curiously mixed with her love for her children, completely dominated and overcame her. She was not distracted from it by handsome men, as Elizabeth was: the thought of God never put the thought of abdication into her head, as it did into Philip's. Her passion was to rule, to negotiate, to supervise, to plot and to write, tirelessly going on and on. 'You feed on this labour,' Henry of Navarre said to her later, 'and you would not be able to live for long without it.'

Catherine was no more religious in the true sense of the word than her uncles Leo X and Clement VII, those half-pagan popes. But she was as superstitious as an Italian peasant-woman. She spent hours with astrologers and soothsayers, seeking encouragement from the stars, from cards and magic mirrors.

In this she showed herself a true Medici. She was a Medici too in

[2] Correro.

her use of magnificence as a means of government, in her squandering of her immense personal private fortune,[3] in the building of the Tuileries and Henry II's noble tomb, in her patronage of Ronsard, Philibert Delorme and Germain Pilon, the founding of museums and libraries and the unceasing collection of works of art.

Such, in 1571, was this princess of the Renaissance—a believer in fortune-tellers, a great ruler, an overwhelming, generous and tyrannical mother, a woman who loved peace and who was a weaver of astonishing plots.

The document in which she best reveals herself is the long letter in which she announces the death of Charles IX to her son, now Henry III: it contains a passionate cry which, coming from such a woman, is very striking. 'If I were to lose you, I should have myself buried alive in your grave.'

In this same letter she provides the new king with an admirable maxim—'Love the French people and do well by them, but never allow yourself to take sides.'

In his twentieth year Francis I was already preparing the political and military campaign that was to culminate in the triumph of Marignano. Charles IX knew this. He was the same age, and he too longed to win glory.

At a first glance one might have thought him capable of it. He was an uncommonly vigorous young man, and at rest his face showed virility and frankness—a somewhat quizzical frankness. He already looked as though he might be thirty, and in his features could be seen something of his father—that obstinate, melancholy look that had marked Henry II since his return from the Spanish prisons in which he had spent his sad childhood. And these features common to both had already been made more pronounced in the son by a life quite filled with stormy emotion.

The king lacked neither head nor heart. He was interested in business and he was already beginning to understand it. As a pupil of Amyot he was happy in literate company; he liked Ronsard and could himself turn a graceful verse. The immense energy he had inherited from his mother, and which in Catherine was devoted to the conduct of the state, found release in the immoderate pursuit of violent exercise. All day long he hunted the stag, the wolf and the

---

[3] She left debts to the extent of eight hundred thousand crowns, which had to be paid by the treasury of Henry IV, her enemy.

bear, hammered iron until his arms almost dropped off and blew the horn until he nearly burst.

It seemed that the French might find in him the prince they had longed for, the warrior who would restore the tarnished glory of the Valois. But alas, there were cruel facts behind this outward show. His Medici ancestry handicapped Charles IX with grave physical and mental defects. The king was tubercular. Furthermore, he suffered from a lack of balance that showed itself in fits of mad fury and a love for sadistic games (before ever Sade was born) as well as a taste for blood. In hunting, he hardly ever used fire-arms, but rather chose the delight of plunging his blade into the living flesh. Nothing amused him more than beating his companions with a stirrup-leather or running about his capital with a mask on, making himself an active nuisance to the passers-by.

This violent young man, infuriated by his own weakness, wished ardently to take action, and to be free at last from his mother's apron-strings.

'After God, he acknowledged no one as he acknowledged me,' wrote Catherine after his death. His feelings for his mother were compounded of love, admiration and fear. And of resentment. Resentment at the too-obvious preference for Henry of Anjou, resentment at the crushing tutelage that was destroying his own personality.

He had been married to the gentle and charming Elizabeth of Austria, the Emperor's daughter, a year before. He did not believe this shy young woman capable of resisting the dominance of her terrible mother-in-law, and he kept his Protestant mistress, Marie Touchet: she came of a modest background, and as she did not belong to the court she escaped the queen-mother's pressure. With her, as with his old nurse, the kind Nanon—a Protestant too—he found tenderness, consolation and peace: he believed that he also found himself.

As soon as he had left adolescence behind, the Duke of Anjou had reached extraordinary heights. Nature and fate had lavished upon him all the gifts that had been so sparingly meted out to his brother: beauty, charm, an unusually acute intelligence, an 'eager and lively spirit', eloquence, courage, popularity and the glory of a 'favourite of Mars and of fortune'. He was already that indefinable character, full of contrasts, who was to become one of the greatest kings of France as well as the least understood and the most execrated.

Henry had shown genuine military qualities, and the Spanish ambassador wrote that he was 'very much of a maiden'. He loved fighting, he fenced brilliantly, and he wasted whole days with the chatter and the childish games of the maids of honour. In council he showed a precocious wisdom, and he wore extraordinary ornaments. He was devout to the point of mysticism and he sometimes thought of retiring to a monastery; but debauchery had already shaken his frail constitution.

'Too sensitive to charm and grace', he possessed the artistic tastes of the Medici to the highest degree; he 'sought the beautiful and the true'; he aspired to happiness. None of this prevented him from having the bloodthirsty instincts of his family. In his heart there was a moving struggle between the man of genius that he was capable of being (and was to become, at the end of his short life) and the neurotic subject to hereditary defects.

Monsieur was violently ambitious, and he found it very hard to yield to a brother whom he despised. The Reformation had fascinated him when he was a child, and it is possible that he had once thought of putting himself at the head of the Huguenots. Circumstance decided otherwise. He was now head of the Catholics and, thanks to his mother, the possessor of a considerable measure of power. A precarious possession, however, for the king's hatred would burst out on the smallest pretext. Once the prince had had to rush from his brother's room, the king's dagger being already out of its sheath.

The Duke of Nevers, his experienced and trusted adviser, had not long before counselled him to let Charles 'rage without interrupting him', to make use of him, to take the weight of business from his shoulders without seeming so to do, to rule him without his knowing it, and so become the real master. But Charles was now thinking of freeing himself, and this policy seemed useless. Unless a foreign crown should offer—and he did not find the prospect attractive— Henry would have to seek other ways.

He had no personal animosity for the Protestants. 'So long as there is no necessity for calling them traitors and punishing them as such,' the Duke of Nevers told him, 'you should order your behaviour for the greater glory of God.' But it was Catholic fanaticism that gave him his opportunity, and his impassioned devotion was well adapted to it.

During that decisive autumn, no one could be unaware of the fact that, of Henry II's sons, the Duke of Anjou alone possessed the makings of a statesman. The foreign ambassadors therefore watched his slightest movement. And Coligny himself, thinking of the past, wondered whether he would not rather have the duke than an unstable king as the mainstay of his great project.

Catherine de' Medici had already lost five of her children. Her second daughter, Claude, was Duchess of Lorraine. The third, Marguerite, then engaged to the Prince of Béarn, had been living at the court for two years, and she had already caused a great deal of trouble.

Brantôme had given her the highest praise as a princess 'versed in learning, both sacred and profane, and delighted by books . . . most eloquent and beautifully spoken in her high, grave conversation, but also charmingly graceful in her kind and pleasant wit'. He was enraptured by her 'perfect beauty . . . together with such a carriage and so high a majesty that she would always be taken for a goddess from the skies rather than for an earthly princess'. She was, in fact, a pretty brunette who often wore blonde wigs, who had a wanton eye, a disturbing bosom and the famous Medici face.

As soon as she left the dismal castle of Amboise, where she had spent her childhood, she dazzled her elder brother, and in her turn was dazzled by the younger. What is one to think of the games and the quarrels of this disturbing trio? When she was middle-aged, Marguerite said that she had been the mistress of both the boys. There is no doubt that both displayed an excessive jealousy in regard to her and until she fell in love with the good-looking Henri de Guise she pushed Monsieur's interest with the utmost fervour.

Her affair with Guise was a hidden, mysterious and passionate idyll. Anjou discovered it. Mad with fury, he denounced the guilty couple to the queen-mother. Catherine was shocked by the idea that Guise might claim a daughter of France in marriage—which was, in fact, at the back of the Cardinal of Lorraine's mind. The unfortunate Margot was called to her mother's room in the middle of the night: she found Charles IX there in his nightshirt: he left her for dead, stretched on the carpet.

His Majesty then commanded the Bastard of Angoulême to shoot her lover down with an arquebus during a hunting-party. Guise was warned in time, and made his escape.

This adventure was to have political repercussions. The young duke married very quickly and kept himself quiet. The Cardinal of

Lorraine was sent as envoy to Rome, in an honourable exile. For a time the encroaching tribe was eclipsed.

Margot, having almost died of sorrow, consoled herself for her lost love with commendable promptitude. A new slave appeared in the person of her youngest brother, François, Duke of Alençon. She treated this brother too with an ambiguous sort of kindness, in spite of his discouraging appearance—for he was a woolly-headed, flat-nosed, negroid freak. He was the most ill-made of the royal children, and his soul was as ugly as his body. Alençon, browbeaten by his mother and despised by the whole court except his sister, counted for nothing. And yet those who contemplated a third force between the Catholic and the Protestant extremists were already looking to him.

Furthermore, Catherine did not hesitate to put him forward as a fiancé for the Queen of England, in the place of the Duke of Anjou. Elizabeth took care not to make a definite reply: one of her means of reigning and of remaining on the throne was to keep matrimonial hope alive in every court of Europe. For thirteen years on end the possibility of her marriage with the most regrettable of the Valois was a matter for speculation.

In comparison with these degenerate youths, Henri de Guise seemed a demi-god. This fair-haired, blue-eyed, athletic young man had so far shone less brilliantly on the field of battle than in ladies' boudoirs, but the combination of his name and ceaseless propaganda had earned him the love of the Catholic masses, particularly in Paris.

He possessed neither the military genius of Duke François, his father, nor the formidable guile of his uncle the cardinal. His splendid appearance masked many weaknesses. So far he had accomplished nothing, but he was nevertheless a person of great importance. By his mother, Anne d'Este, the grand-daughter of Louis XII and Anne of Brittany, he was descended from Saint Louis and a close relation of the king. Both Carolingian and Capetian blood flowed in his veins.

His family worked for him as industriously as a hive of bees. The measureless wealth of his uncle, who had become practically the only bishop in France, was at his command, and it assured him supporters at every social level.

Guise was the focus of all the unbounded hopes that this family had entertained these thirty years past—hopes that Duke François had only partially realised. Like Charles IX and like Anjou, he sought glory and power: he longed to make his name illustrious.

Among these three young men of twenty there existed a spirit of rivalry which would have had a certain nobility, had it not contained the threat of so much misfortune.

Guise had the advantage of a totally uncompromised and unambiguous position: he was a passionate defender of the Church and the Catholic King's favourite; moreover he longed to revenge himself upon Coligny for the assassination of his father. In the meantime he too gave himself up to love and to intrigue.

Such were the players of the chief roles on the Catholic side. Behind them moved a whole world of extras—great nobles, proud and headstrong, preoccupied with their duels and their pleasures; Italian ministers who did their best to ensure the continuity of the royal administration, the Delilahs of the Flying Squadron, astrologers, buffoons and hired assassins.

The unity of the Catholic party was almost at an end. A group of men were gathering round the Duke of Montmorency, the Constable's son, and the Marshal de Cossé-Brissac: these were what we would now call the moderates—at that time they were known as the *Politiques*—for religious fanaticism did not blind them to the horrors of civil war. Had this third force been formed earlier it might perhaps have allowed the queen-mother to avert the worst. In the final analysis it was to triumph; but this would not happen for a quarter of a century. For the moment they only added to the confusion.

And in the background there were the obscure people who were not, however, to be mere supernumeraries: the army of monks and preachers fiercely demanding the extermination of the heretics; the innumerable agents of the Guises, pouring out money, storing weapons in the hidden places of monasteries, making secret contacts, weaving the web of the powerful organisation that was presently to come into the open under the name of the League; the townsfolk and their para-military formations; students eager for the fray, brawlers yapping at the heels of the Huguenots, the dangerous mob of beggars, capable of starting a riot.

It was this court riddled with conflicting interests and this dangerous, excitable populace that Coligny had to face when, leaving his fortresses, he came to guide France towards a new future.

The Admiral appears on the scene already clothed in such a light that it is difficult to judge him objectively. He had transformed a religious minority, apparently doomed to the sword and the stake, into an armed party so formidable that the crown was obliged to treat with it as between power and power. This prodigious feat had earned him the devotion of some, the bitter hatred of others and the more or less open admiration of all.

Gaspard de Châtillon, at fifty-two, had none of that patriarchal air that a certain kind of tradition lends him. He had just married an extremely rich widow, Jacqueline de Montbel, who had loved him without seeing him and who had loved him even more after their meeting: Jeanne de Laval had been dead for three years.

Coligny was a tall man, grave, calm and imposing; he had a most noble air, and called to mind his uncle the Constable by his bluffness, his direct manner of speaking, without subtlety (he also stammered a little), his strictness and his little eccentricities. Just as Montmorency used to run the beads of his rosary through his fingers at important moments, so the Admiral chewed on a toothpick, which became legendary. People had said 'God preserve us from the Constable's paternosters': they now said 'God preserve us from the Admiral's toothpick'.

His grey beard, his old-fashioned clothes and his austerity seemed a reproof to the young, noisy and profligate nobles, covered with jewels and feathers. No one would have believed that he himself had begun his career as a courtier: and yet it was the standing of his uncle and the anxiety of a royal mistress to keep the balance between Henry II's favourites that had made of him colonel-general of the infantry before he was thirty, and, shortly afterwards, Admiral of France and governor of the Ile-de-France.

The wars with the House of Austria had given him the opportunity of competing brilliantly with François de Guise; but his turn of mind was political rather than military. The surrender of Saint-Quentin showed this very clearly. He had defended the fortress like a hero until the battle of Saint Lawrence's day destroyed all hope. He then made no attempt at the final resistance that his soldiers had expected, but was the first to surrender in the breach that he was defending—a breach that no Spaniard had yet mounted. He gave up his sword and at the same time he told his men to point him out, so that there should be no unfortunate misunderstanding—with the result that the Duke of Savoy most insultingly hesitated to believe that he was in fact Coligny.[4]

It was certainly not from cowardice that the Constable's nephew had acted thus, but from policy: if he had vanished, the Guises would

[4] See his *Discours* on the defence of Saint-Quentin.

have become far too powerful. On the other hand, it cannot be said that he had any interested motive when he adopted Calvinism; and this is his principal title to glory at a time when the ambition of great men was only too easily hidden behind the mask of religion. In 1561 the Nuncio bore witness to the fact that unique among the Protestant lords, the Admiral did not subordinate his faith to his political schemes.

In these two respects, Coligny was completely different from the other men of his class and his period: he was upright (though not disinterested, as may be seen from the conditions that he insisted upon before returning to the king); and he was attached to principles alone, without regard for persons and in contempt of that empiricism which was the Medici's only rule. But unhappily for him, and unhappily for his country, these principles were most tragically opposed to one another.

He was a zealous Calvinist: he was loyal to his king: he was deeply concerned for his country's glory. For many years Coligny tried his best to reconcile these three feelings. It was for this reason that Catherine put such trust in him and brought him into her government. It was this that caused him to remain outside the 'tumult' of Amboise and to blame the violent schemes of Monsieur le Prince so often.

But alas, when the civil war broke out in 1562, he found that he was forced to choose between the cause of his religion and the cause of his country. It has been claimed that he had a doctrine whereby the disgusting clauses of the Treaty of Hampton Court could be justified; but this doctrine has so little validity that the Admiral asserted that the fault lay in the Vidame de Chartres, his envoy, who had exceeded his powers.

However that may have been, no casuistry can change this fact: the Admiral of France, governing the town of Le Havre for the king, surrendered it to the English and gave them reason to hope for Calais, Dieppe and Rouen too. He thus rendered his country as vulnerable as it had been in Charles VII's day. And he thus gave an appalling example to the chiefs of the other side, who, while they had certainly never declined a Spanish subsidy, had never yet dared to give away a part of the realm. He had made the choice between his loyalty and his faith.

'A comparison of the queen-mother's correspondence with that of the Admiral for the last days of 1562, January, 1563, and the first weeks of February, silences all argument: Catherine thought only of France, Coligny only of the interests of his party. He presumed to write to the Queen of England on 24th January that he expected his chief help and comfort, after God, from her, knowing that she had virtue and divine succour, and that God had chosen and preserved her against the present time to give her this chance to set up and re-establish the purity of His worship and to destroy idolatry throughout Christianity and even in France. Catherine, on the contrary, was for the nation, and desired national peace. From that time onwards, Coligny sacrificed his patriotism to his religious fervour.' [5]

More than once the Admiral was to try to alter the past or at least to avoid some of the consequences of his agreement with the foreigners. One of the reasons why he was so much in favour of war with Philip II was that this would allow him to serve France again— an admirable servant, an incorruptible minister, a great coloniser, a most accomplished administrator: the prototype, according to Brantôme, of the humanist man of action.

His military talents cannot be so highly praised. Gaspard de Coligny was never a fortunate commander; and his was the direct responsibility for the disaster of Jarnac and the death of Condé. He was also beaten at Moncontour. War might provide him with his revenge for the defeat.

It is one of history's tragic ironies that circumstances should have made a rebel, a rebel under sentence of death, out of this great officer of the crown, who loathed disorder, who had the pilferers of his army hanged and who never compromised. He is more easily imagined as a fierce representative of the royal authority than as the devastator of 1568 or 1570, methodically sacking conquered territory, destroying churches, executing captured garrisons—and all this while proclaiming his horror of useless cruelty.

The scrupulousness that was always active in his Protestant conscience upheld the political reasoning that made a Franco-Spanish war entirely necessary in the Admiral's opinion. If he could lead the king's armies into Flanders to co-operate with his insurgent fellow-Protestants, he would at last have resolved the contradictions within himself, and he would have put his valour at the service of an undivided ideal.

[5] Jean Héritier, *Catherine de Médicis*, p. 337.

PART 2

The Web of Circumstance

CHAPTER I

'WE ARE TOO OLD TO DECEIVE ONE ANOTHER'

ON 11TH SEPTEMBER, 1571, the queen-mother's over-hearty appetite gave her one of her usual fits of indigestion. And as both Monsieur and the Duke of Alençon had also taken to their beds with a fever, the watchful ambassadors thought that some play was being acted— a play full of meaning. But they were wrong.

The Admiral reached Blois on the 12th with fifty gentlemen in his train. A dense crowd watched him go into the castle. While the procession mounted the stairs someone asked, 'To the king's chamber?'

'No,' replied Coligny. 'To the queen-mother's.'

Marshal de Cossé and his son ushered him in. Catherine de' Medici was lying down. In her alcove there were the king, his queen, Madame Marguerite, the Cardinal of Bourbon [1] and the Duke of Montpensier. [2]

Coligny bowed deeply to the king. He was very pale. Charles became paler still and he remained motionless, overcome by a flood of conflicting emotions. Once more the Admiral bowed. This time the young sovereign raised him up and embraced him, while to the intense vexation of those standing by, the former rebel whispered something in his ear.

Turning towards the bed, the Admiral then bowed to the queen-mother. It was a moving encounter. Twelve years earlier these two, such unusual beings and so unlike one another, had thought that they were in sympathy. They had worked together to appease and reconcile the nation; they had worked for the well-being of the state. Then in a few months they found themselves poles apart and presently mortal enemies. Catherine was certain that Gaspard de

---

[1] A Catholic, brother of Anthony of Navarre and the Prince of Condé.
[2] Chief of a Catholic branch of the Bourbons.

Coligny had planned to have her assassinated, 'dispatched', as she put it, writing to her sister-in-law the Duchess of Savoy, in January, 1563.

Six years later she had had him condemned to death, and being unable to bring him to the scaffold, charged the 'king's killer', Maurevert, with his execution. Maurevert made an error, and Monsieur de Mouy died instead of Coligny, who had already been put to death in effigy.[3]

Was it possible to crase such memories? Catherine seemed to be trying to do so as she smiled very sweetly; but she did not give the expected kiss of peace. She made a gesture towards the queen, her daughter-in-law. Coligny, according to etiquette, knelt and endeavoured to kiss the hem of her robe. Elizabeth of Austria drew back, blushing deeply: the touch of a heretic seemed to her intolerable.

The Admiral then visited the Duke of Anjou and the Duke of Alençon. Nothing is known of his interview with the young prince who had defeated him at Jarnac and at Moncontour except that it must have been exceedingly courteous, for each intended to behave with tact towards the other.

The next day the Protestant leader, behaving as if he had never left the court, appeared at the king's levée, at dinner and supper, and even accompanied the king to mass. The past 'was buried in a deep forgetfulness', wrote the Contarini brothers.

The queen-mother's indisposition continued, and she did not leave her rooms. This allowed the Admiral many conversations with Charles IX, and the astonished courtiers watched the grey head bent over the anxious young face of the king in the royal chair.

In a few days the game was won. Charles IX let himself be conquered. He was finding a strength that would help him to escape from his mother's domination; and he, who had lost his father at the age of eight and who had been under a woman's rule since then, was discovering the comfort of a manly authority.

'Father,' he said.

Catherine, still unwell, showed no displeasure. She offered no opposition to the Admiral's attending all the councils, nor, at the

---

[3] It was universally accepted in the sixteenth century that the king had an absolute right to deal thus with a man who, as supreme judge, he had been unable to reach in any other way. As we have seen, Charles IX tried to employ this means against Henri de Guise: Louis XIII was to do so against Concini. The king's killer therefore fulfilled a legal function, like an executioner.

end of a week, to his acting as prime minister. 'The Admiral is governing,' wrote Don Francès de Alava, who also feared the return of Michel de L'Hospital. As the heretic went by, with his pockets full of petitions, he was surrounded by suitors. There were rumours of a new office that would set him higher than the marshals. Perhaps he would even be made Constable.

However, the king did not alter his manner of living. He hunted all day, came back exhausted and staggered off to bed. To his mother's reproaches he answered, 'I have still two years of my youth left—two years of freedom.'

With the queen-mother ill and Monsieur in a state of expectancy, the Admiral had the benefit of something like a vacancy of power. First he took in hand the application of the Treaty of Saint-Germain. A mixed commission was formed and charged with the interpretation of the controversial articles: it was to draw up a document which, fulfilling the hopes of the nation, would be 'the efficient contract for the tranquillity of the realm'. Montmorency, Cossé, Morvillier and the new Keeper of the Seals, Birague, sat on the Catholic side, and the Admiral, La Noue, Téligny, Briquemaut and Cavaignes on the Protestant.

People wondered whether some collision might not take place when the queen-mother became her usual active self again. But not at all. The Medici too displayed a kindness for her former enemy that shocked Alava. 'We are too old to deceive one another,' said the good lady, affectionately.

'A week ago', wrote Don Francès to the Duke of Alba on 5th October, 'he [Coligny] came into the queen-mother's apartments just as she was beginning to hear mass. The Admiral bowed to her, without taking any notice of the altar. He leant on a bench opposite her, keeping his hat on, and he waited for the end of the mass, without, however, troubling to rise at the elevation of the Host. The queen said to him, with a laugh, after the service, "It seems that you take care to hear our mass?" The Admiral replied, "Madame, I can very well see and hear the mass without it doing any harm!" '

Three days later the ambassador, still more disturbed, reported that the austere Huguenot had played tennis for a long time with the king; and worse still, perhaps, 'that he was trying to win over the Duke of Anjou by kindness'.

The English were equally uneasy, for there was question of the removal of the Protestant garrison of La Rochelle.

Full of zeal, the commission finished its work in a month, having in most points satisfied the reformists. The king ordered the stone cross with an insulting inscription that stood on the site of Philippe de Gastines' house to be removed to the cemetery of the Holy Innocents: Gastines had been hanged for having a Huguenot meeting in his house, and the parliament had caused the cross to be set up.

The decay of the royal power now became evident. The parliament refused to annul its decree, and the Provost of Paris declared himself incompetent in the matter. Finally, the king was told that the demolition could not be carried out for want of money, and the matter was held over indefinitely, in spite of the Admiral's insistence.

Catherine begged the Tuscan ambassador to speak to Téligny in order to diminish the Protestants' continued lack of confidence—a state aggravated by this incident. She flattered herself, moreover, that a genuine harmony would be brought about by the marriage of her daughter and the Prince of Béarn.

But this marriage was still remote. It could not take place without a dispensation, and Pius V showed a firm resolution not to grant one. The General of the Jesuits even tried to induce the King of Portugal to ask for Marguerite's hand. On 5th October the Nuncio Caiazzo had a somewhat disagreeable interview with the sovereigns. He was obliged to face the facts: nothing would make them give up the Huguenot marriage, even if it meant doing without the dispensation, in the last resort. One hope remained, and this was the persistent opposition of the Queen of Navarre.

Jeanne d'Albret was indeed very far from pleased, and she continually brought up objections. 'She did not choose to be gulled,' she said to Monsieur de Biron, 'like those who had gone to the court before her and who had there obtained none of those things that they had been promised.' She wanted to be given back her town of Lectoure, which was still held by the royal troops. Her conscience would not allow her to tolerate Catholics either in her train or in that of her son.

Henri de Bourbon—Henry of Navarre—who was then aged eighteen, was even more unwilling. This highlander, brought up among the peasants of Béarn, whose rough and cheerful ways were his, this Nimrod, this pursuer of country wenches, had not the least desire to marry the pearl of the Valois. For her part, Marguerite was no less repelled by the prospect of a yokel, so utterly unlike the splendid Henri de Guise or the exquisite Henry of Anjou.

All this would have been of no importance whatever if only

Catholics and Protestants had at last let their hatred die away: but alas, no such idea ever crossed their minds.

At this point there was a remarkable attempt at relieving the tension by authority. As soon as he woke up, Charles IX would ask for his 'good friend', his 'good lord', his 'father', the Admiral, and discuss matters with him for hours on end. He swore to have the Edict of Pacification, a corollary to the Treaty of Saint-Germain, strictly enforced, and ordered the preparations for his sister's marriage to be begun. On his side, Coligny applied himself to the most difficult problems of the government, and even to financial questions. The crown had a revenue of fifteen million *livres* (about forty-three million pounds sterling today), and its debts amounted to twice this sum. The Admiral asserted that he had discovered a way of making up the deficit without touching the goods of the clergy and without oppressing the people.

By the time the Duke of Alençon's smallpox caused the sudden dispersal of the court, great hopes might well have been justified if only the spirit of conciliation of the rulers had been able to reach the mass of the people.

On All Souls' Day the king, already undressed, was just going to bed, when astonishing news came to banish all thought of sleep from his mind. On 11th October just past, the Papal, Spanish and Venetian fleets, under Don John of Austria, had destroyed the immense naval power of the Sultan at Lepanto. This meant that Philip II was master of the Mediterranean; that the road to Constantinople and Jerusalem was open; and that a second opportunity was open to the Catholic King to obtain complete supremacy in Europe, as he had had after the battle of Saint-Quentin.

For the court of France, said the Nuncio, it was 'a blow on the head'; but there was a noisy pretence of delight, and thanksgiving processions were held in all the principal towns.

Alvise Contarini asked for an audience of their Majesties: he said that France should now break the Turkish alliance and join the Christian League in order to counterbalance Spain within it and to restrain her advance. Circumstances would then allow magnificent marriages for the brothers and the sister of the king, as well as the destruction of the Huguenot party and the end of civil war.

These views were diametrically opposed to those of the queen-mother, who dreaded nothing so much as having a Hispano-Guisard government imposed upon her by the Catholic extremists. Far from wishing to strengthen the Christian League, she was thinking of breaking it up by bringing Venice and the Turk together. But the time had not yet come for her to disclose her plan.

The king and his mother therefore expressed their joy to the Venetian ambassador, to whom Charles IX presented a gold ring, warmly congratulating the Most Serene Republic without mentioning the Pope, the Catholic King or Don John of Austria. France, alas, could not undertake foreign engagements before her domestic peace was re-established. When the marriage of Madame Marguerite had made harmony certain, perhaps his Majesty could think of the ambassador's proposals.

The disappointed Venetian went at once to the Duke of Anjou, whom he found much displeased by Don John's laurels. He urged him to win immortal glory by taking the lead in the great expedition that would certainly follow the battle of Lepanto. The good Catholics thought of him as a hero: they would undoubtedly place their hope in him if the king were to be so misled as to leave the Church. Thus the good apostle took his part too in adding to the kingdom's discord.

Henry did not commit himself. At the council he upheld the Venetian policy, but without arousing the least enthusiasm or agreement. France had exceedingly few ships and indeed when the Turkish fleet was lost, so was hers. It was a disaster. Fortunately Philip II still refused to profit by his victories. He no more exploited this of Lepanto than he had that of Saint-Quentin. Seeing that he made no move, both Catherine and Coligny heaved a sigh of relief.

In fact the Catholic King was not looking in the direction of Constantinople at all, but towards London, where Elizabeth had ostentatiously brought Norfolk, Mary Stuart's unfortunate champion, to his trial. In concert with Pius V, he determined to oblige the Valois to take up a definite position. A papal legate, Cardinal Alessandrino, was sent to bring pressure to bear, to show His Most Christian Majesty how scandalous was his inactivity in the struggle against the heretics and the infidels, and to incite him to a move in favour of the unhappy Queen of Scots. It was, in reality, a question of concluding a great alliance against England.

Elizabeth countered this very quickly. She also sent an ambassador extraordinary, her secretary of state Sir Thomas Smith, with the task of forming a coalition opposed to the House of Austria and consisting of France, England, the Beggars and the Protestant princes of Germany. As a final allurement, Sir Thomas was to speak plainly about the marriage of the Virgin of the West with François of Alençon.

It seemed that the decisive hour had come. Coligny rejoiced, unlike the queen-mother, who was thoroughly alarmed by this state of affairs. The Florentine's enemies pointed out the unworthy reason for her fear—a straightforward attacking policy would prevent her from dividing in order to rule. They pretended to forget that an attacking policy calls for a strong state behind it, and that only by perpetually tacking to and fro could a divided France hope to remain independent.

At this point a curious scandal broke out. Catherine's agents informed her of certain dispatches which proved the Spanish ambassador's subversive activities. He was writing letters to the Holy See which described the queen-mother in the most atrocious terms. He had worked out a plan for the invasion of France, and at the same time he had prepared an insurrection. Not content with lavishing his master's gold upon the extremists, he urged on the Guisards—the supporters and followers of the Guises—in the organisation of the Catholic Holy League, a body of an extraordinary degree of complexity.

Although she was suffering cruelly from sciatica, Catherine summoned Don Francès and demanded an explanation. The hidalgo, who had just let off a splendid firework display in honour of Lepanto, haughtily denied everything. But the restrained voice and the heavy eye of the Medici had terrified his Catholic Majesty's ambassador exceedingly, and the next day, wearing a mask, he fled in the direction of Flanders, without pausing to observe any of the forms of protocol.[4]

At about the same time the Admiral, after strenuous argument, overcame the Queen of Navarre's reluctance. The situation was favouring the Protestants.

Jeanne d'Albret was to leave her dominions on 20th November, but on the 18th, wrote Biron, 'she took some pills for a cold that had affected her teeth and the whole of the right side of her head; and these pills did little until the next day, when she had as it were a looseness of the bowels, together with a high fever'.

Then Henri de Bourbon had a fall from his horse, hurt himself

---

[4] Later he claimed that he had run the risk of being poisoned. This is one of the stories that created the indestructible legend of Catherine de' Medici, the Poisoner. Cf. Pierre Champion, *Catherine de Médicis présente à Charles IX son Royaume*, p. 437, and *Le Jeunesse d'Henri III*, p. 12 et seqq.

seriously and spat blood. In spite of these warnings, the queen, having decided to leave her son in Béarn, began her slow journey to court. 'May God be pleased so to guide my actions that they may redound to His glory,' she wrote to Monsieur de Caumont.

This was a striking success for Catherine, for Coligny and for the cause of domestic peace—that peace which the young king longed for so fervently, but which, alas, seemed degrading to the greater part of the French nation.

CHAPTER II

'THE ROPE IS BEING PULLED
TO THE BREAKING-POINT'

'WITHOUT PARIS, nothing of consequence can be done,' observed the envoy of the Grand Duke of Tuscany. Paris was to give a violent demonstration of its state of mind.

The Admiral attached a symbolic importance to that cross of Gastines whose destruction had been laid down by the Treaty of Saint-Germain. So did the Parisians. In December, the Comte de Retz (Gondi) provided the necessary money and the king ordered the work to be put in hand at once.

It did not go far. The crowd put the workmen to flight, filled up the foundations prepared at the cemetery of the Holy Innocents and then attacked three Huguenot houses in the neighbourhood.

The king was furious, and he bitterly reproached the provost, Marcel, who in spite of being a friend of the queen-mother was also a supporter of the Guises. Charles IX reiterated his command, and on his side the Duke of Anjou urgently called for the monument to be moved. The angry Catholics stood on guard about it. 'The cross of Paris is still defended against the attacks that are made upon it,' wrote Aguilon exultantly to Philip II. Aguilon was the secretary to whom Don Francès had entrusted the embassy.

And the Venetian ambassador Sigismond Cavalli, the Contarinis' successor, wrote, 'The beginning [of the tumult] is such that unless it is dealt with very quickly, the Catholics may one day commit a fine massacre [bella occisione], being incomparably more numerous in the city and being quite determined not to allow the cross to be taken from the spot.'

A riot broke out on 17th December and got beyond control. Other houses belonging to Calvinists were pillaged and burnt. But on the 18th the king's artillery appeared on the Place de Grève, and under its protection the insulting cross at last disappeared.

The king had had the last word. But for all that he had been warned that his capital would never accept either tolerance or a policy guided by the Protestants.

Storm clouds gathered from all sides. For the first time the Admiral, strengthened by his success, definitely suggested war to Charles IX. The young man asked for time before he gave his answer: he had to consult the queen, his mother. Coligny's composure left him. 'These are not matters,' he said, 'that one discusses with women, nor with priests.'

This was a challenge to his old enemy. It was also an extremely unwise move, just at this moment when the Guises were beginning to stir, and when, under the pretext of defending themselves against Duke François' murderer, they were gathering their supporters. One of their captains, La Valette, had already clashed with a group of Huguenots, and a positive battle had ensued.

Occurrences of this kind rendered the poor sovereign, who so longed to restore peace and harmony, quite desperate. Particularly as the ending of the troubles would so markedly have diminished his brother's importance.

After his first skirmish with Catherine, Coligny retired to his estates, leaving the king's heart full of anxiety. Charles now regularly and earnestly took his seat at the council: and afterwards he hunted furiously in the frost-whitened forest. His zeal in running down wild animals satisfied the ferocity for which he was not perhaps wholly responsible; and his hunting fulfilled that part of his nature that might have made him worthy of his ancestors.

Of his own accord, he sent a messenger to the Guises, still buried in the country, asking them to come back, 'to make things up'. He, the king, would act as peacemaker between them and the Châtillons. The Cardinal of Lorraine, who had returned from Rome, begged to be excused: he was well aware that his presence at court would not have the desired effect. But his nephew the duke would come—somewhat later, however; perhaps for Christmas.

Presently it became known that Guise was preparing for his journey by getting a small army together. When he heard this, Coligny summoned five hundred horsemen belonging to his party. The unfortunate Charles was obliged to forbid either the one or the other to move without his orders. And so Penelope's web was unwoven again, and everything was back where it had been in 1570.

Francis I's grandson did not feel himself master in his own house. Snares and pitfalls beset him on every side. The papers of Don

Francès de Alava had revealed the plots of which the Duke of Anjou was the centre. The Nuncio too wrote that Monsieur was the chief support of Catholicism in France, and that it was necessary to be ready to support him, should the king lose his crown.

In the whirl of parties and feasts that the court always allowed itself in spite of the shortage of money, the courtiers watched the two brothers: they were like a pair of swashbucklers, just on the point of drawing.

The fierce Charles IX was nevertheless an ingenuous young man. He had in his service an officer named Lignerolles who used to read him the chronicles of France, and who always emphasised the parts where the monarchs had avenged some insult to their crown. This greatly pleased the restless king, and filled him with confidence in this 'great and noble-hearted' man, as Brantôme, who was also the fellow's dupe, called him.

Here Charles made an error. He committed a still graver one when he 'gave' Lignerolles to the Duke of Anjou, hoping thus to place an observer in the enemy's camp. For the cunning Lignerolles was able to win Henry's favour, and he took care to flatter the prince's ambition. He incited him to claim 'the share in the government that was his due', and then reported to the king the dangerous dreams of his younger brother.

This was more than was needed to bring the hatred of the two brothers to the boiling-point. Catherine took fright. Once again, everything seemed to be overwhelming her at once—her continual lack of health, the dangerous diplomatic situation, the renewal of the troubles, the treasury reduced to two millions. Was a war of the Atridae between her sons going to be added to all this?

The queen suspected Lignerolles. She intercepted his letters and in them found proof that the villain was betraying both princes impartially, and that he was perhaps thinking of a military plot as well.

When he was shown the evidence, Charles roared blasphemies and swore to have the culprit put to death. Catherine took him at his word, and had Lignerolles killed by her guards. The execution was almost public; it took place just outside the royal gate, by way of an example.

The king doubled his guards.

It was into this atmosphere of tragedy that Sir Thomas Smith came to open negotiations between England and France. The ambassadors of the Catholic powers outdid one another in guile to find out what they were about. Presently the important advantages offered to France in the event of a war against Spain became known: four million a year, an alliance with Denmark and several German princes, and the annexation of the greater part of Flanders.

Charles's mind was disturbed by all this. He was shown the undoubted necessity of breaking the hold in which the House of Austria was trying to strangle his kingdom; his grandfather was held up as an example; it was proposed that he should increase his dominions in a manner that would make his reign famous to all posterity.

But Catherine suspected that her 'gossip' was playing a double game. The Spaniards and the Venetians had wind of it too. The perspicacious Aguilon wrote to his master, 'There is nothing that would suit England less than for the French to gain a footing in the Low Countries'. Cavalli was aware that Elizabeth had made known to Philip II her intention of preserving 'the four hundred years of peace that had been observed between Burgundy and England'. He added, 'The English are seeking the closest possible union with France, nevertheless they still wish to keep in with the Spaniards, for they do not yet count the friendship of the French as very sure.'

And then did not their poverty prevent the Valois from thinking of great undertakings?

Yet, to the general surprise, a fleet of thirty ships was assembled at Bordeaux, under the command of Strozzi, a cousin of the Medicis. Was it intended to attack Spain? Or was it one of those distant expeditions, the Admiral's delight, bound for China, the Cape of Good Hope or the Straits of Magellan?

The queen-mother gave the Nuncio the official version of the conversations between France and England. It was a question of a *rapprochement* between the countries, of course, or more exactly of a reconciliation: there was nothing that should make the Catholic King uneasy. Naturally, marriage had been discussed. The Queen of England had to be treated tactfully, after the refusal of Monsieur, and it was for this reason that the Duke of Alençon was asking for her hand.

But the chief subject of debate had been Mary Stuart, that 'walking conspiracy'. The king had intervened on behalf of his sister-in-law, and she had been promised her life so long as she would abstain from intrigue—a point upon which there was a good deal of scepticism, for was not the Queen of Scots Philip II's best weapon against the barely legitimate daughter of Henry VIII?

Catherine's soothing words were but a smoke-screen, behind which the two kingdoms, in spite of their mutual distrust, had laid the foundations of a military and commercial alliance which also guaranteed the independence of Scotland.

This made the Guises still less eager to come to court. The king sent to ask them whether they were prepared to respect his wishes and be reconciled: Guise returned assurances of his loyalty that in fact contained a refusal. Any arrangement of that kind should, he thought, be the subject of direct negotiation, and the king could ask the nobility whether this were not the case. Meanwhile the young duke, being unwilling to stir up any trouble, offered to go and fight the Turks at the head of four hundred soldiers and five galleys fitted out at his expense.

The king forbade this, and then sent him the advice of the most experienced captains. But the haughty tribe would pay no heed: and in any case the moment for the Church's counter-attack had come.

The court had returned to the placid banks of the Loire. Blois, in spite of the approach of many holy personages, once more took on the air of a brilliant bawdy-house, where, under the approving eye of the queen-mother, an ebullient crowd of young people devoted themselves to riotous delights. Masquerades followed one another in quick succession, excuses for fornication and brutish practical jokes. His Most Christian Majesty was to be seen with his face covered with soot, or dressed up as a horse, with a saddle on his back.

The Duke of Anjou was there, always surrounded by women, with his surprising habit of imitating them and scenting himself even more than they did, wearing extraordinarily elegant clothes and earrings of every kind.

In the meantime the new Nuncio, Salviati, arrived; then Francesco Borgia, the General of the Jesuits; and finally Cardinal Alessandrino, his Holiness's legate and his nephew. The Queen of Navarre, still on her road, took advantage of this to stop for a while: she could not expose herself to the contact of the representatives of 'idolatry'.

There was no mystery about the worthy clerics' aims, and no novelty: they were to break France's ties with England and to urge her towards the Christian League—in other words, to Spain. And since the queen-mother was incapable of negotiating without some talk of marriage, she was to be given hopes of an

Infanta for Monsieur and of the King of Portugal for Madame Marguerite.

Pius V, who was then near his death, had written Charles IX an extremely emphatic letter. 'We shall have no rest, either by night or by day, until you have joined this league. If you refuse to take part in it, you will dishonour yourself. Your refusal will be only too clear a proof of the reality of a project that is imputed to you but which we still do not wish to believe, a project suggested to you by the enemies of religion—that of forcibly invading the dominions of one of the confederates [Spain] . . . Our mind is also much taken up by another matter, your insistent desire to unite your sister with the King of Navarre. Although we prize your affection, our duty forbids that we should ever consent to a union that we consider an insult to God and a danger to souls.'

Father Francesco Borgia, commenting upon this message, made it clear that the Pope would never grant a dispensation for the Navarre marriage and that if Marguerite were to persist in it, she would be living in mortal sin, as a concubine. Her children would be bastards.

The talks went on for a fortnight, and at the end of this time Cardinal Alessandrino left Blois in such a rage that he would not accept the gold vases that had been made for him. He had been overwhelmed with outward honours, but this had not prevented people from making game of him to such a pitch that he had found a pair of tailor's shears drawn on his door—a reminder of his father's trade.

The foolish man, as the English ambassador called him, left empty-handed and in a most regrettable state of mind. He stated that the queen-mother was 'a beast', the king a fool, Monsieur an ass and the French a dissolute, frivolous nation, given to 'saying shameful things' and dancing all night. He repeated that trying to do business with women was like trying to negotiate with animals—a point of view, after all, not unlike that of the Admiral.

After this, how is it possible to hold up Catherine as a defender of the Spanish alliance in contrast to Coligny, the champion of the English? Cavalli, the recipient of her confidences, reassured the Republic: what the queen wanted was peace.

The legate's departure took away the Queen of Navarre's last excuse for procrastination. Yet during the weeks of her interminable journey the austere princess had not been wasting her time. Thanks to her keenness, Marguerite de Valois was to be the first daughter of France to be provided with a landed dowry that included such important

5   Catherine de' Medici

Henri d'Anjou   François d'Alençon

Marguerite de Valois

6   The children of Catherine de' Medici

towns as Agen and Cahors, apart from the important sum of three hundred thousand crowns. Jeanne, with a rather surprising simplicity of mind, also counted upon converting her future daughter-in-law.

This was not all. Another marriage had been decided upon, another alliance between the leaders of the two parties. The young Prince Henri de Condé, son of the Condé of Amboise and Jarnac, was to marry Mary of Cleves, Marquise de l'Isle, sister-in-law of the Duke of Guise and the Duke of Nevers. Until a little while before she had been a ward of the Queen of Navarre and she had been brought up a Protestant; but since 1569 the gentle and beautiful Mary had been in the charge of the French court. She would provide a natural link between the immovable Catholics and the son of the man who had been their mortal enemy.

The Queen of Navarre reached Blois on 3rd March, escorted by an impressive train, in which was to be seen Louis of Nassau himself and many lords, of whom the young La Rochefoucauld was one.

It is an important point that the last phases of the marriage negotiations and of those for the English alliance were carried on both at the same time. France seemed to have made her choice. The distressed Aguilon confided to his master's secretary, 'I dare not write to tell His Majesty of the grief and the anxiety that this alliance between the French and the English gives me. I fear that one day we may weep for not having welcomed the English just at the time when it seemed that they must seek to treat with us. And now I fear that the rope is being pulled to the breaking-point ...'

CHAPTER III

'YOU HIDE YOURSELF
FROM YOUR OWN MOTHER!'

THE QUEEN OF NAVARRE was scandalised by the corruption of the court. In letters and conversation she continually said, 'It is pitiable.'

Pitiable to see the king 'making love excessively' and remaining with his mistress until an hour after midnight. Pitiable to see the stratagems of the people round him, for 'here it is not the men who run after the women, but the women who run after the men'. Pitiable to count the cost of this luxury that insulted the wretchedness of the people, this ostentatious display of precious stones.

The strict princess looked at her future daughter-in-law intently, without indulgence. She admitted that Madame was beautiful, intelligent and well-bred, but she did not like the way she drew in her waist. As to her face, it owed too much to art, and that would soon spoil it. The queen detested make-up. Against these beauties painted like Jezebel she held up the naturalness of her own daughter, so pretty 'among the women of this court'.

At first the Medici was very affable to her cousin, and she invited her to supper every evening. Yet the harmony between such very different temperaments seemed but precarious. Both were intelligent, wily and brave; but apart from that there was a whole world between the sceptical, pliant, jolly Catherine and the fanatical, obstinate, puritanical Jeanne.

Each wanted this marriage, and each had set her hopes upon it; but these hopes, unfortunately, were quite opposed. Jeanne wished to bring her son nearer the throne and to win the king's sister for the Reformation. Catherine, on the other hand, sought to draw the prince to Catholicism and thus deprive the Huguenots of the protection of the royal blood.

The queen-mother soon grew tired of her guest's ways. Knowing how to put her out of countenance, she made game of her seriousness, never spoke to her except with laughter and redoubled her jokes and indeed her bad manners. Jeanne d'Albret complained bitterly to her son: 'The queen-mother treats me very ill . . . She does nothing but make fun of me and tell everyone that I say the opposite of what I really say . . . to such a point that I nearly burst, since I am quite determined not to lose my temper here—it is a miracle to see how patient I am . . . I am afraid that it will make me ill.'

She had no intention of yielding to Catherine's insistent demand to make the young Henry come; though there is no doubt that the young man would have been able to cope with the horrors of the Babylonian Blois quite easily. 'If you were here,' she wrote to him, 'you could not possibly escape without God's particular favour . . . That is why I desire . . . that you and your wife should withdraw from this corruption.'

Alas, Marguerite seemed to have no inclination whatever to become a spouse pleasing to the Lord. Any idea of converting her had to be given up from 8th March: in reply to Jeanne's question, the princess replied 'in a sharp and absolute tone' that since the beginning of the negotiations 'it had been perfectly well known what religion she belonged to'.

She took particular pains to emphasise this during the Easter procession. 'I saw her,' wrote Brantôme, 'and she was so beautiful that nothing in the world could be compared to her; for quite apart from the loveliness of her face and her perfect shape, she was very magnificently and richly dressed and adorned: her beautiful pale face, like the heavens in their most splendid white serenity, was crowned with so many great pearls and glorious jewels and above all so many blazing diamond stars that you would have said that the character of the face itself and the jewelled stars did battle with the splendour of a star-filled sky for the honour of giving the likeness of her beauty.'

The young man had no more intention of apostasizing than she had. 'However much they may lie in ambush for me because of this, they will never win me over,' asserted the prince who was one day to observe 'Paris is well worth a mass'.

A compromise had to be arrived at, and nothing seemed more difficult than persuading the intractable and lamenting woman of this necessity. 'It astonishes me how I am able to put up with all my troubles; for I am scratched and pricked and defied and flattered; and they try to worm my secrets out of me.'

But in spite of her complaints, Jeanne forced fresh concessions from her 'persecutors'. Apart from the king's three hundred thousand crowns, the dowry was to include two hundred thousand *livres* given by the queen-mother and fifty thousand each by the Duke of Anjou and the Duke of Alençon.[1]

The marriage of a Catholic and a Protestant presented innumerable difficulties. After several weeks of discussion it was agreed that the marriage should not take place in any church; that the spouses should not hear mass; that the Cardinal of Bourbon should bless them in his capacity of uncle to the husband and not in that of priest; and that the Pope should be asked for a dispensation, it being understood that a refusal would make no difference to anything.

'I hope that God will prevent this marriage,' wrote Philip II. His wishes were not fulfilled. Elizabeth of England was almost equally displeased when the Queen of Navarre, not without irony, wrote to her, 'Yesterday the irrevocable decision to marry Madame and my son was taken: the Devil had incited many minds given to division to oppose it, but since my arrival God has set His goodness against their ill-will, making use of those who love sweetness and union and quietness to accomplish His ends.'

The contract was signed on 11th April, and Jeanne no longer concealed her deep satisfaction. She at last sent for the Prince of Béarn, and provided him with a great deal of good advice. 'I beg you to see to three things: to bear yourself handsomely and well; to speak with courage, even when you are taken privately aside, for you are to observe that at your first coming you will establish the opinion that people will have of you for ever after; and to get your hair used to being brushed upwards, but not in the old-fashioned way. And my last piece of advice, the one which is principally in my mind, is that you should make yourself aware of all the allurements that they may use to lead you astray, either in your life or in your religion, so that you may arm yourself with an immovable steadfastness; for I know this to be their aim—they do not even hide it.'

The good lady did not foresee what a scandalous sight her son's household was to be; nor that this same son, who had already been converted twice, was to change his religion three times more.

Eighteen days after the marriage-contract, the treaty of alliance between France and England was signed. Montmorency, Paul de Foix, Birague and the Bishop of Limoges represented France; Thomas Smith and Walsingham, England.

---

[1] The *livre* was worth nearly £3, and the *écu* usually 3 *livres*. (Translator's note.)

It was a defensive pact, according to which either side was to come to the assistance of the other in case of need. There was to be freedom of trading between the two nations, and the English were to enjoy the same privileges in France as they did in the Low Countries and Norway. Elizabeth and Charles would cooperate in the pacification of Scotland.

All this caused alarm and strong uneasiness in the Catholic world; and this was increased when the plan of marrying the Queen of England and the Duke of Alençon was revived.

Philip II, drawing up instructions for his new ambassador, Don Diego de Zuniga, enjoined him to keep watch in case the French should make any warlike preparations. He required his envoy to undertake the work both of a spy and of an agitator. The Catholic King had some hopes of the Duke of Anjou, and he was quite sure of the Guises. 'This house', he wrote, 'considers itself to be among those that serve me and that are concerned with my interests.' Don Diego also had the duty of visiting all the people 'by whom one might acquire knowledge of what was happening at court and in the kingdom'.

The fleet that had been gathered at Bordeaux under the orders of Strozzi, and which was under the immediate command of the Portuguese sailor André del Bagno, caused a most vexing uncertainty. Aguilon, still waiting for the arrival of the new ambassador, was much preoccupied by it, and he advised the Duke of Alba to guard the coasts of the Spanish possessions. Could the assurance that had been given to the Nuncio, that these vessels threatened neither Spain nor Portugal, be trusted? It was generally rumoured that they were to be used in concert with Louis of Nassau.

Aguilon obtained an audience with the queen-mother, and questioned her. Catherine replied, 'People say that war is near, and this perplexes me extremely, for I would rather die than see such a thing.' It had been mischievously rumoured that the manning of this fleet was a prelude to war. But if the king had authorised a certain expedition, it would in no way be prejudicial to Spain.

The sceptical Aguilon remarked that in that case his master should have been told about it, as was customary between good neighbours. Catherine admitted this, and promised to have it officially put right.

Aguilon had been mistaken in worrying so much. The court really had in mind an 'African venture' designed primarily for the benefit of Monsieur.

At a time when France was allying herself with the Huguenots and when the Duke of Alençon was perhaps about to marry the Queen of England, the position of the victor of Moncontour was difficult, to say the least. The only way of preserving his great reputation, of satisfying his ambition and of sending him away into the bargain, according to the wishes of Charles IX, was to find him that kingdom of his own which his mother so coveted for him. Aguilon himself had noted, 'The Duke of Anjou cannot stay in France: it is essential to find him something outside the realm.'

Just at this time Algiers asked the king for help, being cut off from Turkish protection since the battle of Lepanto and being afraid of falling into the hands of the Spaniards.

Catherine was charmed by the idea of an Algeria under French domination and ruled by the Duke of Anjou. It would be an extension of the occupation of Sardinia and Corsica. The whole younger generation, eager for voyages, and all the seafaring adventurers dreamed of this wonderful expedition.

François de Noailles, Bishop of Dax, ambassador to Constantinople, was charged with gaining the Sultan's indispensable consent. Would one see a Valois ruling Algiers and paying tribute to the Grand Signior? No. The Grand Signior did not trust a vassal of that kind: he made a polite but perfectly clear reply. The French were to wait two and a half centuries before they gained a footing in Algiers: the fleet, meanwhile, remained poised like the sword of Damocles.

No one who knew Philip II well would have expected that he would sit still under such a menace. The ships and the army which he had prevented from attacking Constantinople were still at liberty. Don John of Austria had two hundred and fifty galleys gathered in Sicily: troops were flowing into Spezia. A spy reported from Genoa that the Spaniards had drawn up a map of Provence.

Birague, governor of the French possessions in Italy, raised a cry of alarm. The Duke of Longueville, governor of Picardy, displayed the same anxiety.

And in the meantime, surrounded by the most profound secrecy, negotiations were in progress between the Duke of Alba and the Queen of England.

It was a question of resuming the commercial relations between England and Flanders, which, to the great disadvantage of both countries, had been interrupted not long since. Elizabeth, that past-master at the double game, carried this business forward at the same time as the French alliance. She won her point. The agreement, which was enveloped in mystery but which was nevertheless discovered by the French ambassador, La Mothe-Fénelon, secured considerable benefits for the English. In exchange the queen promised to close her ports to the Beggars, who, since the rising, had sheltered their ships in them. At the time no one imagined what remarkable consequences would flow from this last clause.

The Beggars' fleet, having left Dover, was sailing towards Holland when a storm forced it to anchor before Brill, whose garrison happened at that moment to be putting down the rising at Utrecht. The Beggars profited by the godsend and occupied the fortifications. Flushing opened its gates to them.

The Prince of Orange and Louis of Nassau had scarcely time to blame them for their rashness before the whole of Zeeland was in their hands.

England was in transports of delight. Elizabeth, true to her wily tactics, allowed twelve hundred volunteers to go to Flushing. According to the outcome she could either disavow them, she thought, or make use of them to annex the town.

Mondoucet, Charles IX's envoy at Brussels, instantly sent to say, 'This is not the moment to let such a splendid opportunity go by, but to seize it by the hair. I speak with the greatest earnestness, as one who is here and who sees things as they are.'

At this juncture, France was in a state of unwonted calm. It was as though passion were out of breath: there were no riots, no outrages. Coligny was still at Châtillon, and the Queen of Navarre was getting ready to go to Paris in the company of Nassau. The king—a point of importance—was away from his mother. Together with the princes, he had gone to hunt and to amuse himself, from forest to forest and from château to château. The common people, astonished, began to hope again. And yet already a new storm was brewing.

When he heard of the achievements of the Beggars Coligny was sure that the Spaniards would be thrown out of the Low Countries. He at once sent his son-in-law Téligny to Charles IX; and Téligny had no great difficulty in arousing the weak and hot-blooded young man's enthusiasm.

The king wrote to Nassau, 'Téligny has explained to me the great possibilities there are for accomplishing some enterprise for the freedom of the Low Countries. We are only asked to give them a hand to save them from this oppression, which is a matter in which any generous and Christian prince should use the powers that God has placed in his hands, as I am quite determined to do, as far as the circumstances and the ordering of my affairs will allow it.'

Without waiting for more, several hundred Huguenot soldiers hurried to Flushing. The fever mounted. While the queen-mother did her utmost to soothe the Spanish diplomats, Charles IX was thinking of giving them good reason for having feared his fleet. On 11th May he wrote to the Bishop of Dax, 'I have a fleet of twelve to fifteen thousand men which will be ready to sail anywhere before the end of the month, under the pretext of guarding my harbours and coasts against depredations, but really in order to disturb the Catholic King and to encourage these Beggars to stir themselves as they have already done, having taken all Zeeland and even shaken Holland.'

Louis of Nassau, much bolder than his brother, William the Silent, judged that the time had come to strike the great blow that would give the young king the strength to break his leading-strings. He was with Jeanne d'Albret, and she was not a woman to urge moderation. The brave La Noue, one of the best of the Huguenot captains, brought him his sword and some troops. The two of them swooped upon Flanders, and almost without a blow took Valenciennes and then Mons (24th May).

In the meantime, Don Diego de Zuniga had arrived in France. He had asked for an audience, but Charles IX kept out of his way. In vain the ambassador pursued the royal hunt as it ceaselessly traversed the country bordering the Loire.

As soon as he knew of the taking of Valenciennes, the delighted king told Nassau 'that he would let him secretly draw a certain number of arquebusiers from his kingdom, besides which he would help him with a little money'. For a moment even Catherine herself wondered whether fate had not decided against Spain.

She was soon undeceived. La Noue did not even have the time to fortify himself in Valenciennes. The Spaniards drove him out in a few days, and forced him to entrench himself at Mons. 'I am convinced', wrote the provost Morillon to Cardinal Granvelle, Philip II's minister, 'that the retaking of this place has ruined the plans of the French.'

Warnings and cries of alarm were heard on every hand. The queen-mother received a 'royal counsel' from Marshal de Tavannes: 'I fear, Sire, that your bravery may outrun your strength; and for this reason I am going slowly and cautiously until I know what means you possess for making war.' The old soldier urged His Majesty to fortify his frontiers and to wait before committing himself any further.

On his side the Duke of Longueville wrote, 'I am exceedingly concerned to see you being engaged in war, as you may easily be directly this [the aid to Nassau] is discovered, both on account of the indifferent state of affairs on that side and because of the poverty of the resources that I dispose of to serve you there.'

All of a sudden Catherine panicked. She remembered 1557: she saw Alba's brutal troops overrunning France, and Philip II and the Inquisition masters of Paris. At that moment Charles was hunting the stag in the neighbourhood of Montpipeau. Catherine rushed thither at such a pace that her two coach-horses fell dead at Orleans.

The meeting between mother and son was dramatic. It has been recorded for us by Tavannes. From the beginning Catherine shed floods of tears and held up to the ungrateful Charles her trials, her toils and her sacrifices.

'You hide yourself from me, your own mother; and you take counsel from your enemies!'

She recalled the outrages of the Huguenots, the weakness of the realm, and pointed out the madness of a war against the Spanish colossus. To lose it would give Philip total supremacy and make Guise a mayor of the palace: to win it would hand over power to the Protestants and cause a Catholic uprising.

'If this is to be my misfortune,' she cried, 'let me, before seeing such a thing, have leave to go back to where I was born; and send away your poor brother too—well may he call himself unhappy, having spent his life in preserving yours!'

Charles was not strong enough to withstand an attack like this. He was not convinced, but as soon as his mother made as if to depart he took fright and gave in, at least provisionally.

On 29th May he wrote to the Duke of Savoy, 'My dear uncle: I have just been advised that, contrary to my direct orders, Count Louis of Nassau, together with several gentlemen of the new religion, my subjects, has entered the Low Countries and advanced upon certain towns belonging to the Catholic King, my good brother, which grieves me exceedingly, for as I wish with all my heart to preserve the friendship of the Catholic King and the perfect peace that is between us, I am beyond all measure displeased at seeing myself so ill-obeyed. I have written at once to my cousin, the Duke of Longueville, bidding him gather troops to see to the matter and to proceed against them as criminals guilty of high treason; and I am sure he will do so.'

Pending the transmission of this olive-branch to Madrid by the Duke of Savoy, the queen-mother received Don Diego de Zuniga, who, having given up hope of reaching the king, had sensibly addressed himself to her.

The ambassador at once launched into a bitter indictment: Nassau had prepared his attack on Flanders in France, and every day Frenchmen were joining him, saying that they went on the king's service.

'Does your Majesty not know this?'

Catherine was obliged to admit that she did.

'With so much friendship and brotherliness for the Catholic King, how can you tolerate not having them all punished with the most exemplary severity?'

'The king has ordered the Duke of Longueville to stop anyone crossing the frontier under the penalty of death and the confiscation of his goods. You may tell his Catholic Majesty so.' And then, counter-attacking, she spoke of the Spanish troops concentrated in Italy and intended, it was said, for the taking of Marseilles.

'These are merely excuses,' insolently returned the ambassador.

On 31st May he was at last given audience by Charles IX, who deeply deplored Nassau's deeds. 'I want only one thing—to remain at peace with his Catholic Majesty.'

Don Diego did not allow himself to be persuaded by this. 'It is plain,' he wrote to the Duke of Alba, '. . . that if the undertaking succeeds they will take advantage of it: if not, they will say that it grieves them profoundly.'

The spectacle of Paris made everything obvious enough. War was in the air. Convoys of arms and munitions were setting off towards the north. The prohibition from joining Nassau was not made public. Jeanne d'Albret, who was staying with the Bishop of Chartres (a convert to Protestantism), received many messengers from the count and did her utmost for his cause.

The capital, which had been almost abandoned for the past year, became the political centre of the kingdom again. Everybody came to Paris: first the Duke of Anjou, then the king, then the queen-mother.

Lord Clinton, the Queen of England's envoy, came for the solemn ratification of the treaty of alliance. The Prince of Béarn was on his way. The Guises too were coming, having at last made up their minds to rejoin the court. And finally the Admiral himself was preparing to travel to the city that looked upon him as an emissary of the Evil One.

CHAPTER IV

'SO LONG AS THEY KEEP ON
THEIR MASK...'

ON THE EVE OF Corpus Christi the king and the court took up residence in the Château de Madrid. The Guises reached Paris at the same time. The splendid Corpus Christi procession left Notre Dame the next day and passed through the city among enthusiastic crowds. The Cardinal of Bourbon carried the Blessed Sacrament. The dukes of Anjou and Alençon, the Guises, the Duke of Montpensier and his son—a vast number of great lords—walked in procession after him The Parisians displayed their devotion with a kind of violence that was an indirect way of showing their anger at the arrival of the Admiral.

Coligny came right into his enemies' stronghold, fiercely determined to seize the opportunity and to launch his crusade. It was an immense, almost hopeless contest that he had to win, not only against the opposition of the queen-mother and the Catholics, but also against the vacillation of the Prince of Orange and Elizabeth's duplicity. And against the hatred of Paris—Paris, angered anew each morning by the preachers: Paris, still filled with the memory of that autumn of 1567 when the Calvinist heretics cut the citizens' militia to pieces and set fire to the suburbs.

The Admiral came into Paris like a paramount lord, with four hundred gentlemen in his train. The people, cowed by his defiance, watched in silence as the dark figure went by—already a legend, with his grey beard, his toothpick, his cold, masterful and gloomy eye.

Coligny reached the Château de Madrid. When he had paid his homage to their Majesties he met the Guises, whom he had not seen for five years. The king had insisted that rank should be respected and the Huguenot leader had therefore to bow first to his mortal enemies. It was observed that he had to force himself to obey this

order with a remarkable effort. After this Guise and Coligny took
no notice of one another.

The Admiral at once set about the king and his mother,
and he had long conversations with them. He wanted to bring
everybody round to his point of view, even his personal enemies;
and with this in view he made some surprising moves. He offered, to
the duke's astonishment, to make Anjou 'lord of Flanders'. He went
still farther, and secretly proposed to the Guises that some of the
future conquests, Luxemburg and Gelderland—former family possessions—should be given up to them. But there was little response
to this: the Lorrainers thought the leadership of the Catholic party
more important than these mirages, and they had no intention of
taking part in a reconciliation. As to the king, he seemed to have
fallen under his mother's influence again and to wish to avoid the
domination of 'his father': he lavished his smiles on the Guises.

In fact, he was pitifully undecided. He had written to his ambassador at Constantinople, 'All my desires combine to make me oppose
the grandeur of the Spaniards and I am considering how best I may
go about it.' To his ambassador in Venice he wrote the direct
opposite.

In the meantime, Jeanne d'Albret, whose frail health had been
much shaken by the excitements of the last few months, was wearing herself out in making preparations for her son's wedding and in
doing her utmost for the Beggars. She became ill with pleurisy and
died after five days, with the Cardinal of Bourbon, her brother-in-
law, the Duke of Montpensier and the Admiral round her death-
bed. She was only forty-four.

At first people were stupefied at the sudden death of this almost
masculine queen; then, while the Protestants were still stunned, the
Catholics publicly rejoiced. The letter in which the Nuncio Caiazzo
told the Pope the news was a positive hymn of praise.

Now that the 'evil woman' [1] had gone, the good Catholics had no
doubt that the Bourbon marriage and even perhaps the English
alliance would be abandoned. They saw in this a blessing from
heaven; something like a miracle.

The Protestants, when they came to their senses again, perceived
in this the evidence of a flagrant crime. Had not Jeanne d'Albret received a present of scented gloves that came from the queen-mother's
glover, René? Had she not supped with Monsieur? There was no
possible doubt but that she had been poisoned.

---

[1] 'Mala femina'. Cf. Caiazzo's letter of 9th June.

This constantly reiterated accusation has left indelible traces in the popular memory. Yet even the most fervent of the historians on the Protestant side has been obliged long since to abandon the theory. It is therefore scarcely worth refuting it all over again.

The post-mortem examination showed an abscess on the right lung and 'some little water-filled bulbs between the skull and the dura mater', Jeanne was tubercular. This daughter of Marguerite of Navarre, this mother of Henry IV, so unlike both, was to hand down her disease to her grandson, Louis XIII, together with her hardness, her austerity and her sense of duty.

The welcome with which the English ambassadors were received dispelled the illusions of the Catholic party. The king delayed court mourning, in order to receive them worthily; the queen-mother gave a banquet at the Tuileries, and the princes and the Admiral held splendid festivities. At the same time the Queen of England displayed all her magnificence in honour of François de Montmorency. The treaty was sworn at the Louvre and at Westminster: the two realms now seemed finally bound together, and the spirits of the Protestants rose once more.

They did not know Henry VIII's daughter. Elizabeth attached little importance to helping her fellow Protestants, but a very great deal to maintaining the strength and the independence of her small kingdom in the face of the two giants who were about to confront one another.[2] She thought this an excellent opportunity for weakening both by urging one against the other; but for all that she had not the slightest wish to see Flanders in the hands of the French, who, if they were to win, would be much more dangerous there than the Spaniards, bogged down in civil war. On the other hand, she had never reconciled herself to the loss of Calais; for the possession of the town allowed England to escape from its sea-girt isolation and, to some degree, to level a weapon at the Continent. These various motives caused the formidable queen to carry on a two-faced policy that was to become one of the direct causes, perhaps even the most important cause, of the massacre of Saint Bartholomew.

On 3rd June, while the two capitals were celebrating the Franco-English alliance, the queen sent a secret order to her ministers to

[2] England did not possess Scotland at this time, and was having perpetual difficulties with Ireland: its population was about a quarter of that of France, and its extent did not exceed that of a single province of the vast Spanish empire.

the effect that if the French were to seize part of Flanders, England would help the Catholic King 'by all honourable means', and at that moment—but at that moment only—the Duke of Alba should be told of this.[3]

A few days later, François de Montmorency urged the Virgin of the West to accept the hand of the Duke of Alençon: she gave him a gracious hearing, dressed up and adorned like a heathen idol, in an astonishingly low-cut dress sewn with pearls 'as big as beans'. According to her custom in such cases, she said that she was very old—that were it not for the country's need of an heir to the throne she would blush to think of marriage at all, being one of those whose crown was more sought in marriage than her person. The ambassador's protests were received with an encouraging simper. Her Majesty then raised various other objections, but without in fact appearing to attach much weight to them. Finally, she asked for a month in which to think it over, and left Montmorency full of hope.

But her ministers at once let Coligny know the reason for this delay: before the month was over, the queen expected the offer of Calais. For his part, Lord Burghley made his mind clear to Walsingham, the English ambassador in Paris; 'I could wish that we might have it [Calais] and that the Duke of Alençon might be governor of it for his lifetime, so that our staple there would be secure.'

The Admiral showed no particular indignation. It did not seem to him too great a price to pay to win over the queen-mother, since she was so set upon the English marriage, and to make sure of beating the Spaniards. Yet he still had to discover what Elizabeth's real intentions were.

A secret agent of the queen by the name of Middlemore was then in Paris. This dark figure was brought into contact with Coligny at a supper given in circumstances of great mystery by Monsieur de Champernon, a Huguenot gentleman.

The Admiral pleaded the cause of his war with great fervour and pointed out that both England and France were in danger from Philip II. This was a magnificent opportunity for destroying his power, for if there were a complete union between England and

[3] *Calendar of State Papers, Foreign Papers, 1572–1574*, London, 1876, p. 123. 'If the French proceed to seek the maritime coasts, it were good that the Duke of Alba were informed to assist the king his master by all honourable means in the defence of his inheritance . . . To bring these matters to a good and honourable end, the best way would be for the Duke, upon any entry made by the French into his master's dominions, to demand aid from the queen, according to former leagues. 3rd June, 1572.'

France, victory was certain. Middlemore remained unmoved. 'I am not empowered,' said he, at last, 'to discuss matters of this kind.'

'But what is your own personal opinion, at all events?'

'As for that, in England people chiefly hope that both France and Spain will stay within their present frontiers: people are most uneasy lest France should take possession of Flanders, a state of affairs that England could not countenance at any price.'

'But if your queen were to join with us, she would have her share of the gains that are to be had: the real danger is in missing the opportunity. I am exceedingly happy at the new alliance which has united our two nations; and the surest means of strengthening it would be the marriage with the Duke of Alençon.'

'Yet, of course, one must think of the difference of age and of religion.'

The Admiral understood. The bitterness that he felt shows in that passage in his will which advises Charles IX to regard England and Spain with the same mistrust. Should not this clear-sightedness have led him to reconsider his plan at once? Unfortunately his retreat was cut off—or so at least he thought. He could see nothing but a national war as an alternative to civil war and to that partisan role that had grown intolerable to him—an escape in the form of a charge.

He convinced himself that once operations had begun, Elizabeth would not dare betray her fellow Protestants. There had been so many ties to bind them since the events of Le Havre.

So far from withdrawing he urged the Duke of Alençon to send La Mole, his favourite, to England, and he pressed the king to help the men besieged in Mons. He even made use of Elizabeth's duplicity as an argument: he told Charles that it was necessary to prevent the English from forestalling the French in their intervention. And yet, which is astonishing, this did not stop him passing on the proposal concerning Calais.

In spite of his dislike for this way of carrying on proceedings, it was decided that the matter should be submitted to the council on 19th June, which would give the queen-mother time to recover from a new bout of indigestion and the Admiral time to draw up a paper on the subject. This was contrary to the tradition of the council, for the debates were always by word of mouth; but Coligny was asked to adopt this method exceptionally because of Tavannes' deafness.

The council sat at the Château de Madrid. The Admiral developed his theme—the paper had been written by Duplessis-Mornay, his secretary. 'The cure for civil wars is to employ the warlike part of the nation upon foreign territory; for whereas other nations take up their trade again as soon as peace is made, few Frenchmen will quit off their swords, once they have put them on.'

The leading thought, therefore, was that a war abroad would prevent a war at home. It would be a justifiable war, for the wrongs the King of Spain had done to France were innumerable; it would be an easy war, for the king and his allies had more important forces than Spain and they would go into Flanders as liberators; it would be a profitable war, for the king would become the first sovereign in Christendom.

Charles IX approved. Catherine said nothing.

The decision was deferred until 26th June.

The next day the king received Salviati, the Nuncio Extraordinary sent by Pope Gregory XIII, Pius V's successor, to preserve the peace and to promote the Christian League. His Majesty asserted that his intentions were peaceable. Far from being hurtful to Spain, the English alliance, he said, was a means of neutralising Elizabeth. But the rumour of war grew louder, and filled the Catholic embassies with anxiety, in spite of the calming words that the queen-mother lavished upon them. Every day more soldiers took the road for Flanders.

Zuniga reported, 'The armourers are working even on holidays.'

Cardinal Granvelle, much cast down, wrote, 'Our only hope is that the people of the Low Countries will not want to be French.'

On the 21st, Nassau caused the Comte de Genlis to leave Mons, and with twenty horsemen to escort him he galloped all the way to Paris, where he was at once received at the Château de Madrid. Among his people there was a Spanish spy: he warned the Duke of Alba that the Huguenots counted upon the French army taking the field on the 26th.

There was intense political excitement throughout the week. The Nuncio and the Venetian ambassador preached peace to the sovereigns. Zuniga lost his head. Coligny approached his enemies, one by one, and tried again to win over the Guises. The Duke of Nevers drew up a paper for the Duke of Anjou refuting the Protestants' argument.

This document served as the basis of the discussion on 26th June. Monsieur was called upon for his opinion first, and he argued that the Flemish towns would be difficult to defend against a Spanish counter-attack, that England was not to be relied upon, that the Prince of Orange was wavering, that French Piedmont was lost as soon as hostilities began and that the empty treasury was incapable of maintaining an army. He added—and this came from Tavannes—that the war would last at least eight years, and that even if the king were to win 'he would still be led on a leash' by the Huguenots. 'And so winning would be the loss of everything.'

The ideas of the extreme Catholics on the council were already known: what was surprising was to see the moderates, the men who were called the *politiques*, come round unreservedly to their point of view. Coligny failed to get his way, and peace was maintained. Another entirely military council the next day came to the same conclusions.

The Admiral could not resign himself to it. 'Sire,' he said, 'since the advice of these people has swayed Your Majesty . . . I may no longer oppose your will; but I am certain that you will be sorry for it. However that may be, Your Majesty will not think it amiss if, having promised the Prince of Orange aid and support, I do my best to furnish him with both, with the help of all my friends, relatives and servants and even, if need be, with my own person.' This was a true feudal lord speaking. Going down the steps, Coligny shouted to the Marshal de Tavannes that those who were opposed to intervention 'wore the red cross on their bellies'.[4]

In spite of the decision, the king shared his anger. 'My courtiers and my councillors are no more than brutes,' he told Téligny. He resolved his inner conflict in his usual way and went off to hunt at Lyons-la-Forêt, while the Catholic ambassadors congratulated themselves upon seeing the queen-mother in control of the state once more.

Philip II was less sanguine, as may be seen from his instructions to Zuniga: 'So long as they keep on their mask, we must keep on ours. Nay, let them rather suppose that we trust in their words and let us employ the same dissimulation that they use towards us, at least until they give us some clearer reason to behave otherwise.'

While he was writing this, the queen-mother visited the Admiral, in the rue Béthizy in Paris. We know almost nothing of their interview, which lasted two hours, and which cannot have failed to be moving. Catherine remained firmly attached to peace, to peace abroad and to peace at home—she had just made a new approach to Rome in order to obtain the dispensation necessary for the Bourbon marriage. Coligny could not be convinced that they were not incompatible: he believed that they were. The Florentine used all her per-

---

[4] The emblem of the Spaniards.

suasive sweetness and all her dangerous seduction. But these arms soon lost their edge against the rigidity of the Calvinist. Changing her tone, the queen declared, 'If you and your supporters want to help the rebels, neither you nor your supporters shall receive any aid from my son, the king.'

It was clear that Coligny did not believe this; and his scepticism was an answer filled with menace. It was on this day, 30th June, that the two opponents finally lost all hope of convincing one another and that France was committed to a new and more frightful strife.

CHAPTER V

'GENLIS WAS TO WAIT'

COLIGNY had been unwell since the death of the Queen of Navarre. He went to Châtillon to recover. 'He would have got better earlier', wrote his wife to the Duchess of Ferrara, 'had it not been for the innumerable worrying problems about the religion of the kingdom that afflicted him every day.'

The king was hunting the stag, the queen-mother was travelling, the Admiral was in the country: one might have thought that everything was calm. But not at all—the excitement was mounting. Charles IX did not wish to be ruled again. He wanted to assert himself before his mother and to eclipse his detested brother.

The road to Flanders seemed to be the only one that could lead to freedom. He was in such a hurry to reach it, after his failure on 26th June, that he outdid Coligny himself in blundering haste.

The Admiral would have liked an open declaration of war, a great French expedition with himself the Captain-General. The oblique hostilities and the underhand fighting that allowed his opponents to avoid decision were repugnant to his spirit. So he was not sparing in his advice to Genlis to be prudent, although at the same time he was in the act of mobilising.

Spanish spies intercepted a letter in which he bade those faithful to him to keep their soldiers under arms and to be ready to send them 'anywhere they would be needed'. There was to be no opposition to this, for he was acting on the king's orders.

So Charles IX had given him a free hand. But at the same time the king was listening to Genlis. Charles, like the impetuous captain, did not possess the patience to make a calculated delay; and like Genlis too, he intended to compel fate to favour him. Genlis was able to leave Paris with authority to raise four thousand men for the relief of Mons, and, which was still more valuable, a letter from the king to Téligny which was the equivalent of a pledge to Nassau. The

Admiral was uneasy, and most pressingly advised him to join the Prince of Orange at once—to attempt nothing on his own.

It is difficult to make out whether Catherine was caught unawares or whether she fatalistically accepted a trial that would measure the opposing forces. Whatever the truth may have been, she once more displayed her desire for peace to Salviati—the troops gathered near the frontier were 'few in number and only for defence': the king was occupied solely with the marriage of Madame. And once more she urged that His Holiness should grant the dispensation.

Henri de Bourbon, King of Navarre since the death of his mother, was in fact on the point of reaching Paris after a long delay caused by a bout of fever. His arrival, the departure of Genlis, the Admiral's levies, the movements of the Prince of Orange, whose army had crossed the Rhine—this concentration of Protestant strength spread hope among the victims of Philip II and dismay among the Catholic powers. The Venetians trembled at the thought of Spain being obliged to turn away from the Mediterranean, for then they would be left alone, face to face with the Turks. They sent their best diplomat to the court of France, the aged Giovanni Michieli, to try to save the peace.

While Michieli was riding post-haste—he covered the distance in less than eleven days—the future King Henry IV made his entry into Paris and into history, on 8th July. The Admiral had already joined him. The honours that the king had resolved to pay to this little high-lander brought up among the shepherds of Béarn, this shy orphan who had suddenly become the Protestant symbol, are shown in a letter, whose address and signature have been cut off.[1]

'He was met by the city corporation in their coloured robes with their archers attending upon them: by order of the king, Messieurs d'Anjou and d'Alençon also met him half-way through the suburbs, where there were Messieurs de Guise and Messieurs the marshals of France with a great body of more than four or five hundred horse. The said lord, the King of Navarre, was accompanied by Messieurs the Cardinal of Bourbon, the Duke of Montpensier, the Dauphin, the Duke of Nevers, who had all been in mourning, as far as Palaiseau to meet the king, who had with him the Prince of Condé, the Admiral and the lord of La Rochefoucauld. . . . The Huguenots had rumoured that the King of Navarre would come with

[1] *Bibliothèque Nationale, fonds Dupuy*, no. 349, fol. 63.

more than fifteen hundred horses, but more than half this number was wanting.'

Henry was lodged in the Louvre itself, in the suite which had once belonged to Queen Eleanor, wife of Francis I, together with a great many of his gentlemen. His fiancée took an instant dislike to him, for his sly look, his provincial clothes and his horrible smell. Anjou and Guise, those elegant Catholic lilies, did not scruple to make game of the yokel and of his moody, stunted cousin Condé. Navarre never showed any ill-temper but smilingly put up with it all, bowing frequently in all directions. Condé displayed a touchy sullenness that made his plain face plainer still.

On the other hand, the Huguenot lords were most kindly welcomed by the king. Téligny, La Trémoille, Rohan and above all Comte François II de La Rochefoucauld became Charles's companions at tennis and hunting, and during those nocturnal rambles in which the well-born bullies set upon passers-by and beat them, broke windows and raped women.

This soon became a fashionable amusement. Anjou took to it as well, at the head of his Catholic gentlemen, and often the two gangs battered one another to their heart's content. After midnight, to the great delight of the footpads, the watch no longer dared to intervene.

These brawls added to the fever of the city—a city already sweltering in the dog-days. These hectoring younger sons from Gascony, these sword-rattling squireens from the central provinces and these piratical gentlemen from La Rochelle thoroughly irritated the Parisians, in spite of the sudden prosperity brought by the newcomers. These heretics behaved as if they were in conquered territory, and swaggered about with a great display of insolence. Some openly mocked the king and pretended to recognise no authority other than the Admiral's.

Soon, under the pretext of the coming marriage, the Guises' supporters flocked in. The followers and dependants of the House of Lorraine were beyond counting—innumerable needy gentlemen, bullies and servants lived upon its bounty. A single vassal, Monsieur de Fervaques, had no less than thirty swashbucklers in his train.

All these people put up in the neighbourhood of the Hôtel de Guise, chiefly in monasteries and presbyteries. This meant that in the centre of the town a hard Catholic core was forming, whereas the Protestants were scattered in a haphazard manner, according to where they had been able to find lodging. Many of them camped in the Faubourg Saint-Germain.

Clashes between the two parties were inevitable. Every day blood flowed in the Pré-aux-Clercs as the supporters of the red cross and of the white scarf fought their duels, which in no way impeded the wild amusements that so scandalised the Calvinists.

Once more Charles IX was under Coligny's influence. He was in such a hurry to bind himself to the Protestants that he wanted to unite Madame and the King of Navarre on 10th July 'without any ceremony—let them marry in mourning'. But the queen-mother wanted an act so heavy with consequence to have a greater solemnity. It was therefore laid down 'that it [the marriage] would take place at Notre Dame in splendour and that the banquet should be at the palace, as was customary for the daughters and sons of France'.

The Duke and Duchess of Lorraine determined to be present at this magnificent ceremony. Catherine had a particular tenderness for her lame daughter, the sad and gentle Duchess Claude. She gave up her own rooms to her and moved into those of Francis I.

It was here that Montmorency gave her his report on his mission to England. What he had to say brought her little comfort. Coligny succeeded in seeing her again the next day at Saint-Cloud. He met Strozzi and Brantôme in the antechamber and cried, 'Praise be to God! All goes well. Before long we shall have chased the Spaniards out of the Low Countries and made our king master, or we shall have died in the attempt, and myself the first to fall!'

This was a state of mind very unlike the Florentine's. Once again their conversation ended in complete disagreement. But the Admiral minded it very little, for now he was sure of having tamed the wild young king.

The king had said to him, 'There is one thing, father, that we must take care of, and that is that the queen, my mother, who likes to poke her nose into everything, as you know, should not know about our undertaking, at least for the present, or she would spoil it all.'

The two men were closeted together for several hours on 12th July. When the Admiral came out, looking delighted, he was seen to bow a great many times, as if he were thanking his Majesty for having done all that he could have desired. The Spanish ambassador hurried to warn his master.

Perhaps the moment had come when the course of fate was about to change. Perhaps France was on the point of launching herself into one of the greatest adventures in her history.

Monsieur de Genlis never dreamed that the whole of this depended upon his behaviour. He ought to have followed the Admiral's advice and to have prepared to rejoin the Prince of Orange with his five thousand men. He chose instead to hasten to Mons. The Duke of Alba's son, Don Fadrigue de Toledo, had been well informed of his motions by spies, and had laid an ambush for him near Quiévrain.

While fate rattled the dice, each player tried to save his stake. The Grand Duke of Tuscany, who had set this terrible business on foot, sent money both to the Duke of Alba and to the Prince of Orange.

'The scoundrel!' cried Coligny, when he heard this.

Philip II, writing to Zuniga, summed up the situation very well. 'The state of mind and the intentions of the French in this matter are quite clear. For it may be said, in effect, that they are trying to give the whole world to understand that they want peace and that I want war. And, as you say, there is no doubt that if their dealings with the rebels in the Low Countries should succeed they will espouse their cause . . . You will carry on your conversations upon this basis and you will do your utmost to find out all you can of their designs.'

Don Diego had already found an excellent method of performing this part of his task. Jérôme de Gondi, the master of ceremonies and a member of the council, had formed the opinion that 'the excesses of both sides' should be opposed. He was strongly against the war, and he had promised the Catholic King's envoy to keep him informed of all the discussions in council upon it.

At the same time an emissary of the Duke of Alba named Guaras arrived secretly in London. Walsingham, who was a sincere supporter of the French alliance, urged the queen to fulfil it without reservation, but Elizabeth had resolutely chosen the opposite course. She received Guaras, listened to him, agreed with what he had to say, and suddenly offered him something for which the Spaniards had not even dared to hope: If the French entered Flanders, she would put Flushing into the Duke of Alba's hands.[2]

In spite of their pact, Coligny had helped in taking Le Havre back from the English. Eight years later the daughter of the Tudors repaid this treachery with another.

On 17th July the queen-mother received the Spanish ambassador in audience. Once more she assured him that the peace would be main-

[2] *Calendar of State Papers.* Froude, *History of England*, vol. X.

tained. Had not the prohibition that forbade men to go to the Low
Countries just been published? Don Diego thanked her, but expressed his sorrow at seeing so many Huguenots in her Majesty's
chamber. Catherine, upon this, turned to her daughter-in-law, the
Queen Elizabeth, who was six months with child. 'It is she who can
tell you of what mind they are, both of them! [She and the king.]'

And the young queen emphatically said, 'It will be as she says,
and the peace will not be broken.'

The next day fate threw the dice. Genlis, having clashed with Don
Fadrigue de Toledo, was cut to pieces: his little army was destroyed,
and he was taken prisoner. As these people were not regular bel-
ligerents the Spaniards did not think themselves bound by the rules
of war. They slaughtered them at their leisure. Three thousand
Huguenots were killed. The rest, fleeing in disorder, were attacked by
the inhabitants whom they had meant to liberate but whose houses
they had pillaged and whose crops they had taken. The French were
not loved in Flanders. The survivors made their way back towards
Paris, bleeding, ragged and exhausted, compelled to beg their bread.

In the Spaniards' camp there was thanksgiving for 'the hand of
God'. The Duke of Alba dared to have Genlis tortured in order
to obtain proofs of complicity against the King of France, which in
any case was unnecessary, since he possessed Charles IX's letter,
which was all that was needed to give Philip II the right to declare
war, if he saw fit. Albornos, the duke's secretary, wrote to Cardinal
Granvelle, 'I have in my hands a letter that would fill you with
astonishment if you were to see it; but for the moment it is desirable
to keep it hidden.'

In Paris the news of the battle of Quiévrain caused a sensation. From
the military point of view it was in no way catastrophic—the defeat
did not diminish the forces of either the Prince of Orange or the
Admiral. But psychologically and politically the result was very
different. The Protestants felt their prestige dwindling. The torturing
of Genlis was an insult to the honour of the entire nobility.

'The Spaniards ought to be flayed,' cried the furious Téligny.

Coligny violently blamed Genlis. 'It is his fault! Genlis was to
wait for the Prince of Orange. That was the advice I gave him: he
should never have gone to the relief of Mons.'

He at once went to see the English ambassador, who wrote to the
Earl of Leicester, Elizabeth's favourite, 'The Admiral has asked me

to beg you to intercede with the queen and to learn whether she would come to the help of the poor Prince of Orange.'

This approach shows how little the Admiral was then aware of his ally's real intentions.

The Nuncio thought that peace was saved. The first reaction of Charles IX, however, displayed an uncommon boldness. At his command, Mondoucet protested to the Duke of Alba against the treatment inflicted upon the prisoners and even called to mind the spirit of revenge that would burn in the Huguenots. The duke shrugged his shoulders. He got rid of the ambassador and replied to the queen-mother. He replied telling her that in her son's letter he held a casus belli and that the Queen of England had offered to help the Catholic King. The Medici was thunderstruck, and for once she did not try to hide it. 'The queen-mother is overcome with dread of the Spanish power,' wrote Walsingham.

Catherine saw Spain in a position to attack France, with England's complicity. It was the situation of 1557 again, that conjuncture which the kingdom had resisted so indifferently although it was then the still united and flourishing realm of Henry II. This meant the collapse of that French independence which his widow had so laboriously maintained for the last thirteen years.

Beside herself, the Florentine made Charles comprehend the consequences of his actions; she humiliated him; overwhelmed him. The dashing blade, the boar-killer, the blaspheming hector became a dutiful child again.

As early as 21st July he solemnly renounced his policy. On that day, Giovanni Michieli presented himself at the Louvre. No ambassador had ever received so magnificent a reception. On every step of the great staircase there was a halberdier of the royal guard: attending His Majesty stood all the princes of the blood, including Navarre and Condé, and all the great officers of the realm.

In the name of the Most Serene Republic, Michieli adjured the Most Christian King to preserve his friendship with his Catholic Majesty. In a hoarse, unnatural voice Charles replied, 'Reassure their lordships. I was grieved that the entry of my Protestant subjects into the Low Countries in disobedience to my orders should have given rise to the suspicion that I was going to declare war on Spain.'

Afterwards the Venetian had a private interview with the queen-mother. Catherine ended, 'Send word to their lordships that our deeds even more than our words will show that we desire peace.'

A month later, Michieli must have wondered whether these words had not been an oblique intimation of the massacre of Saint Bartholomew. Indeed, it is not impossible that the Medici, in her extreme distress and exasperation, might then have thought, as she did in 1569, not of massacring the Huguenots but of ridding herself of their leader.

The day after Michieli's reception, Don Diego de Zuniga sent the king a heavily ironic note—'I wished to congratulate myself on the fact that your rebellious subjects who, against your will, set themselves to disturb the Catholic King's concerns, have been punished as they deserved ... I am writing to you, being sure that nobody will be more pleased with this than your Majesty, so good a brother to the Catholic King.'

For his part, Philip II had a similar letter taken to his good brother. When it was handed to him, Charles IX uncovered three times. 'This civility,' wrote the triumphant ambassador, 'must be referred to Don Fadrigue!'

The unhappy king, forced to drink his cup to the dregs, took refuge in a tolerably vile piece of double-dealing. He wrote to Mondoucet, 'You must sometimes tell the Duke of Alba what you know about his enemies so as to give him greater faith in your integrity; for although he may not believe in it, still it will serve my purpose, provided you do it cleverly. It is essential that it should never be discovered that you are in contact with the Prince of Orange and that those whom you send to him should never be discovered carrying anything that would reveal this.' So he did not abandon this war, which, even if it were not to liberate the Low Countries, would set him free.

Nevertheless, at the end of July Catherine could breathe again. She believed she had been able to save the peace, the state and her own power. And now fate offered her a second chance—the chance of taking her kind of revenge against the House of Austria by making sure of a crown for her favourite son.

CHAPTER VI

'IT IS NECESSARY THAT YOU SHOULD LEAVE MY KINGDOM'

SINCE THE COUNCIL of 26th June, there had been a breach between Monsieur and the Admiral. One day the prince had made the Huguenot wait interminably in his antechamber, saying that one had to show what a difference there was between victor and vanquished. What a difference, indeed. There was a most marked discrepancy between the bedecked, made-up, scented young man, loaded with bracelets, and the grey-bearded Calvinist; between the subtle, hidden, dangerous cat and the old lion who never moved out of his road.

Henry, a true son of the Italian Renaissance, surrounded himself with women and favourites. The ambassadors said that he was being corrupted by his women, but the shrewd Duke of Nevers and his young, bellicose, greedy, vainglorious gentlemen were those who really influenced him.

Monsieur was very concerned indeed for his renown, and 'he prized more than his life' his reputation and his place as a statesman. The council of 26th June had won him a very strong position; but it was also a very dangerous one, for, speaking in the name of the Catholic party, he had frustrated the sovereign's designs. In this anarchic realm he stood both for the leader of a winning majority and for the head of the opposition.

As intendant-general he also possessed wide powers, although it is true that they were subject to severe supervision by the old queen. The son's room was between his mother's and an ambassador's, and it would have been most unwise in a captain to go to the one without making an appearance in the other.

Catherine superintended her favourite just as much as her other children. Thanks to the glamorous troopers of her Flying Squadron, she was able to follow them in their thoughts and their hearts, their most private doings. Henry could not escape from this kind of inquisition; though Charles had done so these two years past, by taking a Huguenot mistress.

Both brothers had been initiated by Louise de la Béraudière du Rouhet, one of the Medici's best agents. Then, while the elder sought refuge with Marie Touchet, the younger fell to another Delilah, Renée de Rieux, the lady of Châteauneuf, daughter of one of the first families of Brittany, a magnificent, fiery, dashing thoroughbred.

Philippe Desportes said of this divinity—

> *Comment sans t'éblouir pourras-tu supporter*
> *De ses yeux flamboyants la planète jumelle?*
> *Quelle couleur peindra sa couleur naturelle*
> *Et les graces qu'on voit sur son front voleter?*
> *Quel or égalera l'or de sa blonde tresse,*
> *Quels traits imiteront cette douce rudesse,*
> *Ce port, ce teint, ce ris, ces attraits gracieux?* [1]

And Ronsard—

> *Ce château neuf, ce nouvel édifice,*
> *C'est un chdieuu juli de telle sorte*
> *Que nul ne peut approcher de la porte*
> *Si des grands rois il n'a tiré sa race.* [2]

Renée de Rieux hoped that eventually she might marry this handsome prince, who was more submissive to women than women were to him. Henry was proud of his conquest. Mademoiselle de Châteauneuf was extremely attractive to a great many men, and she was able to provide delights that left the lover tottering, as the watchful ambassadors observed.

Henry was generally considered a cynical libertine—did he not think it amusing, for example, to offer women an obscenely figured goblet?

His mother openly boasted that he was a stallion; but in fact this was not the case, and his heart, filled with contradictory longings,

---

[1] Roughly as follows. How can you withstand the twin planets of her eyes without being blinded by the blaze? How can one describe her native colour or the beauties fleeting and changing on her face? Where is the gold that can rival the gold of her yellow hair? What strokes can draw that sweet asperity, that carriage, bloom, laugh and lovely grace?

[2] This *château neuf*, this castle new, is a castle made in such a way that none may come unto its gate, unless from kings he draws his name. (Translator's note.)

remained untenanted. He was often overcome with melancholy, and this was upon him one evening when he was dancing at a court ball. It was then that the lovely Mary of Cleves suddenly dazzled him, although he had long been acquainted with her.

According to a tale that is difficult to verify, Anjou, in a high state of sweat, retired to a closet and wiped his face with the first thing that came to hand, which happened to be Mary's shift, she too having had to change because of the heat and having left it there. The touch of the shift stirred him deeply.

According to Brantôme, the queen-mother, in her enduring hatred of the Condés, incited Henry to seduce Mary and thus to dishonour the son of the man who was defeated at Jarnac, just before his marriage. The truth of this story is, however, extremely doubtful.

Whatever the truth of the matter, the prince fell most passionately in love. Mary of Cleves was nineteen. It seemed that she was the antithesis of Renée de Rieux. Her loveliness was that of purity, delicacy and gentleness, whereas the beauty of the other at once brought bed to mind. Henry usually boasted loudly of his role of the man of pleasure; but at least some part of him yearned for mystic communion, for the marriage of souls in knightly and religious perfection. The thought of marriage with a person of spotted reputation like Elizabeth of England had filled him with a real horror. He was already growing tired of over-easy, over-skilled women; and four years later he was to abandon them altogether.

With an inconstant sister on one side and a too kind mistress on the other, he sought some unknown ideal throughout his exhausting debauches: Mademoiselle de Clèves showed him what he had gropingly been trying to find.

He was observed to fall into an adolescent rapture, to sigh at the moon, to be writing elegies. Business no longer interested him, and he passed hours on end with the lovely child.

Mary had no defence against this Narcissus, this young man adorned with more laurels than the ancient captains. Did she yield him the treasure that was to be kept for her husband? Brantôme maintains that she did. Mary, until recently, had been the ward of that rigid Protestant Jeanne d'Albret; now she was under the care of a no less rigidly virtuous Catholic, her brother-in-law the Duke of Nevers. Her letters show a modesty and a sense of duty that make her fall at this time most improbable. Besides, Henry could very well have been satisfied with a mystic love. What is certain is that he was consumed with jealousy when he saw his horrible cousin on the point of robbing him of his beloved.

Like a child, he ran to ask for Catherine's help. His mother had never refused him anything: she would certainly take Mary away from that dwarf. He wept, kissing the beautiful Florentine hands. But this flow of feeling did him no service. Had this been one of her 'little eagle's' whims, the queen would willingly have given him all the ladies of her court; but this sudden burning passion shocked her, and she was afraid that she was going to have a rival. She therefore set herself resolutely against her son's request, gave him some pearls by way of consolation and hurried on the marriage. The good of the kingdom was, of course, her best argument: the Bourbons had to be detached from the Admiral, and above all it was essential not to give the trouble-maker an excuse for avenging the failure of his war-policy in France.

At once the Prince's dislike for Coligny darkened into hatred. An event which was shortly to take place caused this feeling to mount to a dangerous climax.

On 7th July, 1572, Sigismund Augustus, King of Poland, died, the last of the House of Jagellon; and his successor was to be elected by the Diet. So began the great interregnum which, in ten months of disorder and contention, was to bring the country to the brink of civil war. And so, too, that 'royal republic' was founded, thanks to which Latin-inspired humanistic politicians could claim to have breathed new life into the institutions of ancient Rome; whereas in fact they had done no more than gratify their deep love of anarchy. And so the unhappy course of Polish history was set in train.

In France, all this was obscure, remote and confused. At that distance the Sarmatian nation seemed scarcely less barbarous than the Muscovite hordes from which it separated the western world, like a strange cross-roads where the blood-soaked memories of the Teutonic Order mixed with the splendour of the Tartar khans. The main thing known about Poland was her fidelity to the Church, although there too the Reformation had progressed and created a numerous and powerful Protestant minority despite the Catholics. Almost nothing was known of her subtle and brilliant civilisation, the charm of her remarkably cultivated upper class, of the pleasantness of life there nor of that tolerance which Europe seemed to have forgotten. Still less was anything known of the paradoxical constitution in which could be found, together with the profoundest respect for the standing of the king, laws which did away with the very essence of royal power and even with the hereditary principle; customs so individualistic that even the hardiest democracy would have found them excessive, and a feudal system which, bringing the lower classes down to an almost servile condition, delivered up the whole country to an unbelievably divided nobility and to an effete clergy.

This 'extreme climate had bred men with the temperament of extremists'—turbulent, eccentric, talkative, lovers of disorder who hurled themselves with joy into struggles between parties, races, religions, classes, tongues and provinces. Continually invoking the love of their country, they continually laboured to destroy it. And in the meantime the Muscovite, the Turk and the Tartar stood at their gates, always ready to make a prey of Poland.

The coming royal election had naturally inflamed their passions. The Grand Duke of Moscow, Ivan the Terrible, the first to have taken the title of Tsar of All the Russias, was a candidate; so was the Archduke Ernest, the Emperor's son. The Holy See was trying to group the Catholics round the latter, in the hope of leading both the Emperor and Poland into the Christian League, a prospect which alarmed the moderates hardly less than it did the Protestants, whose chief was Firlej, the Palatine (the governor) of Cracow.

Nobody wanted the terrible Ivan. It was then that Jean Zamoyski, who had been one of Francis II's pages and a student at Strasbourg, and who was one of the chief creators of the royal republic, pronounced the name of the Duke of Anjou. All those who feared the Habsburg as much as they did the Tsar joined his party. The recollection of the martial glories of Jarnac and Moncontour attracted others who were hesitant. Catherine's agents had been at work in the country for years, and now her foresight repaid her triumphantly. Not only would her favourite reign, but Charles IX and he would hold 'the two ends of the strap' which they would tighten about the House of Austria. The King of France might reach out for the imperial crown that Francis I had failed to win, while his younger brother, uniting with the Turks, would rule the Mediterranean. The hegemony of Spain would be a thing of the past.

In reality the queen-mother and the Admiral were pursuing the same aim. Only their means were opposite and opposed: the Medici, patient and cautious, tried to go round the obstacles; the man of iron, the Calvinist, tried to smash them. The one, a realistic politician, based her policy upon France's traditional allies; the other,

Philip II of Spain
Elisabeth de Valois

Francis II of France
Mary Stuart

Henry, King of Navarre
Marguerite de Valois

Charles IX of France
Elizabeth of Austria

7 Four royal couples

8 Gaspard de Coligny

the uncompromising servant of an ideal, could not bring himself not to place his trust in his fellow Protestants of England.

The clash between these two conceptions had already created a violent enmity. The Polish affair further envenomed it by adding the element of passion.

As soon as he learned of this chance of ridding himself of his younger brother, and saw his mother working to accomplish it, Charles could not conceal his joy. With Monsieur gone, he would really feel that he was the master; he alone would reap the honours of a victory which in spite of everything he counted on winning; and the Catholic party, leaderless, would no longer presume to thwart him.

But this mirage had scarcely formed before it vanished almost completely. The Duke of Anjou held aloof from his own glory. He would not exile himself to a country of ice inhabited by drunkards whose language he did not understand. The thought of leaving the happiness that he had glimpsed with Mary of Cleves maddened him.

His delight turning into fury, the king raged and stormed. Coligny, full of paternal gravity, then intervened between the two young men. He displayed surprise: in one year Monsieur had rejected two crowns, that of England and now that of Poland. Why was he so insistent upon not leaving the Louvre, where he could not but occupy the second rank? Was there not the possibility that evil minds might think that he was hoping to succeed to a brother aged twenty-two, recently married and presently perhaps to be given an heir?

This was enough to bring the anger and the distress of the unhappy king to the boiling-point. He sent for Monsieur. With his hand on his dagger he cursed him violently and ordered him to reign. 'There cannot be two kings in France! It is necessary that you should leave my kingdom and find another crown: as for me, I am old enough to rule myself!'

Henry knew that this time he would not have his mother's support. He gave in. Monluc, the Bishop of Valence, one of the finest diplomats of his time, instantly set off for Cracow to support the cause of the Duke of Anjou before the Diet.

From that time onward Henry nourished an undying hatred for the Admiral; and at the same time he and his brother were possessed by the fury of the Atridae.

CHAPTER VII

'SLAUGHTER ALL THE FRENCHMEN?'

THE NUNCIO SALVIATI was disturbed to observe that, contrary to the general opinion, the king was pursuing his own personal policy.

Since the events in Flanders he had spent seven hundred thousand ducats in support of the rebels—an immense effort for his ruined treasury—and he was still raising troops. Gregory XIII's envoy extraordinary had another just cause for anxiety—the absence of the queen-mother, who, together with Monsieur, had gone to Châlons to be with the Duchess of Lorraine.

Charles IX was following 'the stag that ran before him'. But in Paris the Admiral was disturbingly busy. He was perpetually conferring with the Protestant princes and even with His Majesty's secretaries. Quiévrain and its consequences seemed to have been forgotten: the rumour of war grew loud again.

On 1st August the king returned to Paris and summoned the Admiral, Montmorency and his secretaries. A report that war had been decided upon instantly spread abroad, and indeed it had been decided upon in Charles's mind: Coligny had recovered all his influence over the king. Four thousand foot were sent to the frontier of Picardy. Volunteers were preparing in England, and the queen did not forbid their taking part in the conflict.

The king wanted to strengthen his Protestant policy. He complained that the Church was making his 'fat sister Margot' waste a great deal of her 'good time'. Blaspheming as usual, he shouted, 'If Master Pope plays the ass too long, I shall take Margot by the hand myself and lead her to be married in the middle of a Protestant hymn-singing.'

The Comte de Retz pressed the matter upon Salviati in the king's name. The marriage would be put off until about 20th August. If the Pope had not sent the dispensation by then, it was unlikely that the king would wait for it any longer. The Prince of Condé gave the lead: he openly declared that he had no need of any papal dispensation to marry his cousin, Mary of Cleves. The king's dispensation was enough for him. And the marriage was fixed for 10th August.

On the 3rd, Michieli and Cavalli made another approach in favour of peace. Charles deplored his Huguenot subjects' lack of discipline. 'It is impossible,' said he, 'to restrain them either by threats or punishment.'

But this convinced neither the Venetians nor the Spanish ambassador, in whose opinion the evil was already irreparable. Michieli was even gloomier.

Retz and Birague, the queen-mother's devoted servants, also took fright and sent a messenger to Châlons, where Catherine was lingering with the sick Duchess of Lorraine.

The queen hastened to Paris, without stopping on the way, and she arrived on 4th August. She at once went to see her son, who had just refused Zuniga an audience. Once more she wept, once more she threatened to go away. She exposed the English double-dealing, the trap set for France.

Early the next morning she and the Admiral walked alone in her beautiful garden of the Tuileries, outside the wall and protected against the activities of the seditious by a bastion. The discussion went on and on. Jérôme de Gondi would dearly have loved to overhear some of it. He watched the stout woman in black and the thin lord with wide sleeves as they walked up and down. When at last the Admiral had taken his leave, the queen called for Gondi; but it was only to ask the time.

'Eleven, Madame.'

'My feet told me that it was quite as late as that.'

Already it was being said in the town that she had 'completely undone everything that had been done while she was away'.

On the evening of the same day she received the Spanish ambassador. Don Diego overflowed with vehement complaints.

'Your Majesty may take my word for it . . .' When the king arrived four days before his mother, both sides were so near fighting, that according to the perception that God had given him, it appeared that he must be allowing himself to be drawn towards a definite breach.'

'There will be no war in any circumstances whatever,' asserted Catherine.

Don Diego was very happy to hear it. He deeply regretted Her Majesty's absences: as soon as she left the court there was talk of war! He also regretted the movement of troops and his uncertainty as to the nature of the expedition that Strozzi's fleet was to undertake. And then, letting his anxiety get the better of his judgment, he declared that in order that he should be fully satisfied he, as the representative of the Catholic King, should be allowed to accompany the expedition when it took place. Catherine found the idea so ludicrous that she burst into laughter. She afterwards did her best to soothe and flatter the hidalgo, and sent him away at least half satisfied. Then she summoned Jérôme de Gondi, of whose activities she was well aware.

As soon as he was free again, the Italian hurried to see Zuniga. He was overwhelmed with questions, and answered them in such a manner as to pacify the perpetually worried ambassador. Yes, the queen had saved the peace. In a few days there would be a great council, and she would not fail to have her way once more. Before the end of the week the fleet would no longer be a disturbance to the Catholic King.

'But now, Monsieur,' ended the Italian, in a confidential tone, 'I must tell you something . . . it would be well to have more important pledges for the preservation of the peace.'

'How could there be more pledges?'

'By giving us an Infanta for the Duke of Anjou.'

So that was the price that the Medici meant to have for her good offices. Not without some scorn the ambassador replied, 'The Catholic King would not act wisely in marrying his daughters, since he has only one son.'

Don Diego was incapable of understanding her complex mind and her extraordinarily fertile, but essentially womanly, intelligence, and in imputing to the Medici the baseness of a 'shopkeeper' he judged her as did most of the French lords.

He confirmed this in his report to Philip II. In his opinion, the queen-mother was acting according to strictly personal and selfish motives; she was against the war because she could not bear seeing her son under another's influence, because she could not bring herself to relinquish the power that she had been waiting for these twenty-five years and that she had won with such pains. 'In all of which,' stated the ambassador, 'she puts her private interests before the welfare of the king her son.'

From such a pen, this is an astonishing remark; and it calls for reflection along two different lines. Was Catherine really sacrificing the good of the kingdom to her own personal interests? Did this war really represent the welfare of the king and the nation?

It cannot be denied that a woman completely wrapped up in politics, a dominating mother accustomed to ruling her children, might be repelled by the prospect of a fall from power. But it cannot be denied either that the *gouvernante* of France had passionately guarded the unity and the integrity of the nation as well as the ruling house. The queen-mother was sure that neither the one nor the other could withstand a war with Spain. For her, therefore, there was no question of a distinction between her own interests and those of the public.

Was she right or wrong? Philip II was at that time going through a difficult period, particularly with regard to money, and it may be that she exaggerated the extent of his strength. Yet the experts foresaw an eight years' war. An eight years' war coming after those of the foregoing reigns and the country's fratricidal struggles meant the exhaustion and ruin of the kingdom if it were victorious, and complete overthrow if it were lost. In no way did it guarantee the end of civil war, as Coligny and Duplessis-Mornay maintained. The subjects of Charles IX were not those of Louis XIII. In their opinion religion was far more important than country. The extreme Catholics would have done anything to prevent the crusade against the House of Austria—Henry IV himself fell under their blows when he attempted it. If he were to begin a war, therefore, the king ran the danger of an uprising and of that occupation of the country by foreigners which in fact took place in 1589, as soon as Catherine was dead.

Could a rapid, almost a lightning victory, justify the undertaking? Was such a thing possible? Coligny's military talents were very far from equalling Alba's. And yet a chance of success did exist, a possibility that was controlled by Elizabeth Tudor. If the English, the Flemings and the Beggars all acted in unison with the French armies one might hope for a great Spanish defeat in the Low Countries that would oblige Philip II to come to terms, as Henry II had done after Saint-Quentin. It would be a daring gamble. If it did not, the whole game was lost before it began.

Now Elizabeth, who wanted a Franco-Spanish war, was determined to prevent any triumph on the part of her new allies. Everything urged her in this direction, from the commercial interests of her country to her designs on Calais. She had never forgiven Coligny for his complete change of front in 1564 in the retaking of Le Havre after having given it up, and she had no scruples about betraying him in her turn.

The far-sighted guessed what her intentions were. During these first days of August in Paris, there was talk of the withdrawal of the English troops from the Low Countries. Whether it was true or false, news of such a kind could win the game for the queen: Coligny told Walsingham this very plainly, and Walsingham sent a messenger to Elizabeth's favourite. 'I have written in all haste to the Earl of Leicester,' he wrote to Smith, 'to try to have the recall of our troops deferred, otherwise the whole plan is endangered. If the business of the Low Countries does not succeed, we are clearly in the greatest peril.'

He also told Lord Burghley, 'The king was determined upon war, but the queen, his mother, showed him that without our help it would fail miserably; and by dint of tears, she has made him entirely change his mind. I am very much afraid that without God's hand this may end unhappily.'

'Without our help it would fail miserably.' The Admiral must, in this, have been of the same opinion as the queen-mother; but like a true mystic he believed, he wished to believe, that help would come. Can it be held that strong determination in the King of France would in spite of everything have induced Elizabeth to support the cause of her fellow Protestants? A letter to Burghley from Sir Humphrey Gilbert, who commanded the English contingent of the garrison of Flushing, supplies a crushing rebuttal.

'I have been told,' says this captain, 'that a large body of French troops is getting ready to come here. What am I to do? Leave this town or, if the queen gives me a free hand, provoke a riot between the French and the townspeople and slaughter all the Frenchmen?' [1]

The Admiral did not conceal his resentment when the embarrassed king told him that the matter would be submitted to the council yet again.

'Sire,' he cried, 'this council is made up of lawyers, and from their calling they hate war.'

'Set your mind at rest, father, I shall not summon only lawyers, but soldiers too—Montpensier, Cossé, Nevers, Tavannes. You know them well: there is not one who can stand up to you.'

For this decisive meeting Coligny armed himself once more with Duplessis-Mornay's paper. The Duke of Anjou was now, in relation

[1] *Calendar of State Papers* (1572b, p. 169).

to the king, in a delicate position, and he could not undertake the rejoinder; the queen-mother entrusted this to her faithful Morvillier, a very wise man according to the Catholics, and according to Agrippa d'Aubigné an enemy of innovation and a 'time-server whose prudence was prompted by timidity'.

Morvillier adopted the former arguments of the Duke of Nevers. He brought forward new ones, showed the commercial ties between England and Spain, and proved that the entry of the French into the Low Countries would inevitably bring about the Emperor's intervention. The king would soon have to stand against a coalition which might even include England herself. As for the yearly million in subsidies which the Admiral imagined he would get from the Low Countries, how could they be secured except by plainly and simply annexing a country which it was proposed to liberate? The Flemings had shown after Quiévrain how much they loved the French.

All these things and many more besides were said at this moving council of 9th August, which continued the next day. Tavannes, the old warrior, spoke nobly—'Let us maintain our reputation with God and man, and peace with one and all, above all with our own people, keeping our word in the matter of religion, and let us take breath for a while.'

In a somewhat unexpected manner, Catherine spoke of the immorality of a conflict between France and Spain. Coligny, unmoved, unfolded his plan and guaranteed the raising of a Huguenot army whose size alarmed the Catholics—four thousand horse and fifteen thousand foot.

'There shall be no war,' repeated Catherine.

At the beginning of the discussion she had been in the minority, but little by little she won the upper hand. On 10th August she had her way: the council confirmed its former decision in favour of peace.

Jérôme de Gondi hurried to tell Zuniga. According to the ambassador's report to Philip II of what Gondi said, the Admiral had bowed to the decision and had promised to do nothing without the queen's consent. It seems that Catherine had wished to reassure the King of Spain, for in fact Coligny had no notion of giving in. When the sitting was over but the members of the council were still present, he cried, 'Madame, the king refuses to undertake the war. May God send that another war does not come upon him from which he will not be able to withdraw.'

It was clear. Some historians have been at pains to remove the guilt from this expression. Those who heard it had no hesitation in understanding it: Coligny had locked himself in his tragic dilemma, war abroad or war at home; and he was not to extricate himself.

The queen-mother was deeply moved. But so sanguine was her nature that she saw no immediate danger. Peace was saved, and the Protestants would be kept calm by the marriage of Navarre, now so near. Catherine thought that she could give herself a few days as a mother, and she went to the castle of Monceaux, where the pitiable Duchess of Lorraine, being ill again, had been obliged to interrupt her journey.

For their part, the Protestant lords and princes left for Blandy-en-Brie, the estate of Madame de Rohan, Mary of Cleves' grand-mother. There the Duke of Anjou's beloved was married to Condé according to the rites of the Calvinists. Monsieur, staying in Paris, hid neither his anguish nor his desire for revenge.

Everybody now knew the conflict in which the Admiral was engaged. Friends, sometimes anonymous, showered counsels of prudence upon him. 'Remember', said a letter, 'the maxim that all the Papists observe—faith is not to be kept with heretics . . . If you are wise, you will leave this court, this sewer, as quickly as you can.'

To all these warnings the Admiral replied, 'It is better to die a hundred times over than to live in a perpetual state of suspicion. I am weary of these alarms. In any case, I have lived long enough; and I would rather that my body should be dragged about the streets of Paris than that I should engage in another civil war.'

He was sincere: but alas, he still believed that only war against Spain could spare him from rebellion. Furthermore, he was aware that Charles IX had not given up his dreams of glory.

Neither the one nor the other submitted to the council's decision for a single day. Taking advantage of the queen-mother's absence, they resumed their protracted conferences. 'The Admiral and the court are almost next-door neighbours,' wrote the provost Morillon to Cardinal Granvelle, warning him of 'great preparations for war'. The king sent an order to his ambassador, La Mothe-Fénelon, 'Continue to urge this queen [of England] as pressingly as you can to come out openly against the King of Spain.' The Admiral advised the Prince of Orange that he was preparing twelve thousand arque-busiers and two thousand horse and was 'counting upon coming with them'.

The young Navarre joined in. He asked that his marriage should be celebrated as early as possible, for he meant to take part in the expedition and to bring the many gentlemen of his suite.

The king was delighted by this approach. But what of the dispensation? In Rome Monsieur de Chauvigny had handed over so pressing a letter from His Majesty that at last the Pope 'had been moved to satisfy him on this point'. A courier from the French ambassador travelled at speed carrying the great news. Charles IX knew nothing of it. In his impatience he decided that the marriage should take place on 18th August; and as he expected a refusal from the Holy See he ordered the governor of Lyons to hold all couriers between France and Italy until that date.

On 15th August the queen-mother left Monceaux and returned to Paris with the Duchess of Lorraine. She at once saw the magnitude of the disaster; the whole machine of war was in motion, in spite of all her efforts, and it seemed that nothing could stop it. And all this at a moment when her subtle diplomatic methods were on the point of winning everywhere and when without any war at all they were about to inflict a most painful defeat upon Philip II.

The Polish election was going well. Monsieur de Schomberg had secured the support of the Duke of Saxony for Monsieur. Noailles, in Constantinople, had obtained a more favourable treaty than ever Francis I had been able to negotiate, a treaty in which the Sultan promised to hand over to France all the conquests he should make upon the Spaniards. Finally, the terrible Elizabeth, having yielded to the charm of the Duke of Alençon's envoy, Monsieur de La Mole, suddenly began to think seriously of marrying the young prince.

'Let the duke come quickly. He must come,' said her ministers and her ladies.

If the Valois-Bourbon marriage ensured domestic peace, France, without the risk of battles, might again become the principal kingdom in Christendom.

Catherine saw all this patient, difficult work on the point of being brought to nothing. She also saw herself dispossessed. The power of government was slipping from her and passing into the hands of the man who had been condemned to death in 1569.

Everything in her revolted against this—her love of power and the purpose in life that she had given herself, that of safeguarding their patrimony for the descendants of Francis I, the great king who had let the humble Medici into his family. She had no doubts about herself: she was sure that in taking the rule away from her, Coligny was preparing the kingdom's ruin.

Later, Michieli was to accuse her of having acted out of revenge, of having pursued *sua vendetta*. Certainly the Florentine now hated Coligny, as she hated the Cardinal of Lorraine. But it was not only of this hatred that she was thinking. As she knelt weeping at her *prie-dieu* she thought also Guises' men, those fanatics who were filling Paris and who, to prevent a Protestant victory, might perhaps overturn the throne. She thought of Saint-Quentin, the Spanish invasion, the deadly game of the English.

The lessons of her master, Machiavelli, came to her mind: the prince is not cruel when he uses cruelty for 'the service of the people'; he should not hesitate before the death of one man if that death spares his subjects a world of unhappiness.

CHAPTER VIII

THE 'BLOOD-RED WEDDING'

THE GUISES had taken no part in the debate upon the war. Since May, the Cardinal of Lorraine had been in Rome: the Duke of Guise and his brothers rarely came to the Louvre and when they were there they said very little.

But for all that, their state of mind was clear enough. The Lorrainers hated the Admiral, not only as the leader of the party they had so bitterly fought, but primarily as the murderer of the great Monsieur de Guise. Whatever the truth, nothing would persuade them that Poltrot de Méré had not been set on by Coligny; nothing would persuade them to forfeit their honour by giving up revenge—a revenge that they had merely postponed out of their obedience to the king, or rather out of fear of the queen-mother.

It was a great error, therefore, to suppose that they would sit with their hands folded and watch their enemy take over power and liberate the Low Countries at the expense of the King of Spain, their protector, their ally, their provider of funds.

Certain remarks, certain boasts of the Cardinal of Lorraine, said to have been made just after the massacre of Saint Bartholomew, might lead one to suppose that in about April they had been thinking about the assassination of Coligny and the Calvinist leaders who had come to court with Henry of Navarre. Historians as eminent as Lucien Romier, having vainly searched for some trace of premeditation in the deeds and the writings of the queen-mother, have upheld this contention. Among the arguments on the other side, one must take note of Mariéjol's: the Cardinal would not have tried so hard to prevent the granting of the dispensation if the marriage had been necessary to the success of their plot.

The matter is not clear. But it is certain that the Guises, whether for attack or defence, were making very serious preparations. As early as the end of 1571 Marshal de Montmorency informed the king that the number of their supporters in Paris was increasing and that 'they were hiring rooms in various districts and holding secret meetings by night; that they were doing their utmost to accumulate arms, particularly short weapons, the most effective for quick killing in houses and in the streets'.

The governor of Paris reported that it was believed that among other plans there was one for laying siege to the Admiral in his own house.

The Hôtel de Guise, an impregnable fortress set in the heart of the city, jealously kept its secrets, while outside a perpetual thunder kept up the party's spirits and attracted fresh recruits. This thunder came from the churches, where every day the preachers fulminated against the heretics and the wicked, unnatural marriage of their leader. Some of these preachers had come from Spain and Italy, disguised as students, to fan the blaze of pious wrath. Bishop Sorbin openly threatened the king: by marrying his sister to the Bourbon he would lay himself open to the punishment of Esau, whose birthright went to Jacob—and by Jacob was understood the Duke of Anjou.

The authority of the king and the unity of France would not have survived in 1563 if the two parties had not cancelled one another out. It was natural that the queen-mother should remember this. Alone against so many enemies, she could see only one way of averting total disaster—to have Coligny killed by the Guises and then the Guises by Coligny's avengers.

All the sources prove that this was indeed what she thought. It was a reflection that today would seem unworthy of a chief of state, but there was nothing in it to surprise a man of the Renaissance. Louis XI, Henry VIII, Elizabeth, Philip II and most of the Italian princes thought of much crueller and more treacherous plans, without the excuse of so great a danger.

The methods of the Medici are rightly contrasted with those of Henry IV. But Henry IV would have been powerless if an attempt like that which failed in 1572 had not succeeded in 1588–1589; if the assassination of the Duke of Guise, avenged by the murder of Henry III, had not left him a clear field.

Political crime is still crime: yet one cannot judge it outside the context of the no less criminal atmosphere of fanaticism and rage in which it is almost spontaneously generated. The pressure of malignant forces worked upon this timid, peaceable, procrastinating and sceptical woman and prompted the planning of her diabolical scheme.

It is worth dwelling on this short space of time during which Catherine believed herself in control of events. Fate often provides those whom it is about to lead to perdition with such illusions.

In the light of a report from the Tuscan ambassador, Petrucci, the fatal idea can be seen taking shape just after the battle of Quiévrain.

The queen-mother heard the news on the 20th July. On the night of the 22nd to 23rd she received in secret the widow of François de Guise, Anne d'Este, who had married again and was now the Duchess of Nemours.

According to the then current ideas about the importance of family, Madame de Nemours was a far greater princess than the Medici. In her veins ran the blood of the French kings and the blood of a Pope, for she was the grand-daughter of Louis XII by her mother, Renée de France, and through her paternal grandmother, Lucrezia Borgia, she was a descendant of Alexander VI. She was a proud, noble and remarkably beautiful woman, imbued with a sense of duty towards the state. Yet in spite of her second marriage—or perhaps because of it—she felt it her duty to avenge her first husband.

Catherine gave her to understand that this vengeance, which for the past nine years had been forbidden, might at last be permitted. Anne d'Este, a true Italian, refrained from committing herself. The Guise clan, though mistrustful, nevertheless made plans to carry out the vendetta.

The queen-mother saw the duchess several times after this: the duchess remained very reserved, pretending to be afraid of the king. When Catherine returned from Monceaux on 15th August, she decided to precipitate matters; but, prudent as ever, she first consulted Michieli. The Venetian strengthened her resolution. On 5th August, Philip II, without knowing what was in her mind, had written to her of his own accord suggesting the same idea.

There was another meeting with Anne d'Este, this time in the presence of the Duke of Anjou, whose hatred for the Admiral had reached its height.

Not long before, Her Majesty had said that she would turn a blind eye if the Guises chose to strike at their enemy. Now she incited them to do so. In any case, she wished to know their decision. Madame de Nemours spoke plainly: her sons thought only of punishing their father's assassin, but she, anxious for their safety, asked Monsieur to supply the executioner. The blow, coming from the intendant-general of the realm, would take on the aspect of a judicial execution. And the good lady mentioned a certain Gascon bravo in the service of his Highness who would be eminently suitable for the task. But neither the queen nor the prince saw things in this light, and on that evening the discussion went no further.

While they were trying to find the best way of killing the Admiral, Catherine and Henry spared no efforts to hasten the Navarre marriage. It is clear, therefore, that they really hoped to restore peace between the two parties once the leaders had been removed.

To Charles's fury the Cardinal of Bourbon insisted upon the dispensation. The queen came to her son's assistance. A forged letter was produced in which the French ambassador gave news of the imminent arrival of the document: after the most anxious hesitation the Cardinal announced that he was satisfied. Now it remained to find a bishop who would consent to be his assistant. Jacques Amyot, Bishop of Damietta and the king's almoner, the Bishop of Châlons, the queen's almoner, and the Bishop of Angers, the king's confessor, each in turn refused. The Duke of Anjou made another approach to Amyot, his former tutor, and pressed him strongly.

'My lord,' said the translator of Plutarch, 'the king is the master of my life and my possessions, but not of my conscience. And since he allows the Huguenots freedom of conscience he must allow me the same privilege.'

'Then you do not think that we have a conscience too—that we are Catholics?' returned the prince.

'His Majesty and your Highness are duty-bound to take our advice in matters of conscience: but I am not required to ask it from your Highness.' [1]

The more pliable Bishop of Digne yielded to the royal pressure.

In the meantime an envoy from the Duke of Alba, Monsieur de Gomicourt, had just arrived. He was received in private audience by the queen-mother, to whom he made very strong complaints about the fleet, which was still there at Bordeaux in spite of all undertakings. Catherine promised satisfaction and excused herself on the grounds of her preoccupation with her daughter's marriage. In the public audience at which he offered the engaged couple his best wishes, Gomicourt denounced the new concentration of Huguenot troops on the frontier. Charles swore that these movements were contrary to his orders.

---

[1] Letter of 20th August, 1572, from Don Diego de Zuniga to Philip II. *Archives Nationales*, K.1 530.

'If the Huguenots do not withdraw, will some action be taken?' asked Gomicourt.

'Something shall be done; and in a few days you will be able to estimate the truth of my words by the result.'

It was in exactly these words that the king replied to Coligny when, on this same 17th August, the betrothal having been solemnised at the Louvre, the Admiral urged him to throw off the mask. The marriage was to take place the next day. Charles begged the Admiral to wait for four days. During these four days the marriage would be splendidly celebrated and in the general happiness the Catholics and Protestants would merge. It would be a vigil of arms, and as soon as it was over the dancers would take to horse and the war would begin.

The queen-mother had spies everywhere, and she could not long remain in ignorance of this conversation. No further procrastination was possible. As soon as night had fallen Madame de Nemours returned to the Louvre.

The two Italians came to an agreement. The former 'king's killer', Maurevert, who had failed to kill the Admiral in 1569, had taken service with the Guises and was living under their protection. It was agreed that he should be told to succeed where before he had failed. The Guises were aware of their strength in having this royal complicity, in their troops, in their popularity, and in the anger that this sacrilegious marriage had unleashed in Paris. They agreed to undertake the risks of the venture and to carry it to a conclusion. The queen-mother was delighted to see them walk straight into her net, with their eyes firmly closed.

The people, with an uncanny foresight of something that they could not know, were already saying that this marriage would be 'des noces vermeilles'—that is, a blood-red wedding.

Never had a city provided such contrasts as those which astonished the ambassadors throughout the day of 18th August. In a cloudless blue sky a blazing sun seemed to heighten the passions of a fanatical, untamed and savage populace that saw itself openly defied. The very cobbles appeared to seethe with revolt as the Catholic lords, dark and lowering, stood face to face with the noisy Huguenots, arrogant in their certainty of victory.

The air reeked of battle and of crime, but paradoxically it circulated in a city dressed for a festival, decked out in its most sumptuous ornaments. Triumphal arches stood at every cross-roads;

tapestries hung from every balcony; the merest idler wore his best clothes. As for the court, it dazzled everybody, even the ambassador of Venice, that republic so proud of its wealth, so much richer than this bankrupt kingdom.

Michieli was astonished to see how France had been restored by two years of peace. He could not prevent himself from admiring the magnificence of the nobles who surrounded the king and the beauty of the women. It was as a private spectator that he admired them, however; for following the example of the Nuncio and Zuniga, none of the ambassadors took part in the ceremony.

Their Majesties made their way to the bishop's palace, where the bride had spent the night, and accompanied her to the church. For his part, Henry of Navarre arrived attended by the princes of Condé and Conti, the Admiral, the Comte de La Rochefoucauld and a host of Protestant gentlemen.

Charles IX was dressed 'like the sun'. The queen-mother, having for this occasion left off her mourning, shone with the fire of her famous jewels. Monsieur wore pale yellow satin embroidered with silver and sewn with pearls.

But 'the wonder of heaven and earth', as Brantôme puts it, was Marguerite de France, extremely unhappy in her golden robe and her blue velvet cloak with its train four yards in length.

A complex ceremonial had had to be worked out, for there was no precedent for a mixed marriage. Navarre did not go into the cathedral but went to the bishop's palace. The Duke of Anjou took his place during the mass. As soon as it was over, Montmorency-Damville went to fetch Henry. The married pair, followed by the royal family and the great nobles, took their place on a dais that had been set up in front of the porch of Notre Dame and which stretched from the bishop's palace as far as the choir. It was there that the Cardinal of Bourbon, assisted by the Bishop of Digne and two Italian prelates—'both rather dubious characters', in Zuniga's opinion—gave them the nuptial benediction.

When the Cardinal asked for the sacramental consent, the princess kept her lips firmly closed. With his strong grasp the king forced her to bow her head, and the cardinal contented himself with this enforced assent.

Was this piece of play-acting prepared in advance and intended to provide for the future by creating the basis for a plea of nullity? Did Marguerite, placed there before the two men she had loved,

Guise and her own brother, Anjou, refuse, in this moving instant, to play the part of Iphigenia? It is hard to decide.

The Admiral was not present during this last part of the ceremony. He had lingered in the cathedral and there he contemplated the standards which hung from the roof—standards which the forces of Monsieur had taken from his at Jarnac and at Moncontour.

'Soon,' said he to Damville, 'they will be taken down, and others, pleasanter to look at, will be put in their place.'

No doubt he was thinking of the coming campaign in the Low Countries. But among the various people who heard him, some ultra-Catholics believed, or feigned to believe, that this was an allusion to a fresh outbreak of civil war.

So this unnatural marriage had taken place—this marriage which the pious and the extremists on both sides had refused to believe in. It was designed to bring harmony: its immediate effect was to aggravate hatred.

Standing about their master and waiting for the mass to end, the Gascon Huguenots had made the echoes ring with the noise of their ill-bred joy and their hooting; and this had provoked violent reactions from the crowd.

'We shall compel you to go in,' shouted the Parisians, pointing to the cathedral.

The challenges and the threats spread and grew more frequent throughout the festivities, whose organiser, the Duke of Anjou, had not been sparing in setting traps for the Protestants.

On the 18th, after the ceremony, their Majesties gave a feast worthy of Pantagruel to which they invited the 'orders of the city'. Afterwards there was supper, a ball and a masque. In the great vaulted hall of the Louvre there appeared three waggons carrying 'silvered rocks'. They were driven by the king, Anjou and Alençon. When they stopped, musicians emerged from the rocks and sang beautiful poems set to delightful music. After this the party grew more disorderly: they went on until dawn.

On the 19th, Monsieur gave a dinner and a ball. In the evening there was a tournament at which the ambassadors were present. The king invited Zuniga to take part, but Don Diego begged to be excused, on account of his indifferent health and the coolness of the night air.

On the 20th there was an extraordinary entertainment, the Mystery of the Three Worlds, half pantomime and half tournament, which took place at the Petit-Bourbon. A huge platform acted as stage. On the right there was Paradise with the Elysian Fields below it and twelve nymphs to represent their charming inhabitants; on the left Tartarus, wrapped in sulphurous smoke and grimly lit by Bengal fire. Ghosts moved about within.

Some knights errant—Navarre, Condé and their friends—tried to invade Paradise. But they were violently repelled by the angels—the king and his brothers—who hurled them into Tartarus, where devils held them prisoner. Mercury and Cupid, riding cocks, then descended from the flies, lavished poetic compliments upon the victors and invited them to join the nymphs. For a whole hour the ladies went through the motions of the ballet, and then danced with the angels. Anjou had thought out this way of flouting Condé, who was kept in Tartarus while his wife and his rival held hands and talked of love.

In the end the allegory took a more civil turn. In answer to the prayer of the nymphs the angels went to look for the prisoners. Having opened the gates of Erebus for them, they challenged them, and once more they broke lances together.

During this evening of the 20th tension mounted. The Protestants were infuriated at the way the festivities were going. The Guises, knowing that this was the eve of their revenge, did not hide their feelings. The king was disturbed: he told Coligny of his fear that they might attempt some mischief and ordered the arquebusiers of his guard to Paris.

For his part, the Duke of Montmorency foresaw the explosion. He was the governor of Paris, and it was his duty to keep the city quiet. But he was both a Catholic and the Admiral's first cousin, and he had no wish to find himself in an impossible situation. He prudently decided that he would simply take his leave and abandon the city in his charge to the most appalling disasters. With him all order and good sense departed. Everyone grasped the significance of the situation.

The Admiral, however, had other reasons for uneasiness. According to rumour, the Duke of Alba, a prey to the most acute anxiety, was thinking of having the prisoners taken at Quiévrain put to death. Coligny, no doubt aware of the contact between Gondi and Zuniga, bluntly told the Italian that if this threat were put into effect every Spaniard in France would meet a similar death.

The 'splendours' proceeded despite all this. For the 21st, Monsieur had devised something between a carnival and a tournament in which Turks were to do battle with Amazons. Navarre, Condé and their gentlemen were the infidels: as for the Amazons, they presented the unexpected features of the king and his brothers. The three young men, dressed as women, displayed a single breast and waved a bow. Of course, they triumphed over their adversaries.

This was a fresh humiliation for the Protestants and a profound satisfaction for Anjou, who was taking a bitter revenge for his lost sweetheart—avenging himself on others by making ready a crime, and on himself by revealing his secret nature.

Later, Henry IV would amuse himself in telling how during those feverish days he had chanced to play at dice with Anjou and Guise, and how he had suddenly observed that they saw blood running between their fingers.

The festivities were still dragging on when Monsieur de Chailly, the Duke of Aumale's major-domo, brought Maurevert to a house in the rue des Poulies which belonged to Canon Villemur, the Duke of Guise's former tutor, and which the Admiral usually passed when he left the Louvre. The killer slept there. The next morning he posted himself near a window. A thick curtain hid him. His arquebus was in position.

In the meantime, the indefatigable Catherine, sitting at her desk, suggested to the Queen of England a meeting with the Duke of Alençon 'at sea, on a fine calm day, between Dover, Boulogne and Calais'. She knew very well that her 'gossip' would bear her no grudge for the death of Coligny.

PART 3

The 'Great Madness'

CHAPTER I

'SEE HOW HONEST MEN ARE
TREATED'

AT THE MOMENT when the decisive issue is joined, it is no doubt as well to look at the structure of the Protestant party, that party which had so completely altered the face of a kingdom which, not long since, had astonished the world with its unity and centralisation.

It so happens that Michieli took care to explain its workings to the Most Serene Republic. 'It is said', he wrote, 'that all those of the [Protestant] religion are divided into twenty-four churches which include and share all the provinces of France between them. When some public business is in hand, their ministers are severally charged with taking the personal opinion of their subordinates and with reporting to six others, who are also ministers and are elected as being the most important, from the whole body. These six report to two superiors, who were the Queen of Navarre, during her lifetime, and the Admiral; and everything which these two ordered, according to their wishes, was at once put into effect. Together all these churches, by collections and ordinary contributions, yield eight hundred thousand francs [1] every year, paid without distinction by each as his rate and his share, even by the common people and the wage-earners, such as labourers, artisans, servants and the like. Each rates himself voluntarily, according to his conscience, at a greater or lesser sum, according to what he thinks he can afford, and pays with a marvellous promptness and zeal. With these eight hundred thousand francs they defray their ordinary charges and expenses: the Queen of Navarre, as supreme head, had a hundred thousand francs; the Admiral, for his maintenance and his pay, forty thousand; Monsieur de La Rochefoucauld, ten thousand; the captains, Briquemaut, Piles and other approved, courageous soldiers like them, three and four thousand apiece: the remainder is set

[1] The franc was the same as the *livre*. (Translator's note.)

aside for unforeseen needs. In time of great necessity, the contributions are doubled and tripled. There is such unity and such understanding among them, and they are so obedient to their leaders that, as people say, even the Turk cannot obtain as much . . . In short, the Admiral possesses, in this kingdom, a form of separate state that is independent of the king.'

Unhappy king! Was he to give this separate state the means of dragging the other along behind it, at the risk of a terrible adventure? Would he be forcibly brought back under his mother's control and guidance? Despite his violence he was no more than a weapon that two opponents fought to possess.

Two opponents poised on a tight-rope. Catherine's balance depended upon the skill of a gunman and the daring with which the Huguenots would avenge their chief; that of the Admiral upon the constancy of the half-crazed Charles IX and the loyalty of the treacherous Elizabeth. The latter, the balancing pole, was already no more than an illusion; and at one stroke an implacable fate was to do away with the others.

On 22nd August Coligny attended a council over which Monsieur presided, the king being at mass in his chapel. Nothing remarkable happened during this brief session. As he was going out, the Admiral met Charles IX, who, having heard mass, was going to the tennis-court. The king cheerfully drew his 'father' along with him, but the Admiral stayed only a moment and then made his way towards his house in the rue Béthizy. Chewing on his everlasting toothpick, he read a petition. Half a score of his people were about him. Guerchy was on his right, Des Pruneaux on his left.

He reached the rue des Poulies: he reached Canon Villemur's house. Maurevert marked him from behind the curtain, aimed and fired twice. Exactly at that moment Coligny bent down to adjust his shoe. Never was so simple a movement to have such consequences. For it was enough to preserve the Admiral from death and to reduce Catherine's plot to ruins. It was at exactly this moment that the diabolical scheme eluded the control of its originator and set off on its own insane course.

One ball had taken off the index-finger of Coligny's right hand: the other ploughed through the flesh of his left arm and lodged in the bone of his elbow. The old warrior remained upright. 'See,' he cried, 'how honest men are treated in France. The shot came from that window. There is smoke.'

Some of his companions rushed towards the canon's house. Too late. They found only the arquebus, lying on a table. Through another door, still open, they heard Maurevert galloping away. The others brought the Admiral, bleeding profusely, to the rue Béthizy. One of them ran for the royal surgeon, the famous Ambroise Paré: Monsieur de Piles went to tell the king.

In his rage Charles IX broke his racket, blasphemed and shouted, 'Am I never to have any peace? What, nothing but trouble?'

He hurried back to the Louvre, and without consulting anyone took measures which prove that he was in no way implicated in the affair: he ordered an enquiry, forbade citizens to take up arms and commanded the Catholics living next to the Admiral to give up their houses to Protestants.

The queen-mother heard the news from Jérôme de Gondi just as she was beginning dinner. She rose and went to her room. Her expressionless face prompted Zuniga to report, 'I suppose that she expected it.' Here the Spaniard was completely mistaken: Catherine expected many things, but not a blunder on the part of Maurevert. She was now in the position of a general who is committed to a battle but who finds that it is impossible to make use of his plan.

At the rue Béthizy Ambroise Paré thought that he would have to amputate the arm. In the end he did not do so, but with cruel scissors he cut off the remains of the mangled finger. He then attended to the shattered arm, and having made a number of incisions he extracted the ball.

Coligny had the remarkable fortitude of men of that time. He did not utter so much as a groan, although his people were weeping all around him.

'Friends,' he said to them, 'why do you shed tears? I count myself most fortunate to have been wounded thus for God's name: these are the blessings of God, my friends.' He thanked Ambroise Paré; and when the pastor Merlin expressed his sorrow, he said, 'Why, come now, Monsieur Merlin, do you not wish to console me?'

The Calvinist lords could not preserve the same calm. They hurried in a body to their chief, with Navarre and Condé leading them. Nobody hesitated to accuse the Lorrainers and Monsieur. The fever mounted. Certain captains spoke of going to kill Guise in the presence of the king. The Admiral and Briquemaut restrained them, little thinking that they were thus finally destroying the queen-mother's hopes. But still they could not stop the most impetuous from throwing stones at the Guises' and at Aumale's, accompanied by threats of death. 'Rash threats,' wrote the Tuscan ambassador, 'for threats serve as weapons to those who are threatened.'

At the rue Béthizy the procession of visitors continued—Cossé, Villars, Damville.

'Who can have inspired this?' exclaimed Cossé.

The Admiral replied, 'I suspect Messieurs de Guise. I make no accusation: but by the grace of God I have long since learned to fear neither my enemies nor death itself . . . It is true that this wound grieves me in one respect and that is that I am unable to show the king how much I wished to serve him. I could wish that he would be pleased to hear me for a few moments, for I have things to say that touch him closely and I think there is no other man who dares to say them.'

Damville and Téligny at once set out for the Louvre, where Charles was sending out orders to the governors to keep order in their provinces. The queen-mother and Monsieur emphasised in their messages that they were 'deeply grieved for what has happened to our cousin the Admiral'. The ambassadors of France also had to be told. 'It is essential that I should tell you', the king wrote to La Mothe-Fénelon, 'that this infamous deed arose from the enmity which exists between Coligny and the Guise family; but I shall make sure that they do not drag my subjects into their quarrels.'

On reflection, Catherine decided that she needed to gain time. She lamented and cried aloud that it was shameful. At this point Damville brought the Admiral's message. Catherine took good care that her son would not be alone with the Huguenot. She ordered the whole court to go and pay its respects to the victim of so foul a misdeed.

It was therefore a most splendid train that arrived at the rue Béthizy—the king, the queen-mother, Monsieur, Alençon, the Cardinal of Bourbon, Montpensier, Nevers, Tavannes, Cossé, Retz and many others. Charles was beside himself. 'You, Admiral,' he cried, 'you have to bear the pain and I the shame. But I shall take a revenge so dreadful that it shall never be wiped out of the memory of man.' And upon this he swore the most fiery oaths.

Coligny then spoke. He recalled the course of his life, affirmed his loyalty and so came to the vital point. 'The fidelity and the zeal that I have and that I ought to have for your interests oblige me to beg you not to lose the present opportunity . . . You have made your views on the war in Flanders quite clear. You have pledged yourself to undertake it. If you go no farther you expose the kingdom to an obvious danger . . . Is it not a shameful thing that nothing can be handled in your secret council without the Duke of Alba's being told of it at once?' The tale of his complaints was a lengthy one.

'You move a great deal as you speak, father,' said the king. 'I fear that your vehemence will delay the healing of your wound. I shall take care of everything; I shall revenge the affront and I shall punish those that did it.'

'They are not far to seek,' replied Coligny. 'The signs are plain enough.'

'It is surely unwise for a sick man to talk so much,' broke in Catherine, very sweetly. She asked about the bullet, rejoiced at hearing that it had been extracted and falsely added, 'I remember that when Monsieur de Guise was killed before Orleans his doctors told me that if once the ball was out, even if it had been poisoned, there was no danger of death.'

One of the medical men observed, 'We have not been content with that, Madame, and to provide against the danger, we have given the Admiral a draught to mitigate the strength of the poison, if there should have been any.'

Retz suggested that Coligny should be removed to the Louvre for protection in case there should be a popular rising. The king approved, but the doctors said that it would endanger the patient's life.

Before leaving the house Charles asked to see the assassin's bullet. His mother also gazed for a moment at the copper ball that had missed its mark.

In the mean time, Monsieur displayed another side of the strange Valois-Medici mentality. He remained alone with Coligny, thus conferring on him a signal mark of friendship. Was this an odious refinement of treachery? Or was it remorse, an unreasoning, generous impulse towards an old enemy whose death he had plotted? [2]

When the court had left, the Protestants entered upon a bitter discussion. Some wanted to take immediate action against the Guises and even against the queen-mother and Monsieur. Jean de Ferrières, Vidame de Chartres, urged his friends to leave Paris as soon as possible, carrying the Admiral with them: he felt himself trapped.

[2] Most of the accounts say that Charles IX and Coligny conversed in an undertone, and that when his mother pressed him with her questions the king burst out with his usual fury to the effect that 'He advised me to reign by myself and to distrust you and my brother.' This would have had a decisive influence on Catherine. We, however, agree with P. Champion and Jean Héritier, who do not believe this traditional tale.

Téligny was emphatically against this: he still trusted the king. Besides, there were nearly ten thousand Huguenots, an army of them, in the heart of the city and in the suburbs. Were they to leave the field open to the Guises and betray the cause of the Low Countries now that they had the opportunity of destroying their enemies with the king's support and of taking power? That would be repeating Condé's irreparable mistake of 1562.

Téligny won. Monsieur de Langoiran alone walked out, and without a word leapt on his horse, galloping away as if he fled Sodom and Gomorrah in flames.

Navarre supported Téligny's opinion: perhaps a little too warmly. The extremists of the party wondered if the agile-minded Béarnais had not in mind one of those tricks of which his father, Antoine de Bourbon, was a master. They obliged both him and Condé to sign a formal undertaking to avenge Coligny and charged both with the task of solemnly demanding justice at the hands of the king.

The two young men went to the Louvre, escorted, if not overseen by, a great number of their people. Once more Charles IX asserted his intention of punishing the culprits. He had already entrusted the enquiry to the austere de Thou, president of the Parliament of Paris. He would include a friend of the Admiral, the councillor Cavaigne. Was that enough? He offered more—the hospitality of the Louvre to the princes' gentlemen in order that their masters might be the better guarded and that they themselves should be out of danger. He renewed his order that the Huguenots should gather round their chief, so that the Admiral would be behind a living barrier. He even authorised them to make a store of arms in 'the fief of Béthizy'.

Upon this many of the gentlemen left their lodgings and went to take up others, most of them very uncomfortable, assigned to them near their leader. About sixty others, more prudent, refused to come into the city, 'on the grounds that the air of the suburbs was more suitable for their health'.

News of these happenings gradually reached the over-excited populace, causing terrible waves of emotion. All kinds of rumours flew abroad. Now the Guises were reported to be about to attack the Protestants, now the Protestants the Guises. Warm summer afternoons are favourable to mass-excitement, and 'great upheavals are possible only when the mob-minded urges them into being'.[3]

[3] Gustave Lebon, *Psychologie des Foules*, Paris, 1895, pp. 60–99.

Paris was feverish, restless, rumbling like a storm. It was obvious that the lightning was about to strike.

In the privacy of her room, Catherine de' Medici listened to these terrifying reports. She saw that she was caught in her own trap, and that the monarchy was caught with her. If Charles IX did not know the share his mother and his brother had in the crime, the enquiry would soon tell him. The discovery would cause a double explosion: one on the part of the half-mad king, the other among the Protestants. Charles would be only too happy to find this good reason for striking the brother he hated so: the king would fall entirely under the Admiral's influence; the Protestants would become the masters of France and the Florentine would flee into exile. At the same time war, both foreign and civil, would break out, for neither Philip II nor the Catholics would tolerate the situation.

But perhaps the Huguenots would pretend to believe that the king had had a hand in it, and would try a straightforward assault upon the crown—a development that would not displease the Spaniards.[4] Perhaps the Guises would forestall them and attack: perhaps they would denounce the collusion of Charles and Coligny and raise a Catholic revolt and set up an insurrectional government.[5]

Never had this pupil of Machiavelli had to face so terrifying a situation, and never had this woman, so calm under gunfire, been so little able to control herself. For it was not only the state that was concerned, but that once again her feelings as a mother had overcome those of the queen.

In any event, Henry of Anjou would be the first victim of the disaster. He could not escape the fratricidal rage of Charles and the fury of the Huguenots. If it came to that, neither could he escape the Guises, whose rival he was among the Catholics and who required his destruction to engineer a *coup d'état* in their own favour.

Catherine saw her dearest son, her 'darling eyes', put to death, like so many princes before him. She trembled with horror, wept, prayed and then regained her self-command. She would make a supreme effort to save her son.

[4] The next day Zuniga wrote to Philip II, 'It is to be hoped that the knave [Coligny] will live; for if he lives and attributes this assassination to the king, he will give up his plans against your Majesty and turn them against the one who has allowed this attempt against his life.'

[5] This is what was to happen in January, 1589, after the death of Henri de Guise.

CHAPTER II

'KILL THEM ALL!'

THE TOWNSFOLK having been forbidden to take up arms, the provost and the magistrates ordered the captains of the militia to bring their men to the Hôtel de Ville 'very quietly, without disturbing anyone'. The provost was Le Charron, a somewhat timid person who had only recently undertaken his duties. His predecessor, the goldsmith Claude Marcel, a supporter of the Guises and a friend of the queen-mother, still controlled the body of the people. He paid no heed to the royal order.

Marcel, with the agents of the Guises and a great number of monks, exhorted the Parisians to take care of themselves and handed out arquebuses, halberds and breast-plates.

On the morning of Saturday, 23rd August, the capital took on the aspect that it presented on days of riot. There is nothing more formidable than the union of fanaticism and poverty, and Paris was a half-ruined town whose hatred was directed not only against the religion of the Huguenots but also against their wealth. The Protestants stood for an aristocracy, a military, legal and commercial upper class. They had paid great attention to the words in which Calvin had stated that material prosperity was a mark of the Lord's good will. Their enemies also believed they possessed great treasure derived from piracy and the pillage of churches.

According to the preachers any form of recovery, however violent, was lawful against these hellhounds. What a temptation for the thousands of vagabonds, beggars, ragged workmen, picklocks and carters scattered through the city—a city, moreover, where, in the Cour des Miracles, there camped an army of brigands. In the Paris of 1572 the currency had been debased, prices were continually rising and trade was declining. As soon as night fell the town became a death-trap given over to bands of criminals who would even go so far as to attack houses. An alarm-bell hung at every street corner.

Téligny and Cornaton, seeing that the danger to the Admiral was growing, asked the king to have his hôtel guarded. The king at once agreed, but it fell to Monsieur, as intendant-general, to take the necessary measures. Monsieur appointed a personal enemy of Coligny's, Cosseins, who, at the head of some fifty of the French and the Swiss guards, took up his quarters in the rue Béthizy.

In the meantime the enquiry was going on. Canon Villemur's men-servants confessed, and the guilt of the Guises was no longer in doubt.

The over-excited Huguenots went to extremes: they spoke of leaving Paris with the Admiral, of hurling themselves upon the Guises, of calling upon the king to give himself up. Some uttered threats of death against the queen-mother and even against Navarre, who seemed to them distinctly suspect. It is possible that an order was prepared to bring their troops together at Meaux on 5th September.

Téligny once again set himself against any departure. He sent a gentleman to tell the queen-mother 'that he who more than any other had formerly loved and worked for peace, would do his utmost to break it if justice were not done for this assassination'.[1]

The next day a delegation went to His Majesty and solemnly adjured him to be pitilessly just. The Huguenots, as Albert wrote, were 'ready and armed for the war in Flanders, with the king's consent'. Téligny answered for it that Charles IX was one of them. They must do what they had to do on the spot and not from outside.

These remarks were listened to attentively by a man who was suspected by nobody and yet who was an agent of the queen-mother —Bayancourt, lord of Bouchavannes, governor of Condé.

During this time discussions also took place in the Hôtel de Guise. A servant belonging to the house had just been arrested. The Lorrainers decided to go and see the king. They were the object of the gravest calumnies; they feared that the king no longer loved them and they begged permission to leave Paris.

'Go where you like,' said Charles. 'I shall know where to find you in case of need.'

Guise and Aumale made a show of going towards the Porte Saint-Antoine but branched off and barricaded themselves in their house.

Téligny went to the Louvre. He told the king that Ambroise Paré would answer for the Admiral's life. Charles was exceedingly happy. Catherine, still seeking a way out, appeared somewhat less delighted. The morning went by. After a hasty dinner the queen-mother

---

[1] Cf. Cavriana's letter to F. de' Medici and J. A. de Thou, vol. VI, p. 390.

went to her garden in the Tuileries. She had appointed Anjou and the faithful Tavannes, Nevers, Birague and the Comte de Retz to meet her there: from the height of the bastion some picked guards protected this meeting that they may have presumed to be innocent —a meeting that was to weigh so heavily and for so long upon the future of their country.

It was as they walked about the alleys of this 'earthly paradise' that Philibert Delorme had made, that the advice of Alba, tendered at Bayonne seven years before, came into their minds—to make the Protestant party harmless by suddenly and unexpectedly killing its leaders. The plan, dear to the Spaniards and the Jesuits, had been proposed a hundred times since then. Only Pope Pius V among the unyielding Catholics had refused it, for he, as a former Inquisitor, wanted trial and sentence before punishment. Catherine had never considered it seriously, though this had not prevented her from holding it out as a bait, either to Philip II when she wanted to lull his distrust of her, or to the clergy when it was a question of obtaining subsidies from them. In times of difficulty she had dealt in massacres right and left, laughing up her sleeve at those whom she fooled.

But suddenly this sinister idea, this grim chimera, appeared to her to offer the only road to salvation. Yesterday one death was enough to save the kingdom. This evening, fate had decided that a dozen would be necessary.

The Italians, brought up on the history of the Guelphs and the Ghibellines, agreed: Tavannes, only too accustomed to bloodshed, did the same. Nevers raised objections and pleaded in favour of Condé, who was now his brother-in-law. It was precisely in order to be rid of the repulsive Condé that Monsieur had accepted the prospect of slaughter. In the end nothing was decided.

The queen hesitated before an act so contrary to her nature—an act which would give the lie to her whole life's work. Perhaps she was hoping against hope.

The Duke of Anjou did not possess his mother's sanguine temperament. He was afraid of Charles IX, of the Huguenots and of a tumult in Paris that would make the Guises masters of the situation. In order to gauge the extent of this last danger and of the Catholics' excitement, he decided to go and look at the town. He dared not do this openly, on horseback, so he took a closed coach with his natural brother, the Prior of Angoulême, a violent man who wanted to become Admiral of France.

Creaking and swaying, the heavy vehicle threaded the maze about the rue Saint-Honoré, with its hotch-potch of splendid town houses, little shops and squalid brothels. They were obliged to go at a walking-pace through these filthy streets where the horses' hooves splashed in the stinking mud. The coach had no arms on its door, but the prince, leaning out, was soon recognised. The crowd cheered him, shouting: 'Jarnac! Moncortour!' Anjou bowed, very pale. These cheers were war-cries.

There was a sudden rumour that Montmorency was about to return at the head of his cavalry and put the Admiral's enemies to the sword. Who spread it, the Guises or the Huguenots? In any case, the population reacted violently.

Anjou had just brought this disturbing news to his mother when Bouchavannes arrived unexpectedly and delivered an ominous report: the Calvinists were hatching the darkest plots—they were contemplating violence; they had spoken of killing the queen and even the King of Navarre. Another Protestant gentleman, Gramont, confirmed what he said.

Catherine seemed to be less alarmed than pleased. The suspicion of a plot would give her a reason for taking action, at a convenient moment. At Amboise and at Meaux the crown had only escaped the Calvinists by forestalling them just in time.

Machiavelli's pupil knew very well how different the two cases were. In 1560 and in 1567 the Huguenots had intended to capture the king: they had behaved like rebels. This time they were counting upon Charles IX's support and they would therefore be quite insane to act illegally. What made them particularly dangerous was that they might attempt a kind of revolution under the ruler's own protection. They might do what Catherine had invited Condé to do ten years before.

Today the Medici saw things in quite a different light. At all costs she had to prevent a *coup d'état* that would bring about a foreign war, a Catholic uprising, her own fall and no doubt the death of her favourite son. Did she really believe that a Protestant plot existed? It scarcely matters. Her policy required her to believe in it.

The Protestants seemed determined to relieve her of her last scruples. At her supper there appeared, as usual, many lords, and suddenly there burst out among them a Gascon swashbuckler, Monsieur de Pardaillan. He thundered against the Admiral's assassins, swore that vengeance was imminent and openly threatened and insulted the queen-mother. 'If the Admiral should lose one arm, a thousand others shall be raised to commit such a massacre that the rivers of the whole kingdom shall flow with blood!'

And Piles added, 'If justice is not given us, we shall take it ourselves.'

Catherine showed no outward emotion, but her decision was made. Before the next morning she would forestall the Huguenots by striking down their leaders.

At eight o'clock in the evening, heavy and dark in her mourning black and followed by the Duke of Anjou, ghastly pale, Catherine de' Medici went to the king. She at once struck him a bitter blow, bluntly declaring her share in Maurevert's attempt. Then she talked and talked, knowing very well that the unhappy man's weak brain could not stand up to this kind of eloquence. She recalled the Admiral's rebellions and his crimes, the assassination of François de Guise and of Charry, his so much regretted second in command. She denounced the determined plans that the Protestants had made to avenge themselves and to take over power. She described the Guises raising Paris to oppose them, and the king between the two parties—France hacked to pieces and the crown trodden underfoot. 'You will not have a single town to which you can withdraw,' she cried.

The storm was about to break. They must act before it did so and wipe out the ten or twelve men who symbolised the whole Huguenot party, the party of sedition. With these men dead, the Protestants would be crushed and the Catholics held in obedience: Charles IX would have shown himself worthy of his ancestors.

The king was dumbfounded: he was not at all convinced. Catherine then changed from violence to anguish and shed a flood of tears. She had not the strength to face the coming disaster. Since her son set his face against the 'execution', she would beg leave to go. She would go away with Monsieur, equally ill-requited for his efforts. They would go and live away from France, 'somewhere where they would never hear it spoken of'. This aroused Charles's terrible jealousy. Yet the king did not yield. He retained his 'passionate desire to do justice'.

Unable to make headway, Catherine appealed for help to Nevers, Birague, Tavannes, Montpensier, Morvillier and above all Retz; Retz, Charles's former tutor; Retz, whose 'liberal' spirit was so well known.

According to some accounts,[2] it was this Italian alone who delivered the final attack. The reality was quite different.

The queen-mother summoned the men who were her last resort: they came at about eleven to hold a nocturnal council about the king. The unhappy sovereign was beset and harassed relentlessly. They explained to him once more the abiding conspiracy of the Huguenots; they advised him not to miss 'the excellent opportunity that God had provided to rid himself of this plague and to do willingly what necessity would oblige him to do if he wished to keep both his life and his crown'.

Only Morvillier, taken unawares, did not join in. He sank down in his chair, almost unable to speak. 'Sire,' he murmured, 'it is a vast and important matter which calls not for hurried advice but mature counsel, for it may precipitate a cruel war.'

But the others returned to the charge. They warned the king that the Catholics, indignant at his weakness, were about to appoint a captain-general. They filled him with dread of the Huguenot gentlemen, the best swordsmen in the kingdom, who were living under his own roof.

'The Admiral is storing weapons in his house,' cried the queen-mother.

Charles replied 'that he had given that subject permission to do so'.

'The Admiral hates you, you and your house, me, Monsieur and the rest!'[3]

Morvillier, weeping bitterly, declared that if that were true, the queen's advice must be followed.

Charles's nerves could stand no more: his mind was reeling. Retz, who knew him well, stunned his imagination with the theatrical grandeur of a deed which would impress the whole world, posterity and history with amazement and admiration. The queen played upon his feelings again. The king was afraid to act? He was frightened of the Huguenots? Very good; she would leave him, taking the conqueror of Moncontour, the hero, with her.

In Charles's sick brain, suddenly aroused, bloodthirsty instincts mingled with insane jealousy of his brother and with the old chivalrous feelings that rose up against the betrayal of Coligny.

Then, for the second time, something occurred that nobody had

[2] Particularly that of Queen Marguerite, which we do not follow here, preferring the opinion of Pierre Champion and Jean Héritier.
[3] An English account. *Calendar of State Papers*.

foreseen. Having been unable to cut the Gordian knot by killing one man, Catherine now wanted to sacrifice a dozen. 'Very well then, by God's death let it be so,' her son shouted at her. 'But kill them all, so that not one will be left to reproach me afterwards! '

The road to crime leads to madness and, which is even worse in politics, to absurdity.

Inducing the Guises and the Châtillons to destroy one another was a daring plan that might have worked. Wiping out the Protestant leaders unexpectedly could, at least for the time being, ward off the consequences of its failure. But a massacre made no sense, seeing that as even the Duke of Nevers admitted, it was impossible to kill all the Calvinists—apart from anything else, their troops were camping in the suburbs. It would destroy the unity of France, perpetuate the civil war, discredit the king and put him in the power of one particular faction. In short, with the exception of the foreign war, it was to bring about all the evils that the queen-mother had worked so hard to avoid these thirteen years past.

Catherine was not unaware of this, but she retained a disastrous confidence in her own powers. The essential was the free hand that the king had just given her, thanks to which the Huguenots' counterstroke would be forestalled and her son kept safe. In spite of two lessons in two days she still flattered herself that she could dominate the course of events—the more so as her success with Charles had restored all her self-control.

The king abruptly left the counsellors of death. He fled, shouting, 'Let them all be killed! Let them all be killed ! '

The queen returned to her apartments, sent for Guise at once and held council. Neither she, nor the six men gathered in her room, intended or foresaw wholesale slaughter. With all the confidence of the authorisation that gave her acts the force of law, she worked out a proscription in the Roman manner, the suppression of a certain number of individuals who were harmful to the state.

The meeting deliberately drew up the list of victims and the list of executioners. 'Later, Catherine was to confess to five or six deaths on her own account.' [4] The disappearance of the Bourbons would make the Guises too powerful : Navarre and Condé were therefore spared, to the great chagrin of the Duke of Anjou. [5] The Huguenot

---

[4] Cf. Jean Héritier, *Catherine de Médicis*, pp. 483–484.

[5] The passage in Tavannes' *Mémoires* which tells how zealously the marshal pleaded for the Bourbons and the Montmorencys against Retz must be viewed sceptically. The *Mémoires* were published by his son—under Henry IV.

gentlemen living in the Louvre were a great danger. It did not seem possible to spare them. Guise, Aumale and the Prior of Angoulême would dispatch Coligny.

This work went briskly and they went on to the means of execution. The forces of the king and of the Catholics were of no great consequence—the guards, the Swiss and the Guises' followers. To ensure success and to keep order they had to have recourse to the municipality of Paris.

It was not the provost Le Charron whom they summoned first, but Claude Marcel. When he was told of the king's decision, the goldsmith showed deep satisfaction. The queen asked him how many men he had at his command. That depended upon the time he was given: a hundred thousand and more in a month, twenty thousand in one day. Here it was a question of zealous Catholics, volunteers from the lower middle class and the workers.

Having been sworn to secrecy, Marcel was charged with conveying the king's orders to the heads of districts. 'The next night, there was to be an armed man in each house, provided with a torch and a white scarf about his left arm; there was to be a torch at each window. The bell of the Palace [of Justice] would give the signal.'[6]

The provost came next. He learned of the Huguenots' conspiracy and he was given precise orders: to close the city gates and seize the keys, to remove the boats from the Seine, to arm the city's militia and order it to guard the squares, the cross-roads, the quays, and to gather all its artillery in front of the Hôtel de Ville.

As they left the Louvre, Claude Marcel and Le Charron found a Paris that seemed to have become quite calm again in the last few hours. The burgess of Strasbourg who was to leave an account of the massacre of Saint Bartholomew had gone to bed, relieved at this abatement.

Le Charron disposed his forces with extraordinary exactitude and rapidity. Marcel summoned the magistrates, the district captains and the *dizainiers*,[7] who were also filled with a savage delight at the news.

And for the third time the finger of destiny came to upset the plans of men. The queen's intention had been that Marcel's bands should reinforce the town militia and if necessary add their strength to the royal troops. The Florentine had not realised that she was opening the dams and releasing the wild fanaticism of which Paris had given

---

[6] *Archives Nationales*, registers of the Hôtel de Ville.
[7] Chiefs of groups of ten.

so many proofs in the last fifty years. Claude Marcel shared this fanaticism: it had often grieved him that he had not been able to satisfy it. Now the chance was before him, and he was going to make the most of it.

The former provost interpreted the court's orders in his own manner. He 'told the municipal officers in the king's name that His Majesty allowed them to take up arms, that it was his intention that the Admiral and his party should be exterminated; that they should take care that not one of these impious creatures should escape or be hidden in any house; that this was the king's will and that he would give orders that the towns of the kingdom should follow the capital's example'.

This is how the assassination of one man turned within thirty-six hours into a proscription and then into an enormous slaughter.

'So many mistakes were made,' wrote the Venetian Cavalli later, 'and so many conflicting decisions were come to, that one may easily see that the plan which they carried out had been decided upon without any preparation.'

The queen-mother's *coucher* [8] went on as usual. The new Queen of Navarre, who during the day had been to see the Admiral, was present. She noticed her sister Claude, the Duchess of Lorraine, sitting very sadly on a chest and went to sit by her. Seeing this, Catherine told her to go to bed. Marguerite had already made her curtsey when Madame de Lorraine, unable to restrain herself, cried, 'For God's sake, sister, do not go!'

The queen had not been able to prevent herself from confiding in her dear Claude, and she had never forgiven Marguerite for her affair with Guise: she lost her temper, and forbade the duchess to speak. Madame de Lorraine had the courage to disobey. It was not right, she said, to send Margot off to be sacrificed; for if the Huguenots discovered anything, they would take their revenge on her. In a rage, Catherine insisted upon silence and violently dismissed the Queen of Navarre, who went out 'quite stunned and bewildered', while Claude burst into tears. [9]

Catherine made her final dispositions and then went down to be

[8] *Coucher*, the ceremony before going to bed: the opposite of the *lever*, or levée. (Translator's note.)

[9] The *Mémoires* of Queen Marguerite have often been suspected on the grounds that they tend to exculpate Catherine and Anjou. Judging by this episode, that is scarcely the case. Marguerite was always terrified of her mother, who never forgave her for her irregularities.

present at the king's *coucher*. The Catholic lords stood side by side
with the Protestants, most of them guests of the Louvre. 'For the
last two days Charles IX had been living with them, had had them
at the royal tables, mingled with his household. Abominable fate.
The knife that had served them with the king's bread was to be
thrust into their heart; the officers and captains of the guard, their
boon-companions of the evening, were to be their executioners in
the morning. This was the word of the King of France, a word
respected among the infidels, respected as far as the ends of the
earth! The word of a gentleman, of a feudal host—the ultimate
security upon which one left or unloaded one's weapons on crossing
the drawbridge! All these ancient holy things of France broken and
destroyed and honour itself assassinated! . . . In order to reach
such a level, how terrible must the fear have been.' [10]

Charles, following his father's example, had always delighted in
the worship of chivalry. But since the terrible scene with his mother
the fickle man had changed his personality as he might have changed
his clothes. The hatred for the Protestants which he had shown
during the dramatic ride from Meaux had been revived. He would
play his new part until the end; he would prove that he was the
master, that he was not afraid, that nothing could make him draw
back; he would be the destroyer of the heretics.

Several Calvinists had been his companions during these last
months, and some of them had appeared to be positive favourites—
Téligny, for example, and François de La Rochefoucauld, who willingly joined, as we shall see, in some of the half-mad king's strange,
cruel games.

With his protuberant eyes, Charles coldly watched these former
friends leave, going to their own slaughter. La Rochefoucauld was
one of the last to make his bow. At this something moved in the
half-crazed mind.

'Foucauld, stay with me. Let us talk nonsense for the rest of the
night.'

But the count had an assignation. His mistress, the dowager
Princess of Condé,[11] was waiting for him.

'My little master,' said he (this was his name for the king), 'it is
time for sleep and going to bed.'

'You can sleep with my valets.'

[10] Michelet, *op. cit.*, p. 448.
[11] Françoise-Marie d'Orléans-Longueville, widow of the first Condé, who
was killed at Jarnac: she had married him in 1565.

'Impossible. Their feet stink.'

He disappeared, visited Madame de Condé for an hour and then went to his wretched lodgings in the 'fief of Béthizy'.

The king had let him go. The gentleman on duty drew the curtains of his bed, and he pretended to be resting behind them.

Queen Marguerite had returned to her husband. Their room was full of armed Protestant gentlemen who went on arguing until dawn.

The Admiral, having talked for a long time with Guerchy and Téligny, went to bed at midnight.

The queen-mother suddenly made up her mind that the Palace of Justice was too far away, and that the tocsin, the signal, should sound from the church of Saint-Germain l'Auxerrois.[12]

The night wore on. It was already Sunday, 24th August, Saint Bartholomew's day; and the Louvre, soundless but for the tread of sentinels, seemed to be asleep. Paris, silently arming itself, displayed the same calm. It was a fine summer's night.

Catherine de' Medici and Henry of Anjou slipped out of their apartments. They wanted to see the beginning of the execution of their plan and they went 'to the gate of the Louvre which is by the tennis-court, in a room which overlooks the courtyard'. There the silence and the cool air restored that clearness of mind that they had almost entirely lost since the botched assassination. 'To tell the truth, we had scarcely thought until then,' as Henry was later to admit, about the undertaking, whose consequences now suddenly became glaringly obvious to them. By unleashing Guise and the mob they were launching themselves into an even more dangerous adventure than that which had bewildered them with alarm. 'Struck with terror and dread', they measured the 'great disorders' that they were about to provoke.

They looked at one another in doubt, and exactly at that moment there was a pistol-shot, like a signal. Yet there was not a glimmer of day on the horizon, nor the least sound of a bell. This strange explosion did away with the last of their excitement, and filled both mother and son with horror. One of their gentlemen, called up in the greatest haste, was told to go to Guise 'to bid him and expressly order him to retire to his house and to take care to undertake nothing whatever against the Admiral; this order annulling all the rest'.

[12] According to a tradition that cannot be verified, the bell that started the massacre is at present in the Paris Opera, having been given when *Les Huguenots* of Meyerbeer was first played.

The gentleman hurried away, but he came back with equal speed. Monsieur de Guise sent his apologies: the order had arrived too late: the Admiral was dead.[13]

[13] Tavannes confirms this complete reversal in his *Mémoires*, which is also given in *Discours du roi Henri III à un personnage d'honneur et de qualité*. This document, like Marguerite's *Mémoires*, has given rise to much controversy; and here again we adopt Jean Héritier's opinion in his *Catherine de Médicis*—'It is apocryphal, not a forgery . . . The whole *Discours* strikes one by the exactitude of its detail and of its psychological and moral atmosphere. It was certainly put together, but not invented, except the part that concerns the role of Gondi (Retz).'

CHAPTER III

'HE IS A BOOR!'

COLIGNY, then, had been in bed since midnight. In the next room there were Ambroise Paré, the pastor Merlin and a German, Nicolas Muss. The King of Navarre's Swiss were camping at the bottom of the staircase, and a gentleman, Monsieur de Labonne, guarded the door on the inside. Cosseins and his men were in front of this door.

At about four in the morning, Henri de Guise, his uncle, the Duke of Aumale and the Bastard of Angoulême rushed into the street, with a large number of followers. Cosseins was waiting for them. He knocked. 'Open in the name of the king.'

Labonne had the simplicity to obey and he was instantly stabbed to death. Cosseins invaded the house with Monsieur's Swiss, who, seeing Navarre's Swiss, hesitated. Cosseins brought forward the French guards. They cleared the place with arquebus-fire.

A servant ran to the Admiral's room. He found him already up, wrapped in his dressing-gown, with his friends about him. The pastor Merlin was praying.

'My lord, God calls us to Himself.'

'I have been ready to die for a long while,' said the Admiral. 'My friends, you must escape, for you cannot save my life. I commend my soul to the mercy of God.'

Nicolas Muss refused. The others got away by the roof.

The room of the door gave way and two of the Guises' bullies rushed in, the Picard Artins and the Czech Jean Simanowitz, known as Besme,[1] together, by a grim irony, with a renegade Protestant named Sarlabous, whose brother had once been captain for the Admiral in that town of Le Havre which played so deadly a part in his fate.

Behind them were men whose names have been preserved in

---

[1] Because he was born in Bohemia.

history—Goas, Petrucci, Tosinghi, Josué Studer of Winkelbach, Moritz Grunenfelder, Martin Koch, Conrad Burg.

The killers stopped for an instant, awed by the nobility of this white-haired wounded man. Then to give himself courage Besme shouted, 'Are you the Admiral?'

'I am. Come: you will shorten nothing.'

Besme thrust a pike through his body and the old lord fell, crying with disgust, 'If only it had been a man . . . he is a boor!'

In a blind rage Besme and the others struck at his head.

Guise, below, became impatient. 'Besme, have you done?'

'It is over.'

'Monsieur d'Angoulême will believe nothing unless he sees it.'

The Czech and Sarlabous seized the body and threw it out of the window. The Admiral was not dead. For a second he held on to the window, then fell at the feet of Guise and the Bastard. Blood had made him unrecognisable, and the Bastard wiped his face.

'It is he, upon my honour.'

And he kicked him in the face: the duke did the same, sure of having done his filial duty.[2]

Tosinghi tore off the dead man's chain. Petrucci, a follower of the Duke of Nevers, cut off the head and carried it to the Louvre. A herd of wretches, 'the natural sons of the gutter',[3] hurled themselves upon the corpse, hacked it, mutilated it and dragged it through the streets to the banks of the Seine. Other envious vermin came to seek it and hung it upon the gibbet of Montfaucon and lit a great fire beneath it. The mob cheered them and gave themselves up to a merriment worthy of cannibals.

So vanished Gaspard de Châtillon, for whom everything had seemed to foretell that he would die loaded with honour, having served his king and country gloriously. He died tragically because he had tried to reconcile his patriotism and his conscience, and because he believed that he could escape from civil war by throwing himself into a war abroad. He died of the hatred of the Parisians and their whipped-up fanaticism; of the Guises' revenge; and of Catherine's fear. But above all he was the victim of his pact with England, the victim of a queen whose national selfishness and whose two-faced genius he had not understood, of a woman who betrayed him without a qualm because she thought he had betrayed her before. His blood has stained the memory of Catherine de' Medici: in fairness, it should also darken that of Elizabeth.

[2] Brantôme denies this.   [3] Michelet, *op. cit.*, p. 445.

In the Louvre, day began to dawn. Queen Marguerite had not slept all night; nor had the King of Navarre, nor his companions. There was a knock on the door: a messenger from His Majesty, who wished to see his brother-in-law instantly.[4] Escorted by his gentlemen, Henry went towards the royal apartments, before which he found Condé. The two Bourbons were taken in by themselves: the gentlemen stayed outside, and they were at once disarmed.

The princes stood before Charles IX, who had the queen-mother and Monsieur behind him. This was no longer Francis I's grandson, who only a little while before had lessons from Ronsard and who dreamed of glory. It was a madman whose brain had been turned by the thought of killing. With his dagger in his hand he shouted, 'Mass, death or the Bastille!'

Henry of Navarre did not hesitate for long. If Paris was well worth a mass, as he was to say twenty-one years later, how much more so was life.

Henri de Condé was a Calvinist of another stamp. He replied, 'My king and my lord, God does not allow me to choose the first [the mass]. As for the other two, that is according to your will, and may God's providence moderate it.'

According to the Duke of Mantua's envoy, he presumed to add that there were five hundred gentlemen who would avenge him.

Charles raised his dagger and Anjou, thinking of Mary of Cleves, trembled with a terrible hope. Would the threatening arm strike? No. Catherine put herself between them: it was no time to be killing the princes of the blood when Guise might make himself king of Paris. But the madman, once in a frenzy, could not be easily led. He was fascinated by the prey before him. His mother had to beg and implore him. It must have been an astonishing spectacle to see this terrible woman who had just prepared a huge mass-murder weeping so as to keep on her chessboard a single pawn that she had need of.

Charles gave way. Navarre and Condé were shut up in their rooms. Condé had three days to make up his mind.[5]

In the meantime, archers and wine-gorged Swiss began to hunt the Protestant lords and their many servants who were in the palace from room to room, from gallery to gallery. Some Huguenots were

---

[4] Marguerite says that Navarre had gone to play tennis: this is not so.
[5] According to another version Charles made a long speech and Condé replied with another, equally long, which in such circumstances scarcely seems likely.

killed on the spot. Most were disarmed and then pushed into the court, where troops were assembled. As soon as they were out of the door they were thrust through and through with pikes.

Already the rising sun lit up a heap of bodies. There, among so many others, died the old Beauvais, the King of Navarre's tutor, Pardaillan, Piles, Charles's opponent at Saint-Jean-d'Angély, who had made himself a necklace of priests' ears in that town. Before he fell, this terrible man roared out his curse against the king like a Homeric hero. 'Righteous Judge, revenge some day so monstrous a betrayal and cruelty!'

'Alas, what have I done?' sighed the milder Brichanteau, in a kind of daze.

Many other Huguenots also called up to the young king, the object of their hopes, whom once they had called their Joad. Charles IX showed himself at a window that gave on to this inner court turned into a slaughterhouse. But he gave no mercy. He even threatened the faithful Fervaques who begged for the life of his friend Monneins.

'By God's death, because of what you have done for me I will forget that you have dared ask pardon for that hellhound. But I order you to kill him with your own hands. Do it upon your life!'

Fervaques did not execute this savage order; but Monneins died.

With a disordered gaze, Charles stared at the mutilated bodies, the corpses of these captains he had not long ago yearned to lead to victory.

After her husband had gone, the Queen of Navarre bade her nurse close the door and went to sleep. An hour later she woke up. Someone was knocking violently on the door and shouting 'Navarre! Navarre!' The nurse opened, supposing that it was Henry.

A man covered with blood—a sword-stroke in the elbow and a halberd wound on the arm—rushed in. He hurled himself upon the bed, seized the queen round the body and rolled to the ground with her. Both cried out at once, for the murderers, drunk with killing, seemed ready to strike both one and the other. Fortunately Monsieur de Nançay, captain of the guards, appeared. His composure in the middle of this drama was such that he burst into laughter. He called the archers off, abused them and sent them away, giving the wounded man his life. It was Philippe de Lévis, lord of Léran.

Marguerite had his wounds dressed and hid him in her wardrobe: she took off her bloody shift, put on a dressing-gown and, escorted by Nançay, who had reassured her about her husband, she went towards the Duchess of Lorraine's apartments.

The galleries of the palace presented a spectacle from Dante. Bodies, blood, men who fled, men whose throats were being cut, and who stretched their hands out to her begging for her useless aid. In her sister's antechamber she saw a Huguenot run through the body three paces from her and she fainted. She came to to beg mercy for a gentleman of Navarre, Monsieur de Miossens, and for her footman Armagnac, whom she managed to save.

The noise had also woken the young queen, now seven months pregnant. 'They told her of the pretty play that was acting. "Alas," cried she all at once, "does the king, my husband, know of it?" "Yes, Madame," they said, "and it is he who has it done." "What is this, my God?" she cried, "and what counsellors are they who have given him such advice? God, I beg and pray you to deign to pardon him, for if you do not have pity on him, I greatly fear that this offence will never be forgiven him." And suddenly she asked for her book of hours and set herself to her prayers, with tears in her eyes.' [6]

Some accounts show the king shut up in his apartments on 24th and 25th August: according to some he was terrified, according to others, careless to the point of playing at tennis. Yet it is not impossible that from the very beginning of the business Charles may have wanted to take a direct part in the killing—that this haunted Nimrod went mad at the thought of such a quarry.

In his *Mémoires* the Comte de Vaucluse says that the king, 'having taken them from behind a bolster', showed him six knives, each as long as his arm and very sharp, 'for there were six of them who carried out the said undertaking at the Tuileries, that is to say, His Majesty, seconded by Monsieur de Fontaine, his chief equerry, Monsieur, his brother, seconded by Monsieur de Vines, and Monsier de Guise, seconded by Monsieur de Vaux'.

Whatever the truth of this, the historical image of Charles IX is that of a prince standing at his balcony with his arquebus raised, murdering his subjects. The first to show him firing upon the fleeing Huguenots was Barnaud, in *Le Reveil-Matin*. Brantôme,[7] who had no reason to dislike him, and Goulard in *L'Estat de la France*, both confirm Barnaud. D'Aubigné, who saw the massacre, wrote in the *Tragiques*:

[6] Brantôme (*Œuvres complètes*, Ludovic Lalanne), vol. IX, p. 598.
[7] *Ibid.*, vol. V, pp. 255–256.

Ce Roi, non juste Roi, mais juste arquebusier
Giboyait aux passants trop tardifs à noyer,
Vantant ses coups heureux...[8]

And in his *Histoire Universelle*: 'These letters (by means of which Charles tried to shuffle off his responsibility on to the Guises) . . . were signed by the same hand with which the prince fired from the window of the Louvre at the bodies as they went by.'

Mézeray was of the same opinion. Voltaire, having taken up the accusation in his *Henriade*, brought in the testimony of Marshal de Tessé, who stated that he had known the gentleman who had acted as the king's loader, the gentleman then being a hundred years old.[9]

Some historians have eagerly refuted it, among them Baguenault de Puchesse, Loiseleur, Soldan, Gaston Dodu and many others. As for the window from which the king was said to have fired, and before which the Convention raised a gibbet by way of revenge, it did not exist in 1572.[10] As for the picture of the painter Dubois,[11] who was also a witness of the massacre, it proves nothing. But the king's general behaviour [12]—his solitary act of mercy was to spare Gramont—does not allow one to push the horrible image aside unhesitatingly [13] Remorse was not to overwhelm Charles until later, and, as we shall see, many of his personal decisions, taken quite without reference to his mother, helped to make the butchery greater. It is therefore not impossible that his lust for blood should have led the 'unfair huntsman' to as far as this hideous deed.

[8] Roughly as follows:
> This king, no true king, but a true shot with an arquebus,
> Shot those who drowned too slowly as they went by,
> Boasting of his fortunate hits . . . (Translator's note.)

[9] On this subject Henry Bordier writes, 'The fact was established, and it is incontestable. Voltaire's interference spoilt the story. It provoked some (he meant the Abbé Novi de Caveirac) to contradict it.'

[10] The king's room was in a pavilion in the south-west corner, which was finished in 1556.

[11] Long kept in the museum at Lausanne.

[12] Jean Héritier, in relation to this, recalls his particular sadism, witnessed by several papers in the archives which show, among other things, the compensation paid for the animals which he personally had killed. (*Catherine de Médicis*, p. 487.)

[13] La Ferrière and Armand Garnier, in particular, do not presume to decide categorically.

CHAPTER IV

'DEATH AND BLOOD
ARE RUNNING IN THE STREETS'

AT FOUR O'CLOCK in the morning the tocsin in Saint-Germain l'Auxerrois had begun ringing for what history was to call the Parisian matins. The tragic call woke the Comte de Montgomery,[1] the Vidame de Chartres, La Force, his brother, Geoffroy de Caumont, Fontenay and other Huguenot leaders who were staying in the Faubourg Saint-Germain,[2] either from prudence or because of the crowded state of the houses in Paris itself. Now the tocsin was ringing too early. The queen-mother had had it tolled as soon as the Admiral's death was known, and because of this Claude Marcel had not had the time to surround the suburb as they had planned.

While the Protestants were wondering what it meant, a horse-dealer suddenly appeared, a man 'neither seen nor known since that time'. He was devoted to Monsieur de La Force and he had crossed the Seine, some say by swimming, others in a boat, in order to warn him.

The gentlemen mounted at once. They still believed in the king's friendship and thought that the movement was directed against him. They therefore decided to join him, 'to do him service and, if need be, to die at his feet'. They went towards the Louvre, and, according to a witness who gives the observations of 'men who were intelligent and likely to be well informed', from the bank of the river they saw Charles IX 'denying God' and shouting, 'Shoot, shoot, for they fly!'[3]

However that may be, the Huguenots received the fire of the two

[1] Who had mortally wounded Henry II at the tournament in 1559.
[2] Which was then in fact a suburb, as it still is in name. (Translator's note.)
[3] *Particularités du massacre de la Saint-Barthélemy*, taken from the MSS of A. Conon, barrister at the Parliament of Rouen, quoted by John Viénot, *Histoire de la Réforme en France*.

9   The massacre begins

10 St Bartholomew's Night as depicted by the painter Dubois who survived the massacre

11 The murder of Coligny

hundred arquebusiers set to attack them. Montgomery understood and cried, 'To the Pré-aux-Clercs!'

Soon about a hundred gentlemen were assembled there. But already Tavannes, who had also understood, caused Guise to be asked to throw his cavalry on to the left bank. The duke obeyed. He lost a great deal of time, for he had to reach the Pont Saint-Michel and the key that had been given him to open the Porte de Buci was not the right one. When he came, Montgomery and his friends galloped at full speed towards the west.

If these men escaped, the political operation would be a failure, since the Admiral would have immediate successors; so the Duke of Guise launched into a furious pursuit that was to lead him far from Paris.

The ride continued throughout the day, one of those rides which, much later, were so to delight novelists and film-producers. The Protestants had the better horses. Montgomery, in particular, had a mare 'which ran without drinking or eating, for an unbelievable length of time'. Thanks to this fact the party retained its general staff. At Montfort-l'Amaury Guise gave up.

Geoffroy de Caumont had tried to save his brother and his nephews at the moment when Guise's arquebusiers invaded the suburb. He had measured his strength with the murderers before getting away in his turn. As soon as he found himself safe and sound in his château of Milandes,[4] he wrote to the queen-mother, 'Madame, having reached my house with only one or two of my people, and being somewhat unwell, I think it my duty to tell your Majesties that the tumult which happened in Paris obliged me to leave without having had the honour of being able most humbly to kiss your Majesties' hands and of hearing the orders that your Majesties might have been pleased to give me; for had there not been this commotion among the people I should not have gone, having nothing upon my conscience that could have given any man cause to do other than wish me well.' He recounted his epic journey and ended, not without irony, 'This made me decide to regain my house in order that I might, as soon as I arrived, tell your Majesties and assure them of my unchangeable fidelity and affection for their Highnesses.'

The politic Duke of Nevers very much wanted to be given the mission of clearing the suburbs and above all to be sent in pursuit of those who might escape. But the queen-mother would not let him extricate himself in this way. Each of the princes, except Alençon,

[4] Now the property of Mme Joséphine Baker.

had to lead a troop of executioners. Nevers found himself linked with Tavannes, whose savagery was now quite evident and who said to his men, 'Bleed, bleed! Letting blood is just as good in August as it is in May.'

Their troop first went to La Rochefoucauld's house. Raymond Anglarez, the captain charged with dispatching the king's friend, had been solemnly promised that he would inherit the dead man's office. According to rumours that Brantôme heard, he was accompanied by his son Chicot, later Henry III's well-known jester.

Seeing masked men coming into his room, the count thought that Charles, who loved this kind of joke, was one of them, and that he had come to beat him with stirrup-leathers. 'All right,' said he, 'but you must not hit too hard.'

'He was laughing when they cut his throat.' [5]

Two of his companions, Mergey and Chamont, had not been able to lodge with him for lack of room, and they were staying on the other side of the street. Warned by the noise, they had the good sense not to go out, and they saw the Admiral's house attacked. They escaped by a miracle.

The massacre spread through the whole of the 'fief of Béthizy'. First the lords were struck down, then their companions and their servants. Even the humblest, such as the carpenter Le Normand, were not spared. Guerchy sold his life dearly, Soubise, taken to the Louvre, was killed upon the corpses of his friends. Brion, tutor to the young Marquis de Conti, Condé's brother, was killed in front of his pupil, although the boy begged the executioners to have mercy. Taverny, with one soldier, for a long while sustained a positive siege: so did three Huguenots barricaded in the inn of the Three Kings. They fought until they were killed.

Téligny was able to flee over the roofs. In this way he reached a garret by Monsieur de Villars' house. Unhappily the Duke of Anjou's guards caught sight of him. They hurled themselves after him, reached him, stabbed him and threw him into the street like his father-in-law.

This was the end of the prologue. Now from all parts came the shout, 'To arms! Kill! Kill! ' mingled with the rallying-cry, 'Glory to God and the king! ' And if it is not true that scarlet streams poured down the gutters, yet 'death and blood ran in the streets'. With their white arm-bands and the cross in their hats, the slaughterers did not

⁵ Michelet, *op. cit.*, p. 455.

spare themselves. The Duke of Montpensier, a Bourbon, distinguished himself by his pious rage.

The Duke of Anjou, at the head of eight hundred horse and a thousand foot, was supposed to keep order. But his men did not long refrain from joining in the hunt. Presently they attacked the jewellers and the gem-dealers of the Pont Notre-Dame and sacked their shops. Money-changers and goldsmiths were, as a matter of course, treated as heretics. The best known, Le Doux, Dupuy and Bourselle, were among the first victims. It is said that Henry settled a dispute between two of his soldiers by taking possession, for ten crowns, of a 'very beautiful clock' looted after the murder of Mathurin Lussant, the queen-mother's own goldsmith.

The Spanish ambassador afterwards claimed, in order to prevent his election as King of Poland, that the prince had raped Madame de Téligny: it was not true—the thought had not entered his mind. On the other hand, he did save Marshal de Cossé-Brissac's life, although it is true that this was to please Mademoiselle de Châteauneuf.

Caumont-La Force was still in the rue de Seine with his two sons, the elder being too unwell to mount a horse. He offered Martin, the captain who had come to execute them, the enormous ransom of two thousand crowns. Martin yielded to the temptation, gave Catholic badges to the three gentlemen, their page, La Vigerie, and Gast, their valet, and took them to his own house in the rue des Petits-Champs. The valet did not go in. He hurried to the Arsenal and there reached one of La Force's sisters-in-law, Madame de Brisanbourg, who undertook to pay the sum if she were allowed two days. Martin agreed to wait until the 26th.

'I give you my word of honour,' said Monsieur de La Force to Martin, 'that neither I nor my children will move from here.'

The little Baron de Rosny, later to become Sully, was awakened by the tocsin. His tutor and his valet went to find out what was the matter: they provided themselves with scarves. The boy put on his school gown, took a large missal and with this safe-conduct walked unharmed through the horrors of the pillaged town. He reached the Collège de Bourgogne: the door-keeper insulted him and turned him back, but he succeeded in bribing the fellow and was able to speak to La Faye, the headmaster. La Faye took him out of the reach of the fanatics who lusted for the death even of sucklings, and for three days he secretly fed Henry IV's future minister, hidden at the bottom of a dark hole.

In expectation of a day of wrath, fanatics in the municipality had long since made a secret census of the Huguenots. At that time Paris had sixteen districts or quarters. Each of the sixteen *quarteniers*, district chiefs, who were responsible for the quarters, had a list of the names of the Huguenots living in his district, taken from the tax-rolls. The court may have improvised the massacre, but the town had been thinking of it for a long while, and the preachers had prepared their parishioners' minds for it.[6] This explains the great scale and the methodical character of the butchery, which could never have been achieved without a deep and persistent thrust of popular feeling. For this was a positive eruption.

On the Pont Notre-Dame, zeal for loot did not calm the ferocity of Monsieur's soldiers. The houses of the Huguenot merchants were cleared of their people as well as their goods. Nicolas Le Mercier saw his family and his servants hurled out of the windows before he was killed in his turn. It was the same with Mathieu, the ironmonger. At the sign of the Pearl and of the Golden Hammer the killers left nobody. 'A little girl was dipped naked in the blood of her massacred father and mother and with horrible threats she was told that if ever she became a Huguenot they would do the same to her.'[7]

Antoine du Bois, governor of Corbeil, the Constable's chief provost, was killed there: his flight in disguise did not save him.

Madame de Popincourt, the most beautiful woman in the quarter, the wife of the king's *plumassier*, was stabbed and thrown into the water with her maid. The wretched women, still living, clung to the pillars of the bridge: they had to be finished off with stones. Madame de Popincourt's body remained there for four days, held by her long and beautiful hair.

At the Pont aux Meuniers, between the Châtelet and the Conciergerie, the horror was no less. Madeleine Briçonnet, widow of d'Yverny the judge, who was escaping disguised as a nun, was there discovered by her coloured skirt showing under the habit. She was called upon to recant: she refused and was stabbed and thrown into the water. The same fate awaited a countess who 'was so pregnant that her child could be seen to move'. (Pregnant women seem to arouse a special fury in a massacre.)

The enameller Bertrand and his assistants, dragged thither from the rue aux Ours, there ended their days. It was from the Pont aux Meuniers that the victims from the quarter of the Louvre were hurled

---

[6] Gustave Lebon was therefore right in attributing a terrible responsibility to the mob.   [7] *Mémoires de l'Estat de France.*

into the river. A great many people came to watch the sight, and mocked and insulted the dead.

In the rue Saint-Germain-l'Auxerrois, Françoise Baillet, wife of the unhappy Lussant, the queen-mother's goldsmith, broke both her legs in jumping from a window. A neighbour hid her in his cellar. The killers found her there, cut off her hands to get her gold bracelets and left her in front of an eating-house, whose proprietor dispatched her with his spit.

At the Banner of France, near the Croix-du-Trahoir, everybody was killed, men, women and children, masters and servants. At the Great Stag in the rue Saint-Honoré the daughter of Coligny's standard-bearer died. Round the cemetery of the Holy Innocents, a great many merchants paid the penalty for their religion or simply for their wealth. Nearly thirty persons died at the sign of the Royal Chest, a cutler's shop. In the rue Saint-Martin a pregnant woman was killed on the roof of her house. The Iron Cross was a hecatomb —three young women from Orleans, Jean Robin and his wife, the widow Marquette and two of her children.

The bookseller Jacques Kerver, captain of the town militia, had his colleague and son-in-law Oudin killed; they had quarrelled. Spire Niquet, a bookbinder in the rue Judas, was grilled alive in the middle of his books. René, the scent-maker, who was accused of preparing the queen-mother's poisons, slew a young lame goldsmith. The wife of the haberdasher Jean de Coulogne was given up by her own daughter, who afterwards married one of the murderers. One Aubert, a commissary, threw his Huguenot wife into the street, and later he thanked those who, with sticks and stones, had made him a widower. It was a wife, on the other hand, who destroyed the old joiner who was thrown alive into the Seine. He managed to save himself by swimming and spent the night on a beam: in the morning he ran home to his mate, who slammed the door in his face. He was seized again, and again thrown in, finally this time.

The romantic hero Bussy d'Amboise brought a drawn-out lawsuit over an inheritance to an abrupt end by stabbing his cousin, the Marquis de Renel. The president Pierre de La Place, a highly respected judge, bought his life for a thousand crowns. Alas, the next day the provost Senescay ordered him to go to the king: archers would escort him. La Place understood, stopped his wife from throwing herself at the provost's feet, refused to put on the badge of the Catholics, and left his house with a firm tread. He was struck down at the corner of the street.

There were many children among the victims and, which is perhaps still more revolting, among the killers. A group of ten-year-olds dragged a little creature in swaddling-clothes along the cobbles with a strap. Infancy was no safeguard: a baby played with the beard of the man who was carrying it up until the moment the monster stabbed it and threw it into the river.

The history of mankind is filled to overflowing with horrors of this kind. The centuries that followed were to see infinitely worse. But the massacre of Saint Bartholomew was set apart from the others by this: that the murderous drunken frenzy, the greed and the lechery were let loose in the name of the Lord. Giovanni Michieli saw it and it appalled him. He wrote, 'One could then perceive what the strength of religious passion might be; and it seemed strange and barbarous to see people in every street composedly, deliberately committing acts of cruelty upon inoffensive fellow-countrymen, often acquaintances, even relations.'

In crises of this kind, the moderates are in great danger. Monsieur de Biron, who had negotiated the most recent treaties, knew it and shut himself up in the Arsenal, of which, as grand master of the artillery, he was governor. He was right. A band arrived. Biron, who had armed his people, pointed his guns at the murderers and put them to flight.

Meanwhile pillage and butchery continued unabated. The example was given from above, the king having given the Swiss 'for the dutifulness that they had shown in this affair, the sack and pillage of the house of the very rich jeweller named Thierry Baduère. I have heard tell,' adds the author of Le Réveil-Matin, 'that what was taken was worth more than two hundred thousand crowns . . . The pillage of the lords, gentlemen, merchants and other Huguenots killed was performed by private authority, or given and shared out by the king to his courtiers and others, his faithful servants: of whom any finding something uncommon among the booty of the dead would come and show it and offer it to the king or his mother or some other of the princes to whom he was more bound.' [8]

'With my own eyes', wrote the Duke of Mantua's envoy, 'I have seen soldiers of the king's guard leading away horses, carrying off money and valuable things.' While the mob stripped the corpses, nearly six hundred houses were sacked. 'Many people,' observed Salviati, 'had never believed it possible that one day they would possess the horses and the silver that they own this evening.'

[8] Le Réveil-Matin, pp. 66–67.

In the end the citizens found that they were in greater danger than the gentlemen, so much so that the authorities of the Hôtel de Ville, burgesses too, began to react.

Le Charron, a moderate in comparison with Claude Marcel, decided to take steps to put an end to the excesses. Between eleven o'clock and noon the magistrates made their way to the Louvre.

At this time Charles IX was still in the grip of his bloodthirsty madness. It was in vain that the queen, his wife, had come to throw herself at his feet.

'Pick up the Germanic goddess,' he said to a chamberlain, 'and take her to her rooms.'

Yet in order to avoid any difficulties with the Emperor he forbade 'the killing of any German or any foreigner whatsoever, under pain of death'.

The queen-mother was far from sharing his high excitement. She was exceedingly angry at seeing the capital given over to the mob. She was no less displeased at seeing Guise play the part of the Church's champion.

The magistrates arrived and were shown in at once. They represented to His Majesty that both the soldiers of his guard and all kinds of people mingled with them and under their protection were pillaging and sacking many houses and killing many people in the streets'. They asked for a return to order.

The queen-mother seized the opportunity, and her son, like a horrifying automaton, once more moved in the direction in which she thrust him. He ordered the magistrates to go through the whole town, to stop all the executions and to disarm the Parisians. After this the best that could be done to provide an explanation for the governors of the provinces and for the French ambassadors abroad was to be done.

Catherine had not given up hope of seeing the surviving Huguenots rid her of the Lorrainers. Charles IX gave out that the old Guise-Châtillon quarrel had broken out most tragically once more, that the two sides had clashed, and that one had tried to wipe out the other. He, the king, 'has had enough to do in guarding himself in his Louvre . . . orders having been given throughout the city for the abatement of the sedition, it is at present, thanks to God, subdued'.

For his part, Monsieur wrote, in his letter to Matignon, the governor of Normandy, 'You will see by the letters of the king my brother what passed last night between those of the House of

Guise and the gentlemen and friends of my cousin the Admiral de Châtillon, to my very great regret and as the king's intention is to change his Edict of Pacification in no way.' [9] (!)

Thus the court washed its hands of the massacre. The Duke of Guise, who was not there, bore all the responsibility.

The Duke of Montmorency could at that moment have entered Paris, snatched their arms from the killers and treated them as they deserved. Unfortunately he did nothing of the kind. The unrestrained rioters therefore made game of the trumpeters who published the new royal decisions. Laverdin, Conti-Francourt, Madame de Châteauvieux and her three daughters, and a great many ordinary people were still to die on this Saint Bartholomew's day, together with their families and their servants.

Darkness brought a respite. On the morning of 25th August the sensible Catholics showed their anxiety, and the zeal of the extremists slackened. The Frenchman is a jurist to the core, always careful of legality; and since the afternoon of the 24th murders had been illegal. Could one carry on with them without the sovereign's backing?

Suddenly there was no further need for it, for here was the backing of God Himself. A Franciscan brought the news : at the cemetery of the Holy Innocents a hawthorn had just flowered again, 'a dead thorn, dry and quite spoilt, has green twigs and is covered with flowers'. It was a miracle, a proof that heaven was pleased, that it blessed the rooting-out of the heretics. Innumerable bells rang their loudest to celebrate the event.

'This frightful storm of unexpected noise which crashed over the whole city poured a kind of intoxication into it, a vertiginous madness of blood and death.' [10]

The tree was guarded closely by soldiers who would not allow the crowd near enough to see for themselves. But who wanted to verify it? Hysteria spread through the crowd and presently the cemetery was full of men having fits and howling women. Soon after there was talk of new stars seen and statues that wept—with tears of joy, naturally. The slaughterers forgot the earthly king and returned to their work in order to please the King of Heaven.

The queen-mother was not at all pleased. Charles IX maintained

---

[9] *Bibliothèque Nationale, fonds français*, no. 3 193, fol. 23.
[10] Michelet, *op. cit.*, p. 467.

his position of the day before and ordered the Huguenots to be counted and protected. This is his mandate:

In the King's Name,
His Majesty being desirous of truly knowing the names and appellations of all those of the so-called reformed religion who are in the houses of this city and its suburbs, most strictly commands the provosts of the merchants and the magistrates of the said city that by the *quarteniers*, each in his own quarter, they cause officials to be sent into all the houses within their district, there to make each one of them a true list of the names and appellations of the men, women and children being in the said houses, without any omission, on pain of death, and at once to carry the said lists to the said provost of the merchants, who will instantly bring it to His Majesty, whose further pleasure it is that the said *quarteniers* command the masters and mistresses or those who live in the said houses to preserve all the said persons of the [reformed] religion, so that no annoyance or wrong should be done to them, but that they should be well and truly guarded.

Signed: Charles.

26th August, 1572,

At the same time the king provided London with a second version of the events, and spoke of a dreadful conspiracy that he had only just escaped.

Salviati sent a brief account to Rome: 'All the Huguenots have been hewed to pieces', the cause for it having been the 'impertinence' of the heretics during the last few days and the Admiral's provocative attitude: the king had ordered the executions and the pillage to stop. The Nuncio concluded, 'If the Admiral had died from the arquebus-ball that was shot at him, I cannot bring myself to think that so great a slaughter would have been made . . . When I wrote some days ago . . . that the Admiral was presuming too far and that his knuckles would be rapped, I was sure that he would no longer be tolerated and I was still persuaded of the truth of this when I wrote in my ordinary dispatch that I hoped soon to be able to give His Holiness a piece of good news;[11] but I did not believe a tenth of what I now see with my own eyes.'

Catherine, too, had not foreseen the extent of the massacre nor its magnitude. But since it had taken place and since she clung to the

[11] This phrase, divorced from its context, has often been quoted as a proof of premeditation. It is obvious that it is nothing of the kind.

hope that the Guises' party would bear the odium, she thought it would be ridiculous not to make the best of it or to leave it unfinished; and in this the duplicity of a sixteenth-century ruler for whom human life was of no importance was amply demonstrated. And what monarch of that time would have reasoned otherwise?

Charles IX commanded that no further 'offence' should be given to the Protestants. At the same time his messengers were hurrying to seize Coligny's children at Châtillon-sur-Loing and to give a *verbal* signal for the massacre in the provinces.

The Swiss whom Captain Martin had entrusted with the guarding of La Force and his sons were ready to let them escape. Gast, the valet, urged his master to take the opportunity. It was already being said in Paris that he was alive and a prisoner; if the rumour reached the Louvre all would be lost. La Force replied, 'I have given my word: I shall not break it.'

This was the position in the evening of that Monday the 25th, when the exhausted Guises came back from their vain pursuit.

The Lorraine princes, and above all their mother, had political sense. They saw themselves loaded with the momentary glory and the lasting guilt for a crime that was officially disavowed; they saw themselves exposed to the Protestants' vengeance and to the abhorrence of decent Catholics. They grasped the significance of the queen-mother's machinations.

Madame de Nemours was an Italian too; and she too had read Machiavelli. Far from letting themselves be acclaimed by bloody-handed fanatics, her sons suddenly displayed a noble magnanimity, as though all passion had left them now that their father was avenged. Henri de Guise offered asylum to those who were proscribed, and about a hundred of them found safety in his hôtel. Outstanding among these was the terrible d'Acier, chief of the Protestant bands of the south, who later attached himself to his leader's murderer and 'in exchange for his body, gave his soul'. The king 'thought this very wrong': the Parisians were dumbfounded. The handsome duke's popularity was very near extinction.

The Lorrainers would see to that later. They first had to forestall the timid Montmorency, who might at last make up his mind to fall upon them in the king's name. They therefore hurried to the Louvre, stormed and insisted upon their terms: the king must dissipate all doubt and solemnly take upon himself the responsibility for the execution carried out according to his orders.

With only the guards and the Swiss the court was powerless against the frenzied populace that Guise, by changing his mask, could unleash against a criminal king who had turned protector of the heretics. Catherine was finally beaten. Nothing remained to her but to save her face and to give her defeat the appearance of a victory.

CHAPTER V

'IF ONLY HE WERE THE LAST
OF THE HUGUENOTS!'

ON TUESDAY, 26th August, the splendid royal procession went from the Louvre to the Palace of Justice as it did upon days of high solemnity: the king, followed by his family and his entire court, was going to dispense justice [1] in the parliament. Dead bodies and pillaged houses lined his road, and he acknowledged the cheers of the crowd with a savage expression. The queen-mother was attended by the ravishing young ladies of her Flying Squadron who, far from turning pale, showed a lively interest in the grim spectacle. The Protestants said that 'they indulged themselves in the lewd pleasure of gazing at certain signs of masculinity on the naked corpses'.

High upon the cushions covered with fleurs-de-lis, from the place where his father had ordered Anne du Bourg to be seized, Charles IX, having denounced the Huguenot conspiracy, declared himself the sole author of the execution. He even stated that it was a premeditated act. All this blood had flowed because it had been his wish that it should flow.

'All that has been done in Paris has been done not only with my consent, but at my command and of my own mere motion.'

The parliament had had a great many heretics burnt, but nevertheless it was filled with terror. That evening the president de Thou, a moderate, wrote of his indignation in his secret diary; but this did not prevent him speaking in the assembly's name, congratulating and thanking His Majesty, and reminding him in Latin of Louis XI's remark, 'Who cannot dissimulate cannot rule'. The Admiral's memory was damned and vilified.

---

[1] *'Tenir un lit de justice.'* When the king came to procure the registration of a law by the parliament (which was sometimes refractory) he was said to hold a bed of justice: the term was also loosely used in the sense of dispensing justice or making a legal pronouncement. (Translator's note.)

As he came out into the sun to the cheers of the people, the unfortunate Charles might well have supposed himself a powerful king, worshipped by his subjects. The taste of popularity, even of a popularity of this kind, turned him into an odious demagogue. There was a sudden cry of 'After the Huguenot!' and a man was seized and stabbed before his eyes.

'Ah,' cried the half-mad king, looking at the victim, 'if only he were the last of the Huguenots!'

Still another unforeseen accident! In spite of the king's announcement to parliament his order to stop the killing remained essentially valid. But now these words of his annulled it. This, at any rate, was how the murderers understood them, and they set off again on their heretic-hunt light-hearted.

No doubt the queen-mother thought the best course was to try to direct this irresistible movement. At all events, the court launched out with fresh fury. The Duke of Anjou, completely contradicting his words of the day before, ordered Monsieur de Puy Gaillard to write to him 'on the subject of the massacre of the Protestants which was also to be carried out in the provinces'.

This day was to witness yet more hideous spectacles. To make it less tiring, the Protestants were brought to the bridges and thrown into the water. One man emptied a huge basketful of babies into the Seine. Carts filled with bodies were unloaded in the same way.

France lost one of her most illustrious sons, Pierre Ramus, the former professor at the Collège de France, who, after following Coligny during the wars, founded the Collège de Presles, which had a considerable influence throughout Europe. This had unleashed the formidable wrath of the university against him, the wrath particularly of Charpentier, that fanatical supporter of Aristotle, whose doctrines Ramus had assailed. Jean de Monluc wished to give him shelter and to get him away to Poland. Ramus refused.

On 24th August, Charpentier, who had become a captain in the citizens' militia, charged some of the killers who had been sent to the assault of the Montagne Sainte-Geneviève with dispatching his rival. But they drew a blank, for Ramus had agreed to hide in a cellar. Unhappily on Monday he went back to the Collège de Presles, which was attacked and overrun as the Admiral's house had been. The philosopher was run through the body and hurled alive out of a fifth-floor window, then his head was cut off and his body was thrown into the river to float away with the rest. The triumphant

Charpentier later celebrated 'that resplendent, gentle sun which beamed over France in August'.

In the rue des Petits-Champs, La Force awaited his ransom and his release. One of the most savage of the killers, the handsome Annibal de Coconnas, the Duke of Alençon's favourite and a great friend of Larchant, a captain of the guards, came to see him. The death of the young La Forces, who were his wife's [2] half-brothers, would be to the advantage of Larchant since their inheritance would come to him.

'I have come to fetch you,' said Coconnas to La Force, 'at the order of Monsieur, the king's brother, who wishes to speak to you.'

As soon as they were in the street the soldiers of the escort un-sheathed their swords. La Force and his elder son fell, pierced through and through. The younger boy, Jacques Nompar, who was twelve, pretended to have been struck dead and went down. La Vigerie, the page, escaped and succeeded in reaching the Arsenal. All day long Jacques Nompar deceived the killers and the thieves and lay there motionless, bleeding, between the bodies of his father and his brother. Towards the evening he heard a man sigh as he went past and say, 'Oh, God will punish this.' It was the marker at a tennis-court. The child rose and said, 'I am not dead.'

He wanted to be taken to Larchant, but fortunately his preserver refused and brought him to his own house. There he hid him in the straw of his bed, but not before he had taken his rings.

Meantime, as invariably happens in such circumstances, the dregs of the population had risen to the top. It was now less a question of serving God than of squaring private accounts and of making a profitable thing out of it. Some shrewd men had quickly struck a quantity of medals with the inscription *Jésus-Maria*. They sold them at a high price before the doors of churches, for they served as a talisman against threats of violence.

This was a comparatively innocent racket. Michieli estimated the booty that arose from pillage at two millions in gold.[3] At the Louvre the offices formerly held by the dead were being turned into money: according to the Protestant accounts the royal treasury made nearly three millions out of this.

By the time things had reached this state, the original motive for the turmoil was forgotten, and the religion of a man others wished

---

[2] She was born of their mother's first marriage.
[3] As far as these things can be estimated, this would be between five and five and a half million pounds sterling today. (Translator's note.)

to be rid of was but a fragile armour. Michieli was very much surprised not to find more Catholics among the victims. However, some of them perished, and not the least important; there were personal enemies of the Guises like Salcède or of the municipality like Canon Rouillard of Notre Dame,[4] or tradesmen who were irksome to their neighbours: the names of the last are to be added to those of the very many Huguenot competitors whose death was so convenient to pious businessmen.

We now come to the morning of 27th August.

The young La Force, dressed as a beggar, and the tennis-court marker made their way all along the ramparts as far as the Arsenal, where the page La Vigerie hesitated before recognising his young master. Biron had both of them hidden and gave the marker thirty crowns. But the story spread. The horrible Larchant came hurrying. In the queen-mother's name he asked for his brother-in-law, in order to protect him, as he said. He was refused, and saw his prey elude him. The child got away the next day, furnished with a passport from Biron, and after an adventurous journey at last reached his uncle Caumont. He later became Marshal de La Force and lived for almost a hundred years.

Five days had passed since Catherine saw in her mind's eye an arquebus-shot that would rid her of both Coligny and the Guises, save the dynasty and prevent a war that was lost before it was declared. Only five days. But the series of unforeseen events had followed one another at such a rate that the situation as it had been on the 22nd seemed to belong to the remote past. With her chessboard overturned, the queen-mother found herself faced with a corpse-strewn field; and she wondered what kind of a harvest this wreckage would yield. She had recovered her self-control, her clearness of mind and her remarkable intellectual resources, all of which had left her for one fatal hour. She no longer had to fear the war, the Admiral, the loss of her own power, the Protestant party, nor, above all, the threat which had a little while before hovered over the head of her favourite son.

The relief that she felt from this mastered her other feelings, and it even reawoke her customary joviality. 'What has been done was more than necessary,' she said to d'Elbène, the Duke of Savoy's representative. The diplomat noted, 'She looks ten years younger,

---

[4] Although the chapter had decided, on the morning of the 24th, that each canon should fortify his house.

like someone who has recovered from a serious illness or who has just escaped from a great peril.'

To Cavriana she artlessly confided, 'It was much better that it should happen to them than to us.'

She was less frank with Gomicourt, the Duke of Alba's envoy, but she did not refrain from joking. 'Am I such a bad Christian as Don Francès de Alava claimed?' she asked. 'Go back to your master and tell him what you have seen . . . The blind see, the lame walk. *Beatus qui non fuerit in me scandalisatus.*'

The popularity that her admirable work for the unity of France had never gained was earned for her by her crime. The enthusiastic Parisians acclaimed her as the Mother of the Realm and the preserver of the Christian faith.

It was not mere vanity that made Catherine rejoice at this. She knew that it was essential to ward off the immense danger of the fanatics' victory, and to do so by appropriating it to herself. It was equally necessary to bring back an appearance of balance and to reestablish domestic peace. These considerations, which gave rise to many other anomalies, explain the curious 'Declaration and Ordinance', that was meant to put an end to the massacre of Saint Bartholomew.

In the first place the king wished to make known to his subjects 'the cause and the occasion of the death of the Admiral and others, his supporters and accomplices . . . inasmuch as the said fact may be hidden from them and disguised for something that it is not'. The execution had taken place at his direct command 'and not for any reason of religion whatsoever nor [to] contravene his Edicts of Pacification, which he has always meant to uphold and maintain as he still wishes and intends that they should be observed'. It had been a matter of forestalling a vile plot of the Admiral against the king and his people. His Majesty now informed 'all gentlemen and others whatsoever of the allegedly reformed religion that it was his will and desire that they might, in complete safety and liberty, dwell with their wives, children and family in their houses under the protection of our said lord the king'. He ordered the governors of provinces 'not to permit any persecution of the Protestants, upon pain of death for the offenders and culprits'. In order to prevent any disturbance, he forbade the Protestants to hold any assemblies or services until he should 'have provided for the tranquillity of his kingdom'.

This document was drawn up with great difficulty and signed on the 27th.

The governors were also required to calm the passions in their provinces. Charles IX sent to the Vicomte d'Orthe in particular, 'I beg you to give orders for the safety of the town of Bayonne. It is to be feared that some, under cover of this pretext, may attempt to carry out their revenge, which would cause me unbelievable sorrow, and for this reason I ask you to make it publicly understood . . . that the people are to remain in peace and quiet without taking up arms or provoking one another upon pain of death.'

The town criers brought the royal order to the knowledge of the Parisians; and they, it seems, paid little attention to it. In the glorious summer weather the city was ringing with pious joy. There were thanksgiving ceremonies, processions in all the convents and all the churches. The clergy announced a jubilee and an extraordinary procession for the next day. The king decided to take part in it.

Salviati sent the Declaration to Rome. He attributed the change of policy of the court to its fear of 'alienating England and Germany'. He was convinced that the queen-mother was about to restore religious unity. 'It cannot be doubted since the death of the Admiral and so many other important men, which, moreover, is consistent with the talks I had with her at Blois on the occasion of the King of Navarre's marriage.'

The last phrase may look like a proof of premeditation. But the 'talks' seem rather to have been about religious unity. In any case, even if there had been questions of Coligny's death, it could not be asserted on that basis that there was a premeditated plan. From 1569 onwards Catherine had contemplated her enemy's disappearance a hundred times.

Salviati also wrote to Cardinal d'Armagnac at Avignon: it was impossible that the papal city should show less zeal than Paris, and the cardinal owed it to himself to toll a bloody matins too.

On 28th August the royal declaration appeared in print, published by Jean Dallier, bookseller, dwelling on the Pont Saint-Michel at the sign of the White Rose. The text was not exactly the same as that which had been cried the day before. There was a particularly important addition: 'All those who for the above-mentioned reason [religion] may have taken or may retain prisoners, are expressly forbidden to take any ransom from them and are at once to inform the governors of the provinces or the lieutenants-general of the said prisoners' names and qualities, who are to be released and set at liberty by His Majesty's order . . . His Majesty furthermore orders that from this time onwards no man should presume to take or arrest

any prisoner whatsoever for the aforesaid reason without His said
Majesty's express command or that of his officers or to be so bold
as to go about to take in fields, farms or other tenements any horses,
mares, oxen, kine or other cattle . . . nor to ill-treat or abuse the
labourers but to let them do and peacefully exercise in entire
security their labours and whatever pertains to their calling.'

It is clear what kind of rapine had been going on during these
four days.

An ordinary reader of the Declaration might have supposed that
clemency was now the policy of the court. But Charles IX was far
from having regained his mother's calmness of mind. He was still
under the domination of that terror which had made him say 'Kill
them all!' His conscience was torturing him, and for this very reason
he wanted to be finally rid of the Huguenots. So, still only by word of
mouth, he now gave the order to dispatch all those who were not in
their houses.

The procession wound its splendid length across the town, not without finding forgotten corpses here and there along its path. The
people noticed the difference between the glowering, angry king, with
his scarlet face and his furtive look, and the calm, open-faced, smiling
queen-mother.

The court prayed at each stopping-place, worshipped the hawthorn and finished by visiting Montfaucon. The brilliant lords and the
ladies in their splendour crowded to see the shapeless thing that had
been Coligny, and from which drifted the stench of death. The
pamphleteers attributed to Catherine the Roman emperor's remark,
'A dead enemy always smells good.'

Coligny's sons were brought: they were made to look at the
hideous sight. The elder sobbed most bitterly; the younger, a mere
child, seemed unmoved.

The 29th was still a day of confusion, with killing, pillaging and
ransoming still going on. But the zest was diminishing: even
Tavannes was growing disgusted. The queen-mother was afraid of
angering the Protestant powers to such a pitch that she would find
herself completely bound to the Spanish chariot.

She had already freed Philip II from his long lasting anxiety about
the fleet; for on the very first day of the massacre she had written
to Strozzi, 'Today, the 24th, the Admiral and all the Huguenots who
were in Paris have been killed. However, do your best to make your-

self master of La Rochelle and deal in the same way with the Huguenots there.' [5]

On the 30th the king published and sent forth a new declaration, much clearer than the others before it: he cancelled all orders given for the punishment of the Huguenots and forbade attacks upon them under penalty of death.

This time the exhausted, sated Parisians obeyed and once more became upright citizens and worthy fathers of their families. Only a few madmen and, of course, the scum, went on until the month of October—people such as Crucé, in the pride of his four hundred murders, the butcher Pezou, captain of the town, who could count a hundred and twenty, and Tanchou, the killer of prisoners, thanks to whom Retz had Loménie's office transferred to himself, without saving the unfortunate man in return.

As always happens during persecutions, the chief persecutors had each plucked some people from destruction. But by far the most striking example was that of Vézins.

Monsieur de Vézins had a very particular enemy, his neighbour, the Protestant Régniers. On 24th August he seized him and carried him off to his château in Quercy. Then, wheeling about, he said 'I leave you free to love me or to hate me. I have brought you here to enable you to make this choice.'

The king was only able to stop the butchery for good when he had caused gibbets to be set up at the cross-roads. The envoys sent specially by the Pope and the Catholic King to glorify the massacre were not a little surprised to see them.

But alas, if the capital had quietened down, the provinces were ablaze.

[5] Strozzi confined himself to suggesting, without success, to the people of La Rochelle that he should transplant them all to Florida, with their families.

CHAPTER VI

'I BEG THAT I MAY CONTINUE
TO BE OBEYED'

HANS RÖTZE was a Swiss captain in garrison at Lyons. He sent a report to the council of the city of Freiburg in which he wrote, 'The news has reached here (the 27th). The governor Mandelot has at once increased the guards on the gates and has taken possession of the chief places in the town . . . It has also been ordered, to the sound of trumpets, that the Huguenots are to stay in their houses and to give up all their weapons; and the Catholics have also been forbidden to molest them or touch their goods.'

Monsieur de Mandelot had taken these measures on his own authority. On Thursday, the 28th, the Catholics became extremely restive. They remembered that the Protestants had sacked the town in 1562, and they dreamed of revenge. Messieurs de Rubys and de Masso, two natives of Lyons 'then residing in Paris on behalf of their city', had sent the municipality an account of the massacre of Saint Bartholomew. Their letter arrived that Thursday and in it there was the explosive phrase, 'His Majesty's intention being that it should be done in this town as in Paris . . .'

But on Friday, the 29th, at ten in the morning, Mandelot received by Maurice du Peyrat, knight of the order of Saint Michael, a completely different royal letter dated 24th August—that is, after the reversal which occurred at about noon on that day. 'There being nothing in this', wrote Charles IX, 'to break the Edict of Pacification, which on the contrary I wish to be upheld as firmly as hitherto, I beg you to make it understood that all are to remain in peace and quiet in their houses and are not to take up arms or provoke one another under pain of death.'

The governor had a long talk with Peyrat and then summoned the magistrates. It was decided that the Huguenots should be protected and that the town militia should safeguard them. But the fanatics did not give up the hope of the vengeance that they had nourished for ten years; the tumult increased, and spread. Mandelot was afraid 'that the whole population might take part in it'; he lost his head, and leaped from one extreme to the other, ordering the Protestants to come to his house.

Those who did so found themselves arrested and imprisoned in the archbishop's palace and in the monasteries. The possessions of all Protestants were sequestrated and many outrages were perpetrated during that night.

On Sunday, the 31st, menacing groups of armed men gathered at the cross-roads. Mandelot nevertheless managed to keep order until the beginning of the afternoon, when the news came of an uprising at La Guillotière a considerable distance away and he was obliged to go there at once.

The prisons were at once invaded and seven or eight hundred of their occupants were murdered. The massacre was perpetrated 'without noise or rioting', as Jean de Massot wrote to his brother, who was then in Paris. That is to say, without opposition.

Goudimel, one of the glorious sons of France, Goudimel the composer, the man who gave us the music of Clément Marot's psalms, fell there, among soldiers, lawyers, carpenters and goldsmiths.

Captain Rötze gives the details: 'Monsieur de Lyon [Mandelot] had them all massacred, stripped and taken into boats on the water, murdered in the houses, wherever they could be found, and thrown day and night into the Saône and the Rhône. There are still a great many in the prison called Roanne and others at the convent of the Celestines from which some have been freed, having been converted to the Catholic religion.'

A certain number of these unfortunate people managed to escape from the citadel and to take refuge either in Bresse or behind the ramparts of Montluel.

The city, however, was not at ease. The people were afraid both that they would be accused of moderation and that they would be punished for their crime. The magistrates protested against the clemency with which the heretics in the citadel seemed to have been treated; and at the same time they wrote to their delegates, Masso and Rubys, 'In order that the people should not later be molested nor found fault with on account of the tumult, we are of the opinion that it is essential to obtain from His Majesty such declaration as you think fit to ensure that the people do not find themselves in difficulties hereafter; and it would be as well that what has been done in the said city should be avowed.'

The delegates replied that the king complained of the softness of Lyons: things had not been carried out on the banks of the Rhône with the same comprehensive thoroughness that they had on the banks of the Seine. The frightened magistrates remonstrated with Mandelot, who sent two dispatches to the Louvre and wrote directly to Charles IX, 'Sire, I am in no way to blame, knowing nothing of your Majesty's wishes except from orders which arrived late and were incomplete. I fear your Majesty may be angry that the people have done so little, the more so as nothing has happened in any of the neighbouring provinces.'

His messenger had only just left when new orders arrived. In a letter of 14th September the king commanded that the seditious Huguenots be 'kept under good guard' and the others left to live in peace. As to the killing, 'His Majesty is displeased that the people should of their own authority have carried out such an undertaking and the said Monsieur de Mandelot will give orders that hereafter nothing of the kind should occur.'

It must be admitted that supernatural powers were needed to know what the king's real intentions were.

At Meaux, part of the domain of the queen-mother, there was no uncertainty, no qualm of conscience. The *procureur*,[1] Louis Cosset, hearing of the Parisian matins on the evening of the 24th, at once had two hundred Huguenots arrested. The next morning he called the roll, and according to the usual custom, each man was struck down as he came out of the gate.

The people of Meaux made the most of the opportunity and dispatched a good Catholic at the same time, one who was particularly unpopular among them, the tax-gatherer who collected duty on wine and cloth in the name of the queen-mother.

On the night of the 25th the people of Orleans received a royal message merely ordering that the Catholics should be armed and that they should wait. The next day there came a letter from the dreadful Bishop Sorbin, exhorting his flock to proceed with the slaughter. The legal officials maintained a cautious attitude, but the municipality thirsted for blood and in three days some five hundred Huguenots perished.

Later the Duke of Anjou assured the Poles that he had prevented

[1] A legal official, not unlike a public prosecutor. (Translator's note.)

these horrors in his town of Angers. This was not exactly the case; though his changes of attitude no doubt limited the damage.

On the other hand, wholesale slaughter followed the barbarous orders of the Duke of Montpensier at Blois, Beaupréau and Saumur. Monsieur de Montsoreau's unrivalled savagery extended as far as Bas-Poitou.

In general the attitude of the governors proved to be the decisive factor. The stand of the Vicomte d'Orthe and the reply that he was said to have made to the king was long quoted—'In Bayonne I have found no hangmen: I have only found soldiers.'

In fact Orthe did prevent massacre, but his actual letter, of 31st August, is in a less heroic tone: 'I have heard of the happenings in Paris on the 22nd and 24th of this present month of August, and as these are private quarrels, I hope to give you so good and faithful an account of those you have placed under my care as to make them behave themselves in such a manner that your intentions will not be frustrated in any way.' [2]

It is rather the courage and the nobility of the Comte de Tende, governor of Provence, that should be recorded for posterity. He told envoys of the court that he had no written order, and that even if he had, he would not obey it.

In Normandy, Monsieur de Matignon also did what he could to keep the fanatics under control. He was at his château of Lonray, near Alençon, when the news came, and he gained some days by having Protestant hostages sent to him. This was long enough to allow for the announcement of the appeasing Declaration of 28th August, which he published at once. In this way many lives were spared; although at Mortagne there was a tumult in which an important royal official, the *Grand Bailli* of Le Perche, was murdered.

In Rouen the governor, Carrouges, shared Matignon's ideas, but here it was a question of a town in which there were many Protestants and in which Catholic resentment ran very high. In the preceding March there had been a riot which had cost many Huguenots and two Englishmen their lives. Catherine had been very angry at this and had insisted upon exemplary punishments 'because of the evil consequences that such a deed brings in its train'.

At first Carrouges employed 'feigned severity'. He ordered the Protestants to be arrested for their own protection. His plan seemed to be succeeding; the crisis passed without an explosion and Car-

[2] *Bibliothèque Nationale, fonds français*, no. 15 555, fol. 47.

rouges, on the 17th September, thought he would be able to leave the town. The next day those who had been merely exiled for their part in the March riots, returned. Under the leadership of Captain Maronne they burst into the prison and murdered the Protestants. The gaoler tried in vain to save even a single one. The lists had been carefully drawn up, and none escaped.

After this the murderers went to Dieppe, where peace had so far reigned. Governor Sigogne would not let them in: he saved the Huguenots, but afterwards he obliged them to abjure their religion.

When Charles IX heard that there had not been more victims in Normandy he fell into one of his frenzied rages. He violently reproached Matignon with having published his own royal orders for mercy. 'I find it wonderfully strange that you should have allowed the letters and dispatches that I have sent you since the death of the Admiral, which should have been kept secret and not made known —that you should have allowed them to be printed and published everywhere, as you will see from a copy that I send you, printed at Caen. I send you this dispatch to tell you that I am exceedingly displeased that this should have been done, all the more so since the said printings are being sent out of my kingdom; and to beg that you will not omit to find out what printers have made the said printings in order that all they have printed may be seized and burnt . . . but this must be done instantly and quietly, lest in remedying this another and worse error should be perpetrated.'

Anne de Vaudrey, *bailli* of Troyes, did not lay himself open to such rebukes. On 30th August he had the Protestants arrested: on 4th September he caused them to be murdered in the usual way. Among the killers the cooper Caclot boasted of having killed thirty heretics with his own hands. It was only on the day after, 5th September, that Vaudrey published the Declaration of 28th August.

The Duke of Longueville, on the contrary, maintained order and civilised behaviour in Picardy: so did Saint-Hérem at Clermont-Ferrand, Captain Combelles at Issoire, Monsieur des Bories in Périgord, the magistrates at Limoges, Montmorency at Senlis, Glandage at Die, Archbishop Grimaldi at Vienne and Bishop Hennuyer at Lisieux.

In the Vivarais there arose 'a unanimous feeling of disapproval at the massacre in Paris'. Men such as Leugères, Peloux and Chalenday de La Motte prevented all bloodshed in that region.

Provence remained fairly peaceful, thanks to the Comte de Tende.

The Duke of Montpensier bade the city of Nantes follow the lead of the capital. The town council met, prohibited any ill treatment of the Protestants and swore a memorable oath of which this is the text—

'In the year 1572, on the eighth day of September, the mayor of Nantes, the magistrates and the city councillors, with the judges of the mercantile court, being met at the town hall, take oath to uphold their earlier promise not to go against the Edict of Pacification made in favour of the Calvinists, and they forbid the citizens to offer them any violence.'

In 1623 the then mayor caused an inscription to be painted on a panel in the council chamber of the town hall: 'To the memory of Master Guillaume Harrouys, of La Semeraye, mayor; Michel Le Loup, of Le Breuil, deputy-mayor; Pierre Billy, de La Gree; Jean-Paul Mahé; Nicolas Fiot, of La Rivière; Jacques Davy; Gilles Delaunay; Jean Hovic; Guillaume Le Bret; Jean Quantin and Guillaume Brétaigne, who refused to obey the letter of the Duke of Bourbon-Montpensier, dated from Paris on 26th August, 1572, and received on 8th September, requiring them to massacre the Protestants.' [3]

The Comté de Cabot-Charny, governor of Burgundy, having received two royal letters, ordered the arrest of the Protestants of Dijon and then held a council. In the course of this Jeannin, who was then a barrister at the Parliament of Dijon, made his first appearance in history.[4] On the advice of the young jurist the envoys of the court, Messieurs de Comartin and de Ritan, were asked to confirm in writing the verbal orders that were contained in their messages.

Comartin and Ritan proved haughty: their word as gentlemen was quite enough. Jeannin then recalled the story of Theodosius: after that emperor had been excommunicated because of some over-hasty executions, he made a law according to which any governor who received an unjust order was to wait thirty days before complying with it. Comartin's brother, Monsieur de Ruffé, was sent to Paris. By the time he got there the wind had changed and so the Huguenots of Dijon escaped death, except for their leader, Monsieur de Traves, who was killed belatedly on 21st September, at the king's express desire.

La Guiche, the governor of Mâcon, saved the Protestants there;

---

[3] Cf. P. le Noir, *Histoire ecclésiastique de Bretagne*, 1851.
[4] He later played an important part as minister under Henry IV, Marie de' Medici and Louis XIII.

but at La Charité the Duke of Nevers' Italians indulged in the vilest cruelty.

In Dauphiné there were many Protestants, and they were strong: this made the governor, Gordes, cautious, and he declined to believe officially in the king's murderous intentions. He forbade the Protestants to leave their houses and entrusted their safety to the moderate Catholics.

In Montpellier, which had been in a great turmoil since the beginning of the month, Monsieur de Bellièvre put the Huguenots under a strong guard 'without injuring anybody', until he was able to publish the Declaration of 28th August.

The Duke of Anjou had told Caylus to make sure of the towns of Montauban, Millau and Saint Antonin. The Protestants moved first and 'went to work so briskly that they were in these towns four days after the Admiral's death, so that they could not be taken: and all those of the lowlands took refuge there'.

In Nîmes the news from Paris produced a unique phenomenon: with the approval of Joyeuse, the governor, Catholics and Protestants combined to guard the city gates and to forbid the entry of the royal troops. In January, 1573, Charles IX was obliged to order Damville 'to use force, since kindness cannot prevail'.

A frenzied band went to Le Vignay, the chancellor de L'Hospital's house.

'If the little door is not unlatched so that they can get in, let the big one be opened,' said the old man, who saw the final ruin of the work of a lifetime that he had hoped to have linked with his name.

His friends did not listen to him, however, but barricaded the house and sent a messenger to the queen-mother. At Catherine's orders a company of archers hurried thither and relieved the siege. Yet L'Hospital is to be counted among the victims of the massacre of Saint Bartholomew, for he died of sorrow.

The *capitouls* [5] of Toulouse argued furiously over the way they were to behave. In the end they too sent to Paris to ask for orders. His Majesty answered only at the end of September: the Protestants were to be counted, 'kept under good and certain guard' (that is to say arrested), 'but still to be treated with humanity'.

Everything was orderly until 3rd October. On that day a rich merchant of Toulouse, one Delpech, arrived from Paris. He gathered together a troop of men and declared that they should follow the example set in Paris. In vain the magistrates opposed him: that very

[5] The municipal magistrates of that city. (Translator's note.)

evening the prisons were opened with the connivance of two members of the parliament, and two hundred Protestants were killed. Among them was Coras, the jurist. The next day two Huguenot members of the council were hanged, wearing their red robes. The anonymous author who describes these bloody events ends, 'The people must not be accused of this massacre, for it was the rich burgesses [he gives their names] who took it in hand.'

In Guyenne, Monsieur de Montpezat kept everything quiet during the first weeks of September. The king congratulated him on it. 'I beg,' he added, 'that I may continue to be obeyed . . . in defending those who remain quiet from all ill treatment.' On 20th September, Montferrand, the governor of Bordeaux, stated, 'Here the people live in peace with one another and they have all promised Monsieur de Montpezat to remain quiet and to obey your Majesty's wishes.'

Alas, the preachers set themselves to destroy this quietness. On Michaelmas day Father Auger, a Jesuit, announced wonderful news —the Parisian matins had taken place at the archangel's command. Another, Father Emond, went so far that the parliament wished to remonstrate with him.

Montpezat, fearful of stirring up public opinion, opposed this Thereupon Montferrand, for reasons that have never been discovered, let himself be won over by the fanatics. On 2nd October he spread about the rumour that the king had ordered him to execute forty leading Protestants: he brought troops into the town and obtained the officers' consent.

Then he sent for the *jurats* ⁶ and without showing them any kind of document, required them to attend the punishment of the heretics. The parliament summoned him to its bar, but in vain. Montferrand ran through the city and let loose his pack while the parliament was sitting. Eighty people were killed, among them three members of the court. After this the troops proceeded to the usual massacre of prisoners: there were two hundred and sixty-four of them.

Lagebaston, the first president of the parliament, did not feel himself safe, as he had married a Protestant, and he took refuge in the Fort de Hâ. He wrote to the king, 'Sire, it is inconceivable that it can have entered into your heart to order such deeds to be done in so peaceful a city . . . It appears to the most clear-sighted that here there was nothing at all comparable to the situation that presented itself in Paris, in that there the plot was ready to be carried into execution and the need was so pressing that it could

⁶ The aldermen of Bordeaux. (Translator's note.)

not wait on the ordinary processes of the law, and because there it was better to begin by striking before being struck, as you declared in your court of parliament . . . but in this city, distant from you some six or seven score leagues, nothing of the kind obtained.'

At this time Charles IX earnestly desired to be done with it. On 30th September he had written to Longueville, 'I beg you, the moment this is received, to renew your express orders that forbid all persons, of whatsoever quality and condition they may be, to kill, pillage or sack in any manner whatsoever under colour and pretext of religion upon pain of the offenders' being summarily put to death without any form of trial.' [7]

On learning of what had happened at Bordeaux he fell into a rage and furiously blamed Montpezat for not having prevented it. The jurats threw the responsibility on to Montferrand. Anjou took the side of Montpezat, who wrote piteously to him on 22nd October, 'Your Grace, I find that I am passing from one very bad state to another even worse: I thank you most humbly for your kindness in sending me news of His Majesty's displeasure at what took place at Bordeaux, and for the kind opinion that you are pleased to have of me in declaring that it was not my fault.'

Thus Matignon was blamed for that moderation for which the Duke of Longueville was congratulated, and Montpezat for his weakness towards the fanatics. In 1572 it was not easy to govern a province in the name of King Charles IX.

The majority of these high officers were nevertheless able to keep their heads, to resist the pressure of the extremists and to preserve their honour before history.

Far removed from them, at the very bottom of the social scale, another class of men earned the same praise: these were the hangmen, who, with a very few exceptions, refused to play the part of murderers.

Among the characters in this inhuman tragedy some remained human; and it is strange to find that one of these was the Duke of Alba himself.

The fierce hidalgo still had the prisoners of Quiévrain in his power, and Mons could not hold out against him much longer. Philip II urged him to make a memorable example. But the duke was subtler than this: the duke was the first to benefit from the massacre of Saint Bartholomew, and he also wanted the whole odium of it to

---

[7] *Bulletin de la Société de l'Histoire du Protestantisme*, vol. XXXIX, p. 414.

fall upon the King of France. He therefore adopted a chivalrous attitude, exactly the contrary of that of Charles IX, treated with Louis of Nassau as equal to equal, allowed him the honours of war and lavished attentions upon him after the surrender of Mons, and finally set free the soldiers of Genlis.

What was to become of these unfortunate men? Mondoucet wrote to the king, 'They thought they were acting at your orders, but now, seeing the demonstration that your Majesty has made in France, they no longer know where to go: on leaving Mons, they ask no more than to come and throw themselves at your Majesty's feet and obtain pardon.'

This letter is dated 18th September. Catherine was already calmly trying to win back the Protestant rulers. Charles, on the other hand, was still hag-ridden—'Let there be not one left to reproach me with it afterwards!' Even if no word was said, what reproaches would he not read in the eyes of those whom he had sent to the help of their Flemish brethren? If they were to do no more than tell what had happened to them it would be enough to give the 'unfair hunter' over to hatred and mockery.

This idea gave the Valois the heart of a Nero. He ordered Longueville to set upon these guiltless soldiers; and from town to town, village to village, they were harassed, run down and destroyed.

A single man was spared, the brave La Noue. He was summoned to the court, and before he left Longueville advised him to be careful. 'Take care to act prudently, and to speak prudently, for you will no longer be speaking to the kind, favourable, gracious king that you knew. He is quite changed. At this moment he has more severity in his face than he has ever had kindness.'

What was the number of the victims? There has been doubt about this since the first day of the massacre, and it has rarely been argued calmly. The most exaggerated estimate is that of Péréfix, Louis XIV's tutor and later Archbishop of Paris, who speaks of a hundred thousand dead. Bossuet, writing at about the same time, gives the lowest figure—six thousand. Sixty thousand, stated Sully: forty thousand, asserted de Thou, and ten thousand of these in Paris: the Jesuit Bonamy reckoned four thousand in Paris and twenty-five thousand in the provinces, thus going beyond the figure of fifteen thousand that the Protestant Crespin gives in his *Martyrologue*— which the abbé Novi de Caveirac later contradicted with great care and no impartiality. Papyre Masson, the king's historiographer,

Conon, Geizkofler and the reports in the English archives all arrive at results that are very close to one another—two to three thousand Huguenots killed in Paris, about ten thousand throughout the provinces. Petrucci and Zuniga speak of three thousand in Paris.

According to Brantôme, Charles IX 'took very great pleasure in seeing pass under his windows more than four thousand bodies of people killed or drowned, floating down upon the river.'

Sauval, the historian of the *Antiquités parisiennes*,[8] has two informative texts: these are they—

1. 'To the grave-diggers of the cemetery of the Holy Innocents, 15 *livres tournois*[9] ordered to be given to them by the said masters in their directions of 9th September, 1572, for having, with their fellow grave-diggers numbering eight, buried the dead bodies which were in the neighbourhood of the convent of Nigeon, in order to prevent all infection and unhealthy air in the said town and its surroundings.'

2. 'To the grave-diggers of the cemetery of the Holy Innocents, 20 *livres*, ordered to be given to them by the provosts of the merchants and the magistrates according to their directions of 13th September, 1572, for having in the last eight days buried one thousand one hundred dead bodies in the neighbourhood of Saint-Cloud, Auteuil and Challuau [Chaillot].'

It is natural that many of the corpses should have been stranded at the bend of the Seine near the village of Passy, where the convent of the Bonshommes de Nigeon stood; at the bend between Sèvres and Saint-Cloud near the former Ile de Monsieur, which has now disappeared; and at the mouth of a stream coming out at Chaillot and converted into a sewer. The grave-diggers having been given twenty *livres* for one thousand one hundred bodies, the first bonus of fifteen *livres* corresponds to the burial of some eight hundred others. About one thousand nine hundred victims, therefore, must have been taken out of the water in the neighbourhood of Paris. The *Bulletin de l'Histoire du Protestantisme* concludes, 'However low the river may have been, it must have carried on at least half of those who were thrown in. One therefore arrives at a result not far from Brantôme's figure.'[10]

---

[8] Vol. III, p. 634.

[9] The *livre tournois* was worth 20% less than the *livre* minted at Paris. (Translator's note.)

[10] *La Seine et le nombre des victimes parisiennes de la Saint-Barthélemy*, by N. Weiss, in *Bulletin de L'Histoire du Protestantisme*, vol. XXXVI, p. 474.

In fact so much doubt remains that the objective historian cannot presume to make a decision, but calls to mind the last lines of *A New Song Against the Huguenots*, which came out a little after the event—

No one can tell
The number of dead.
Endlessly, endlessly, the bodies,
Men's bodies, women's bodies,
Were hurled in the terrible fury
Down into the river
To carry the news
As far as Rouen with never a boat.

PART 4

The Unforeseen Consequences

PART 1

The Unforeseen Consequences

CHAPTER I

'MADAME LA SERPENTE'

OUTSIDE FRANCE the massacre of Saint Bartholomew caused an extraordinary sensation. But the men of the sixteenth century did not feel things in the same way as do those of the twentieth: according to circumstances, the reaction was that of enthusiasm, fury, admiration, alarm, indignation, envy, and a very generally felt amazement or stupor; no one, anywhere, raised the cry that such an act would evoke today.

Apart from the few people who knew the matter from within, neither Catholics nor Protestants had any conception of the court's distracted state of mind nor of the improvised nature of its crime. The one side acclaimed, the other denounced, the guile and the dissimulation with which the operation had been first conceived and then carried out. Honourable men blamed the Most Christian King for having broken his word; but nowhere is there to be found that horror or contempt which should, as it seems to us, have overwhelmed Charles IX. Far from it: for the first time the half-demented man took on the appearance of a genuine ruler—he was now believed capable of using his subjects as Philip II and Elizabeth used theirs; capable of using deceit and of hurling the thunderbolt. In a few days his prestige rose to such a pitch that it caused the overshadowed Anjou the bitterest chagrin.

The queen-mother was preoccupied by totally different anxieties, although indeed she was still uneasy at the enmity between her sons. Catherine, so long a true Penelope of peace, had at length lost a preventive battle: she had begun it unwisely, and the control of it had been out of her hands from the beginning. But it was some time before the 'great madness', as the Tuscan ambassador called it, bore its poisonous fruit. For the moment the fact that war had been avoided and the Protestant party rendered powerless kept the Florentine in a fine humour and emboldened her to undertake the remarkable task that the state of affairs required of her—to make the Catholic powers pay the price of blood and to forge new links between France and the Protestant world.

The Nuncio Frangipani had once written, 'This queen no more believes in God than does any member of her suite'; and indeed Catherine believed in nothing but reasons of state, or political expediency. She felt not the slightest remorse at having anticipated Coligny's warlike intentions. She had not the slightest scruple in playing a quite remarkably double game, now ordering three medals to commemorate the massacre and announcing the restoration of religious unity, and now asserting that liberty of conscience would continue and that the treaty of Saint-Germain would be respected. The duplicity of Madame la Serpente, as the Spaniards liked to call her, took on almost awe-inspiring proportions, whereas Charles remained in his state of bloody-minded hysteria and the Duke of Anjou, extremely downcast, 'did not speak a hundred words in a day'.

Salviati's dispatches were not the first to bring the news to the Holy See. Mandelot's secretary had sent a messenger to Monsieur de Jou, who first told the Cardinal of Lorraine. This was on 2nd September. The Cardinal, beside himself, hastened to the Pope, together with Férals, the ambassador.

Gregory XIII burst out in enthusiastic delight, and paying no attention to Férals, who advised him to wait for the official dispatches, he ordered bonfires to be lit.

The letters began to pour in on the 5th: the king's letter, Montpensier's, with a thoroughly detailed account of the Huguenots' conspiracy 'to raise up a king of their own kind and to do away with all religions but their own', and Salviati's of 25th August.

Beauville, Charles IX's messenger, was brought to Gregory XIII by Lorraine and Férals. The Holy Father greeted him emphatically: 'Noble envoy, Charles, King of France, bears his name of Most Christian not only as an old title belonging to him, but as a right that he has lately earned and deserved by his destruction of heretics, the enemies of Christ.'

Salviati's second dispatch, which showed the queen-mother determined to 'restore the Catholic religion', carried joyfulness to its height. The Medici, whose lukewarmness had so often been decried, had raised herself to the height of a Mother of the Church. The Pope ordered a Te Deum to be sung in the chapel of his palace.

However, the Cardinal of Lorraine was uneasy at seeing all the glory for this being attributed to the Valois; and at the same time he wished to avoid the possibility of any return to toleration. He had an inscription set up over the porch of Saint-Louis-des-Français which said that Charles IX had, to his glory, followed the counsels that had been given him. This both compromised the Holy See and at the same time bestowed the most important role upon the Guises.

The cardinal knew that he was not loved at court. He resolved to make the world believe that the massacre was the culmination of a policy that he had set afoot and which had been pursued for a long while. At his instance Camille Capilupi brought out a pamphlet that upheld this thesis as early as 18th September. The massacre of Saint Bartholomew became the *Stratagème de Charles IX*.

The Protestants thought that this controversial pamphlet showed the very face of truth. For centuries they remained convinced that a plot had been hatched between the Holy See and the French court, just as generations of extreme Catholics believed without reserve in Coligny's conspiracy. Historical criticism has had little difficulty with the latter, but it has proved much harder to deal with the former.[1]

On 8th September, Gregory XIII came to Saint-Louis-des-Français to thank heaven solemnly 'for having delivered not only the King of France, but also his whole kingdom and the Holy See from the danger which threatened them if Coligny had succeeded in his design to murder Charles IX, to have himself proclaimed king, to uphold the rebels in the Netherlands and to march upon Italy, there to destroy the States of the Church and the metropolis of Rome'. Such was the fertility of the Cardinal of Lorraine's imagination.

No event was ever celebrated in Rome with greater splendour. A thanksgiving jubilee, commemorative medals, salvoes of artillery, Te Deums sounding from one church to another, a magnificent procession, a fresco commissioned from Vasari to perpetuate the scenes of 24th August—nothing was lacking.[2]

At this juncture Gregory XIII and Catherine displayed an almost equal simplicity of mind. The Pope thought that Charles IX was

---

[1] In the second edition of Capilupi's work, which appeared in October, the cardinal had already begun to withdraw a little.

[2] It must be acknowledged that these raptures became distinctly cooler when exact accounts of events in Paris arrived. The Pope refused to see Maurevert. He even said, 'I weep that among so many dead there should be innocents as well as the guilty.' But he did not cancel the order for Vasari's fresco.

ready to join the Christian League, now that the Protestants had disappeared from France; and the queen-mother hoped not only that the Holy Father would uphold the Duke of Anjou in Poland but above all that he would ask the French clergy to grant the important sums that the treasury needed so badly.

'Bishop,' said she to Salviati, 'now you have a chance to show me whether you and our lord the Pope are of the same mind; for you tell me all day long that he will always be found willing to procure anything splendid and profitable for me and for my children too.'

She soon altered her tone. The Church blessed her new policy, but declined to pay for it. The Florentine therefore did not conceal her anger when a special legate, Cardinal Orsini, was charged with bringing their Majesties the Holy Father's congratulations.

This last sign of the Pope's good will threatened to upset the delicate balance of her schemes.

Gregory XIII was surprised, disappointed and shocked when he learnt that objections had been raised against the coming of his representative, and that the chief of these was that it might vex the Protestant powers. Cardinal Orsini kicked his heels for a long while in Avignon before his embassy was considered flattering.

It was not until 23rd November that he made his solemn entry into Paris. The people welcomed him rapturously, but the king was at the château of Monceaux, having had to escort his sister of Lorraine upon her way. By this time the position had already developed considerably, and when at last the legate was received he had subtly to mix reproaches with his praise of the king.

The real object of his mission was to enrol France in the Christian League. In spite of six weeks of effort he had to return empty-handed. Even before his arrival Catherine had taken care to reassure the Sultan: her son would in no way change their old alliance.

Delighted at being rid of this exasperating purveyor of compliments, the queen one day spoke her mind. 'From now on,' she said, publicly, 'I shall not allow the Pope to meddle in the affairs of France.'

'As I write, they are killing them all. They are stripping them and dragging them through the streets; they are pillaging the houses and not sparing a single child. Let us bless God for having converted the French princes to His cause! May He inspire their hearts to go on as it has been begun!'

Zuniga's letter, with this passage in it, reached Philip II on 2nd

September. As he read it the impassive king for the first time lost his self-control: he could not contain his joy. The next day he received the French ambassador, Saint-Gouard, and to the general stupefaction he burst out laughing. His hyperbolical congratulations were a little sly, however, for he praised the disinterestedness of the Church's new champions.

'Happy the mother who has such a son! Happy the son who has such a mother!'

Saint-Gouard adopted a cynical tone for his reply. 'You will admit, Sire, that you owe your Low Countries to the king my master.'

He too maintained that there had been premeditation. Philip II and even the Duke of Alba believed in it at first. The latter, writing to Zuniga, recalled his conversations at Bayonne and 'what she [Catherine] had offered him.' 'I see,' he ended, 'that she has kept her word very thoroughly.'

Her word! If she had given it (and that seven years ago!) Machiavelli's pupil had never dreamt of keeping it. She had remembered it only at the time of her greatest confusion.

Of course, she was delighted when Zuniga, giving her the Catholic King's most cordial letter, congratulated her upon 'having performed that which the Duke of Alba had discussed with her at Bayonne'.

Don Diego, moreover, was not deceived. He took pains to disillusion the king and the duke. 'The assassination of the Admiral was *caso pensado* [a considered act] that of the other Huguenots *caso repentino* [a sudden decision],' he asserted. And in another dispatch 'They only desired the death of the Admiral, and that the blame should fall on the Duke of Guise, but the Admiral not having been killed by the arquebus-shot, and knowing where it came from, they determined upon what they did from fear of his vengeance.'

Nevertheless, Philip II, who had escaped a terrible danger, was exceedingly pleased. 'This has been one of the greatest satisfactions that I have ever had in my life,' he wrote; and he too sent an ambassador extraordinary to France, the Marquis of Ayamonte, charged with complimenting all the authors of the massacre from the king down to Retz.

Charles IX solemnly told Don Diego, 'I love the Catholic King like a good brother. I shall always keep the peace, and that with all due affection.'

Catherine bore witness to her pious zeal, and, swearing him to secrecy, told Saint-Gouard the reward she expected. 'The king my son has shown his intention of serving God in the matter of those of the new religion, and I could wish that this might persuade the Catholic King to give his eldest daughter to the Duke of Anjou in marriage.' Her ambition did not stop short at an Infanta for her darling boy, but embraced a kingdom for him too; and in that case the Polish crown would go to François d'Alençon.

Once again the Medici was blinded by mother-love. The Spaniards were not in the least grateful for her services, and they continued to cherish ill-feeling towards her. When Granvelle received the false news that L'Hospital and his wife had been put to death he told Morillon how pleased he was, and added, 'I dare not say that I wish another woman [Catherine] was in the place she deserves to be in.' Morillon replied, 'A good riddance to L'Hospital and his wife. Would to God that this Jezebel we know so well might follow them soon.'

The Marquis of Ayamonte came to the court of France, distributed good marks all round and looked attentively into the state of the realm. A little before he left, the queen-mother struck a great blow. During a banquet she turned to Don Diego de Zuniga, who was sitting by her, and said, 'I have just done what you asked me to do: I have ordered the governors of the provinces to declare that all, without exception, must live according to the religion that the king my son professes.'

The ambassador spoke of kissing her hands and her feet.

Presently Charles I confirmed his mother's words. He swore 'Cordieu!' that 'everyone should go to mass'. His will would be expressed in an edict.

Henri de Guise, drunk with happiness, told Madame de Nemours of the session of the council. 'The king was divinely inspired, and he does not mean to allow anything that offends the Christian faith: he is completely determined . . . to exterminate and utterly wipe out all that remains of the seditious vermin.' For his part, Salviati wrote, 'There is good reason to hope that the king will expel all the Huguenots from his realm.' All this evoked the feeling of being back once more at 24th August. The assassination of William of Orange was being considered, as well as an enterprise against Geneva.

At this point Catherine showed her hand. Overflowing with a mother's feelings, she told Ayamonte and Zuniga of her matrimonial plans. Alas, she was obliged to recognise the facts: Philip II was no more willing to enter into a new alliance with the Valois now than he had been in 1565. France and Spain remained natural enemies.

The Italian princes themselves conveyed reproof and above all uneasiness delicately concealed in their elegant phrases. 'The Spaniards will rise up and make the most of the opportunity,' said the Tuscan Cavriana, and the idea that he expressed alarmed all Europe—an alarm that is to be seen reflected in the dispatches of most of the French ambassadors, admirable in their courageous condemnation of the massacre.

Du Perrier, who represented the king in Venice, was violently indignant that 'by such means such great and obvious harm should have been done to his Grace the Duke of Anjou and so great a benefit to the King of Spain, who may now call himself the only prince in Christendom, the one who gives orders to all the rest'.

The Emperor Maximilian, Charles IX's father-in-law, confidently expected his son, a candidate for the Polish throne, to profit by the occurrence. He nevertheless told Montmorin, the ambassador, 'The king and the queen-mother have done the worst thing in the world —and very ill-considered. They will realise this in time to come.'

Francis I's policy had therefore to be taken up again. The King of France, an exterminator of heretics in his own dominions, was to secure their friendship abroad.

It is not difficult to imagine the outcry among the Lutheran princes of Germany, France's friends, and in the Protestant cantons of Switzerland, her best allies. Nobody could any longer place the slightest trust in the French king's word. His Most Christian Majesty was called 'treacherous, criminal, heartless'; his representatives were insulted and threatened. Pictures made for the populace glorified the Admiral and displayed hideous scenes of the massacre in Paris.

As for the Prince of Orange, who only a little while before had thought himself within reach of obliging the Duke of Alba to yield, he gave up 'all hope that rested upon mankind' and expected the total application of the so-called Bayonne plan.

But already the queen-mother's agents, particularly Frégose and then Retz himself, were in action. By autumn the princes, those great suppliers of mercenaries, were talking of overcoming their indignation if Charles were to send them two or three hundred thousand crowns. By the spring of 1573 Frégose, having shown that his master would never ally himself with the Pope or Spain, was able to guarantee the benevolent neutrality of the German states, if not their former devotion.

At this point the massacre of Saint Bartholomew had an unforeseen result: it was the recall and disgrace of the Duke of Alba, soon to be replaced by a moderate governor, Requesens. Such was the outcome of the secret understanding engineered between the King of Spain and the Prince of Orange on the morrow of the tragedy. But William the Silent was well aware that it was only the exhaustion of Philip's treasury that caused him to take up this attitude. William turned towards France again without delay and acknowledged Charles as the protector of Holland, while Louis of Nassau, Coligny's intimate friend, supported his murderer's candidature for the imperial crown.

The English attitude, it is true, had not been one that would urge them to make an unyielding stand, nor to bear an undying grudge.

In the course of the massacre the English ambassador had seen two of his servants and a minister of religion killed. Until the Duke of Nevers set a guard on his house he was in danger himself; and at the first lull he left his exposed embassy in the Faubourg Saint-Germain and hurried to seek the protection of Don Diego de Zuniga, of all people, taking up lodgings in his vicinity. It was there that he offered asylum to old Briquemaut, one of Coligny's officers, who had miraculously escaped.

On 26th August Walsingham sent to thank the queen-mother for having protected him, and asked what were the real reasons for the Parisian matins. On 1st September Lansac and Mauvissière, with twelve guards, came to escort him to the Louvre.

Charles IX declared his affection for Queen Elizabeth and said that he hoped these events would not lead her to doubt it. He promised to punish those who had killed the three Englishmen. The ambassador next visited Catherine, who told him of the plot that it had been necessary to forestall. She assured him that the Edict of Pacification would be maintained. And the very next day Mauvissière asked him not to interrupt his efforts to bring about a marriage between his sovereign and the Duke of Alençon.

'I am hardly encouraged by what I see about me,' replied the ambassador.

This observation earned him a second audience.

'Our treaty,' said Catherine, 'was concluded with your queen, and not with the Admiral. Have we failed in it in any way?'

Walsingham, no longer master of himself, cried that the massacre was a direct challenge to the Protestant rulers. Had it not taken place by reason of the covenant of Bayonne?

In her turn the Medici lost her calmness. 'You refer to Bayonne which is one of the devices of the Admiral, designed to make us appear odious. Understand this thoroughly: your queen has no reason to be pleased with him.' And with this she waved the will that had been seized among the dead man's papers. In it, as we know, Coligny advised the king to distrust both the Spaniards and the English equally.

'In that, Madame, he showed himself a very loyal servant of the French crown.'

Checked, the Florentine changed the subject at once and began to speak of the Alençon marriage. Walsingham asked her to confirm that it was her desire to maintain the Edict of Pacification: she replied that the newly-discovered intrigues no longer allowed the authorisation of the practice of the reformed religion. 'Still, the Huguenots will have the same freedom as the Catholics in England.'

'Our queen has not published any edict. If she had she would keep her word.'

'She is free to do what she pleases, as we are free to do what we please.'

The ambassador went to the heart of the question. 'In the event of war with Spain, can England still count upon France?'

'Certainly. Even in the event of an attack by the King of Spain— I am not afraid of naming him. Our only wish is to keep our kingdom tranquil.'

At this juncture two things happened to poison the atmosphere. First, in defiance of the law of nations, Briquemaut was carried off; then, as the ambassador's wife fled from this inhospitable place, she narrowly missed seeing two clergymen of her suite cut to pieces as she passed through the gates of Paris.

At almost exactly the same moment Elizabeth was receiving the French ambassador, La Mothe-Fénelon, in a somewhat theatrical audience. According to the usages of an ancient and uncommon ceremonial, the whole court was gathered at Woodstock, and all the courtiers stood massed behind the queen, who was dressed in mourning. The conversation was disagreeable and harsh.

'I fear,' ended Elizabeth, 'lest those who have made the king abandon his own subjects make him also renounce our friendship.'

The English were beside themselves with anger and alarm. The Bishop of London called for Mary Stuart's head by way of reprisal.

Elizabeth announced Walsingham's recall; and she told him to deliver an extremely strong protest to the king and the queen-mother before he left. The ambassador accomplished this task, but he showed no particular hurry to leave Paris.

Elizabeth could hardly avoid giving some satisfaction to public opinion, but in fact her feelings had little resemblance to those which her representatives and her speeches expressed.

Henry VIII's daughter and Catherine de' Medici kept up a secret correspondence under false names,[3] of which, unhappily, almost nothing has survived. The two 'gossips' could in this way speak to one another with great freedom, and it appears that they did not disguise their thoughts.

Neither really cared what methods the other used towards her own refractory subjects. Catherine's remark, 'She is free to do what she pleases, as we are free to do what we please' exactly reflected Elizabeth's, 'Each does as seems to him by his estimation best.'

The Queen of England felt no scruples at having had so great a share in her fellow Protestants' disaster. She wished to keep the French out of the Low Countries, and that was what she had done. She had never forgiven Coligny for the affair of Le Havre and she was not in the least sorry for his downfall. As an autocratic ruler, very free with the gibbet and the block, she could not side with a subject, a rebel even if he was a pardoned rebel, against another despot. As the spiritual head of a church, she disliked the democratic tendencies of the French Calvinists. And lastly, it was in her interest to go on playing that waiting game which, after some thirty years of trimming, was to ensure her triumph.

[3] The Spanish and Tuscan ambassadors were nevertheless aware of its existence. They sometimes referred to it.

CHAPTER II

'SOME DO NOT THINK IT PRETTY'

CATHERINE proposed to her 'gossip' a meeting that would do away with misunderstandings. But Elizabeth too was a master of the double game and she evaded it. Philip II thought that this was a favourable time for causing England and France to break for good, and she did not wish to discourage his advances. Already there were conversations going on with Spain 'for the resumption of trade'. The Duke of Alba's agent, Guaras, whose discreet role had had so much importance some months before, came back to Windsor.

When the news of this was known at the Louvre, it aroused a great uneasiness. Was an isolated France going to pay the cost of reconciliation between the Habsburg and the Tudor? In order to ward off this peril Catherine thought it necessary to justify the massacre of Saint Bartholomew by a solemn affirmation of the existence of the Protestant plot.

Cavaigne, the judge and Coligny's friend, had been saved by the Duchess of Ferrara, Renée de France, who had rashly entrusted him to her daughter, Madame de Nemours. Madame de Nemours betrayed him.

Catherine determined to force from him and from Briquemaut a confession that would serve her purpose. During the trial Briquemaut, on the rack, showed little courage and even suggested a means of taking La Rochelle. The fearless Cavaigne reproached him for being 'faint-hearted'.

Both refused to make a confession that, in any case, would not have saved their lives: they were nevertheless declared guilty of high treason.

As for Coligny, who was judged after his death, he was proclaimed 'guilty of high treason, a disturber and violator of the peace, an enemy of the public quiet and safety, chief head, author and conductor of a conspiracy against the king and his state'.

The parliament decreed that his body 'or what remained of it' should be hanged in the Place de Grève, then dragged at a horse's tail and finally gibbeted at Montfaucon; 'that all his portraits should be broken and trodden underfoot by the hangman, his goods confiscated, his arms erased, his children proclaimed base-born, low, infamous, unworthy and incapable of making a will or holding any condition, office, dignity or possessions in France'. The castle of Châtillon was to be pulled down and in its place a pillar set up, bearing a copper plate inscribed with the text of the decree. The parliament decided, furthermore, that each year on 24th August there should be public prayers and solemn processions to thank God for having allowed the discovery of the horrible plot.

Fortified by this fine sentence, Catherine tried a bold approach: she sent Mauvissière to ask Elizabeth to be godmother to the child that the Queen of France was soon to bear.

Elizabeth, flattered without showing it, deferred her reply. She observed ironically to Mauvissière, 'You find me in an embarrassing position, after what has happened. If I turn to any great man and ask him to represent me, he will think that I wish to be rid of him.'

When Henri de Bourbon became Henry IV he would sometimes tell his particular friends of the happenings at the time of his 'blood-red wedding'. He would interrupt himself. 'Look,' he would ask, 'is my hair standing on end?'

He often told the following story, 'A week after the massacre, a great host of crows came and settled on the pavilion of the Louvre. Their noise made people come out to see them, and the ladies sent to tell the king how frightened they were. The same night the king, two hours after he had gone to bed, leaped up, aroused all the people of his bedchamber and sent for me, among others, to come and hear a great din and noise in the air, a concert of shrieking, groaning and howling voices, just like those that were heard on the nights of the massacres. The sounds were so clear that the king, believing that there was a fresh outbreak, had the guards called out to hurry into the city and stop the killing. But they came back and said that the city was at peace and that only the air was troubled; and he too remained troubled, chiefly because the noise went on for seven days, always at the same time.'

Troubled: and so the dangerous, horrifying puppet was to remain to his last moment. Later he was to begin his battle with remorse: he was not yet at that stage, but already he was trying to escape from the appalling reality, now by a fresh attempt at 'killing them all', now by searching for an impossible oblivion. He hunted more than ever, exhausted himself in his mistress's arms, rushed about the town in a mask by night, indulging in frantic excesses: and afterwards he would spit blood.

He was still just as distressed by the sight of Monsieur; and now he had a new bugbear before him—his youngest brother, François, the ill-favoured creature whose soul was as ugly as his face, did not scruple to propose himself to the 'malcontents' as their leader.

On 24th August the young prince had cried, most appositely, 'Oh, what treachery!' Then, while the queen-mother was going through the Admiral's papers, Alençon stood up for his memory: and this was certainly not from chivalrous motives.

As to the two other princes, Navarre and Condé, their conversion was slow. A former Protestant minister who had returned to Catholicism, Hugues Sureau du Rosier, had the task of instructing them. Navarre, once his first alarm had passed, wished to be given a formal order, which Charles had no intention of providing: but his submission was taken for granted. Condé, on the other hand, resisted fiercely and to such a degree that one evening Charles, in one of his haunted fits, took up weapons to go and kill him. After this crisis, Condé's uncle, the Cardinal of Bourbon, was able to show him the futility of resistance and to persuade him to recant. All the members of his family followed his example, including the gentle Mary of Cleves, whose beauty had been one of the indirect causes of the massacre. In the end, Navarre was the last to obey.

On 28th and 29th September, the feast of Saint Michael, the patron of the French town bands, was celebrated at Notre Dame with exceptional splendour. Saint Michael also gave his name to the order of knighthood founded by Louis XI. After the mass dedicated to the memory of the former knights their Majesties took their place in the choir under a canopy of cloth of gold. The living knights attended them, dressed in white and wearing cloaks with long trains of cloth of silver. Their hoods were of crimson velvet embroidered with gold and pearls. 'They prayed', wrote Simon Goulard, 'for the souls of many for whom their own consciences were deeper dyed than their hoods.'

The king, with candles going before him, went up to the offertory. Monsieur followed him, then the King of Navarre. The queen-mother stood up to see what her son-in-law would do. Henry made a genuflexion before the altar, came back and bowed to the king and the ladies. At this Catherine could no longer contain herself: turning towards the astonished ambassadors, she burst into laughter. It was not only the apparently final crushing of the Huguenot party that her mirth saluted, but also the humiliation of the detested young man to whom both Nostradamus' prophecy and Ruggieri's magic mirror had promised the crown.

At this moment there arrived a messenger who, without disturbing the ceremony, was able to tell her of the extermination of the Protestants who had been made prisoner at Mons and then liberated by the Duke of Alba. Charles IX's court was indeed a court 'of blood and silk'.

The next day, Catherine offered to 'un-marry' her daughter. But Marguerite had forgiven neither Anjou nor Guise, and she knew that she was isolated in this fierce world. What sovereign would wish to marry the sister of the 'unfair hunter'? So it was better to remain with the first prince of the blood.

'You put me with him,' she replied, 'and I must stay there.'

The conversion of the Bourbons led to a host of others. 'The Nuncio had piles of ready-made bulls, forms of abjuration which only needed a signature. Everyone wore the white cross and carried a rosary.' [1] The queen-mother's best friend, Madame de Crussol d'Uzès, not long before governess of the royal children and accused by the Spaniards of having brought up the princes in the Huguenot way, yielded to the pressure as early as 19th September.

The young Rosny received a letter from his father requiring him to imitate the King of Navarre and to share 'the fortunes of that prince to the end, so that he might never be reproached with having abandoned him in his distress'. Besides, the stiff-necked Huguenots were going to lose their offices and their goods.

The majority of the great nobles who had survived renounced Calvinism. The only Protestants who remained at court were humble people, Ambroise Paré and Nanon, the surgeon and the former nurse, who was essential to Charles's happiness.

It is surprising that the Church should have been satisfied with conversions that did not even have the outward show of sincerity. The new Catholics called the mass 'the compulsion'.

The *Mémoires de l'Estat de France* provide interesting details upon this subject.[2] 'The cruel and furious massacres having so utterly

[1] Pierre Champion, *La Jeunesse d'Henri III*, p. 118.
[2] Quoted in the *Bulletin de l'Histoire du Protestantisme*, vol. XL, p. 420.

astounded those of the [Protestant] religion who were left alive, the
memory of these dreadful storms remained with them for many
weeks after, and they were bewildered and distracted, to such a
degree that in all parts of the kingdom there were strange recanta-
tions, and particularly by the formulary spoken of before; [3] those
who could get away in time avoided this danger. The others, having
been once or twice to mass against their consciences, and then
finding some way of escaping, straightway left the realm of France.
Others, having escaped during the time of the massacres, came back
soon after, upon the plea of their goods and their families, and
abjured. But a very great many did not move: they presently began
to forget their religion, went often to mass, and made much of the
murderers and the priests. So much so, that soon after the massacre
it seemed that many of them, who six weeks before had made loud
profession of their religion, had never had any knowledge of it.
But there were also many who stayed and who, having gone once
or twice to mass, sorrowfully exiled themselves later, protesting their
desire to follow their religion.'

In the meantime, fear and devotion to their faith had sent a host
of Protestants out of the kingdom. In tragic procession they arrived
in England, the German states and above all Geneva. Tragic also for
France; for having lost a great many excellent captains she now
found herself deprived of some of her best minds and an important
proportion of her most industrious tradesmen.[4] For those who left
France belonged in general to these two social groups. The gentlemen, the rich citizens and the peasants were too firmly attached to
their country.

The court had never foreseen the consequences of the improvised
crime, and they hesitated for a long while as to how they should
treat these people.

The Duke of Nevers drew up a long dissertation for the Duke of
Anjou, and, through him, for the council. It is an instructive document and one that reveals the state of mind of the extreme Catholics
immediately after their bloody victory.

The massacre of Saint Bartholomew, stated the pious mentor, was
the result less of human wishes than of 'God's simple leave . . . to
bring a greater good and a greater splendour to His Church'. The
king did not bear the responsibility for the massacre: it had been

[3] The formulary drawn up by Gondi, the Archbishop of Paris.
[4] 'Tradesmen' in the widest sense, the original is *petits bourgeois*. (Translator's note.)

accomplished by 'the common people of the towns, unarmed and with nothing more than their little knives'. God had made use of this rabble 'to clean and ennoble His Church'. It was for the prince to finish the work by imposing religious unity and by obliging everyone to live 'after the Catholic manner in fact and not only in appearance'.

What of the Huguenots? Whether they were 'brought back to the Catholic religion' or whether they remained 'obstinate' it was necessary to distinguish between those who were seditiously opposed to the crown and those who were misguided believers. None among the first was worthy of keeping his nobility, whereas the second class might be allowed its privileges. Both classes should lose part of their possessions, the gentlemen a sixth, the bourgeois a tenth.

But this was no longer the time for thinking of measures of this kind. Already, in the provinces, the Huguenot resistance was taking shape.

Strozzi had been unable to seize La Rochelle, France's only port upon the Atlantic, an almost independent town, allied with the English and the Dutch, 'fortified by nature and by art', the nurse of 'a race of coarse and hardy men, much given to trade and seafaring, rich and by their nature proud'.[5]

This citadel received the refugees of the neighbouring provinces. Urged on by the mayor Jacques Henri and the citizen Jacques Salbert, the people protected the town by making a desert for ten leagues all round it. Wives, children and fortunes were sent to England, victuals stored up and a garrison formed of one thousand three hundred old soldiers and two thousand ferociously determined townsmen. Montgomery fitted out a reserve fleet at Guernsey. Nobody imagined that the Queen of England could remain deaf to the appeals with which she was assailed on every side.

Nîmes, Montauban, Montpellier, Sancerre and Somnières in the Languedoc became so many Protestant bastions, in which the royal authority was of no account.

At the same time two factors of immeasurable importance came into being—factors that Catherine had certainly never foreseen when she caused Maurevert to raise his gun. The Protestant party became imbued with republicanism; and the hideous triumph of the fanatics became that of those *Politiques* for whom the state was more important than the Church.

Those two contradictory promises that served to keep the Floren-

[5] Cavriana.

tine poised, the destruction of Calvinism and the maintenance of the Edict of Pacification, were equally illusory. A fourth civil war was in train, and in this, for the first time, the Huguenots would not fight in the name of the king, but against the king. In this war there would no longer be any question of loyalty being linked with duty towards God.

In Geneva, the royalist Calvin's disciples were giving 'full scope to all the democratic possibilities implicit in Calvinism'.[6] Hotman was writing a book, *Franco-Gallia*, that was destined to have a profound influence upon men's minds and to give rise to a first attempt at collective government in France. 'A natural inversion of values at the time when the Catholic argument stopped putting the rights of the prince and the rights of God in opposition and set itself to merging them.'[7]

This ideological revolution got under way just as religion was suddenly withdrawing before 'a pallid god with a livid mask',[8] named politics. Crowning irony: the centre party represented that of the queen-mother, the party she had tacitly formed and which should have upheld her since her Edict of January, 1562. The belief that the public safety was more important than the safety of souls, was not this the true doctrine of that somewhat pagan, realistic Florentine?

A natural reaction against the horrors of 24th August brought the mass of reasonable Catholics to adopt this view at last. But this movement of opinion, which a few months earlier would have been a great triumph for Catherine and which would certainly have prevented her from committing her desperate act, was now to place her in the utmost danger. For far from strengthening the throne, as it appeared that they must, the *Politiques* were already thinking of an alliance with the Protestants and even of a rebellion.

Their leader, Montmorency, who had not reappeared at court, was a moderate man, incapable of setting off an explosion. His brother Damville, on the other hand, caused the greatest uneasiness. As for the Duke of Alençon, the hope of the party, he had sent an envoy to his 'fiancée', Queen Elizabeth, and dreamed of being carried off by the English fleet.

Biron, who had survived the massacre, was appointed governor of La Rochelle; but he was not accepted. Charles IX then turned to La Noue, who had survived Mons, that royalist Protestant who,

---

[6] Henri Hauser, *La Prépondérance espagnole*.   [7] *Ibid.*
[8] Michelet, *op. cit.*, vol. X, p. 4.

according to Cavriana, had the triple fame of virtue, steadfastness and military talent.

Negotiations were set afoot, negotiations that were sure to fail. As early as October war seemed to be unavoidable. It was essential, therefore, that the Queen of England should remain neutral; and it was necessary yet again to justify the Parisian matins in her eyes by proclaiming the gravity of the plot that had been forestalled.

On 27th October the good Queen Elizabeth of Austria was brought to bed of a princess. In spite of the disappointment that the birth of a girl always causes, there were the usual rejoicings at the Louvre.

In the evening of the same day the ferocious crowd that attends all great religious or revolutionary killings filled the Place de Grève, lit by the sinister light of smoking torches. At a window in the Hôtel de Ville stood the king, the queen-mother and the King of Navarre, behind a curtain.

An immense clamour arose when there appeared the cart with Cavaigne and Briquemaut, chained and covered with filth. The din grew monstrously loud at the sight of the straw-stuffed figure that stood for the Admiral and which had been dragged from the Conciergerie at a horse's tail.

Three gibbets stretched up into the dark sky. The condemned men reached them with difficulty, for the hysterical mob wanted to cut them to pieces. The decree of the parliament was read. Then Briquemaut began to climb the ladder. The provost's lieutenant asked him whether he did not wish to make a last disclosure. The old man had by this time recovered a stoicism worthy of the Admiral, his friend. He said, 'I pray to God, at whose judgment seat I shall presently appear, to forgive the king and all those who have caused me to die unjustly, as I hope that He will forgive me the sins that I have committed.'

He reached the last rung, and spoke again, 'I should indeed like to speak to the king, but . . .'

The hangmen had already grasped him, and that was his last word. Cavaigne died without having opened his mouth.

The figure wearing the clothes and the badges of Coligny swung in its turn from the gallows. Where the face should have been a humorous lout stuck a piece of wood to represent the famous toothpick.

Although for these many years past Catherine had been entirely callous,[9] there was nothing of the sadist in her, and her presence served merely to emphasise the importance she attached to the conspiracy. This was not the case with Charles.

The Most Christian King, surrounded by torches, went to see the quivering bodies close to, and the hanging effigy of the man he had venerated three months earlier. 'Some do not think it pretty,' as Brantôme was to write.

Charles then went to the Hôtel de Ville, where a splendid banquet celebrated both the execution of the victims and the birth of his daughter. While the court was at this banquet, the populace overturned the gibbets, hacked the corpses to pieces and fought over the pieces. 'Of all these tragedies,' wrote Walsingham to Leicester, 'this last is the most astonishing and extraordinary. To go in person to watch the execution of one of his subjects and one of his oldest soldiers is a most rare and uncommon instance among Christians. God will not allow a prince of such a temper to remain for long over his people.'

[9] Her kindness had long been held up for praise and even more for blame.

CHAPTER III

'THE WRETCHED HUGUENOT PARTY
IS STILL IN EXISTENCE'

ALBERT DE GONDI, Comte de Retz, was indispensable. Co-author and beneficiary of the massacre of Saint Bartholomew, he had yet been able to calm the fury of the Lutheran princes. Once more Catherine sent him abroad, this time to help Mauvissière in London in his efforts to beguile Elizabeth.

Retz, a most accomplished player in the *commedia dell' arte*, had quite overwhelmed Charles IX on 23rd August by his moving words. Now, with the Queen of England, he displayed all his talents as a charmer and all his powers as an advocate. He pleaded his master's cause, guaranteed his good intentions and above all, did his utmost to demonstrate the weakness of a decimated, scattered and disorganised party. A great sovereign was well aware that it would be folly to sacrifice the friendship of France to the cause of the defeated. The king and his mother were most pressing in their offers of friendship and asked for a similar demonstration in return—even going so far as to ask for a loan. Retz added to this many specious observations and much flattery.

On the other hand, Elizabeth had in her possession a letter received shortly after the massacre in Bordeaux in which the Protestants of La Rochelle asked her to take back the inheritance of the Plantagenets. 'Your Majesty neither can nor should be allied with those who seek to destroy your people of Guyenne, who have from all eternity belonged to you and whose arms Your Majesty still does them the honour to bear. May it please Your Majesty to help them with your forces and all means at your disposal, and they will devote their cities to you and risk their lives and their possessions to acknowledge you as their sovereign queen and natural ruler.' Elizabeth lavished marks of friendship upon Retz and pretended to be as yet undecided. In the event she sent only trifling help to

La Rochelle and towards the end of December she agreed to be godmother to the daughter of Charles IX.

In the meantime a ship was waiting at Dover, ready to sail with all speed to the coast of Normandy, there to take aboard Alençon and perhaps Navarre and Condé.[1]

Did Alençon lack the heart for it? More probably it was Catherine, warned by Mauvissière, who caused the romantic plan to fall through. The whole matter is obscure.

But in any case, the Medici gave nothing away, and without having to feign, she displayed all the happiness of a grandmother.

On 1st February, 1573, the Earl of Worcester, the Queen of England's ambassador extraordinary, made his solemn entry into Paris, as Cardinal Orsini and the Marquis of Ayamonte had done before him. But the honours and the civilities that were showered upon him had nothing of that ill grace which had so grieved his predecessors.

'I desire that the friendship between us should last for ever and that the whole world should be aware of it,' said Charles IX to him.

Catherine, very cheerful, said that one day she hoped she might be godmother to a child of Elizabeth.

Worcester was a Catholic, although according to Zuniga the Inquisition would have had excellent reasons 'for making him sweat a little'. Nevertheless Salviati refused to meet him, and pretended to be ill. He regretted it later, when the very pious Empress, Maximilian's wife, agreed to be second godmother.

On 2nd February, Candlemas, the baptism took place at Saint-Germain-l'Auxerrois with the prodigious splendour that made all Europe envy this blood-stained and ruined court. When the ambassadors paid their compliments to the young queen, Don Diego thrust Worcester aside and went in front of him, conscious of maintaining his Catholic Majesty's honour.

A few days later the entire nobility, even the newly-converted members of it, went off to join the Duke of Anjou, who had already taken command of the army intended for the reduction of La Rochelle. Alençon, Navarre, Condé and Montmorency rubbed shoulders with Guise, Nevers, Retz and the vilest murderers of 24th August.

Wishing to bless their undertaking, the Pope spoke of sending the king 'the sword of honour and the hat'. An untimely mark of favour:

[1] Cf. Maisonfleur's correspondence, published by H. de la Ferrière in *Le XVI*e *siècle et les Valois*, Paris, 1879.

the Most Christian King let the Holy Father know quite clearly that he did not choose to compromise himself any further in the eyes of the Protestant world. It would be time to think of the sword of honour after victory had been achieved.

In spite of the efforts of the honest and honourable La Noue, subtlety had not persuaded the men of La Rochelle to come to terms. The siege began; a long, cruel and disappointing siege in which many of the Admiral's assassins were killed, particularly Aumale and Cosseins, who had been filled with foreboding, and who had never ceased to repeat, 'Curse the massacre of Saint Bartholomew.'

The English fleet appeared, fired a few broadsides and vanished; but the town refused to surrender, although it was also attacked by the plague and by famine. Any man who even spoke of surrender was hanged within the hour.

In Monsieur's camp plots would be hatched between two assaults. It was here that the Montmorencys firmly knit together the central party of the *Politiques* and the *Mal-contents*, and placed it openly under Alençon's patronage. It was here that they made their first contacts with the Huguenots. The Catholic leaders loathed one another, and the regiments guarded themselves from their fellows even more carefully than they did from the enemy.

After the failure of the fourth assault upon the 'bastion of the Gospel' the *Politiques* secretly suggested to the besieged that they should try a sortie. Taking advantage of the disorder, the Montmorencys would fall upon the Guises, and Alençon upon Monsieur's very headquarters. The Huguenots were so astonished at the enormity of this fratricidal plot that they could not believe that the suggestion was sincere.

While the men of La Rochelle were fighting like martyrs sure of winning a heavenly reward, the Polish Protestants were zealously supporting the cause of the prince who longed to destroy them. In Cracow, Monluc displayed the renowned Duke of Anjou as a hero who loved tolerance, who was innocent of the massacre of Saint Bartholomew and who was determined to respect the liberty of conscience of his future subjects. The dexterous ambassador also promised a policy of appeasement in France, the mediation of Charles IX between Poland and the Sultan and between the Sultan and Venice. The dazzled Poles saw their corn, their salted meat and their leather travelling across the Turkish dominions to reach Venice, where all goods would find a purchaser.

The Diet assembled on 5th April in a plain beside the Vistula. On 9th May, Henry of Valois was elected King of Poland to the cries of 'Gallum ! Gallum !'

Catherine wept with joy. This diplomatic victory not only realised her most cherished maternal hopes; she could also, as a sovereign, be proud of her work. Coligny had wanted to put the future of France in jeopardy by attacking Spain. Nine months later the Medici had contrived, entirely by peaceful means, to inflict a terrible defeat on the hereditary enemy.

In reconciling Poland with the Sultan, who was at that time master of a great part of Hungary, she blocked the path of the Emperor and prevented him from joining Philip II. William of Orange had just acknowledged Charles IX as the protector of the Low Countries. Many of the German princes wished to set the imperial crown aside for him. In order to complete the ring round the Habsburgs it now only remained to conclude the marriage between Elizabeth and Alençon.

Without firing a single gun, Machiavelli's pupil had paralysed Philip II and had prevented him from attacking France, which, emerging from the blood-stained shadows, suddenly reappeared at the height of its influence. 'Master,' wrote Saint-Gouard to Charles IX, 'by strength or by intelligence, you will make yourself master of the world.'

'Such was Catherine's great work—to lose all the ground gained by two years of intrigues and labour in a single day, to break so many hard-won alliances, and then to turn this Europe, simmering with indignation, inside-out like a glove: this was indeed the most striking triumph of her diplomacy!' [2]

The King of Poland could not compromise his standing before the impregnable walls of a city in its death-throes. When the eighth assault had been thrown back, Catherine gave up. As if her conduct during the last year had been concerned only with her foreign policy, she did not hesitate for a moment to adopt the German princes' earnest pleas as her own and urge Charles IX to make peace with the Huguenots.

What kind of a peace? The same as that of the Treaty of Saint-Germain and the Edict of 1570—the same peace as that which existed before the massacre of Saint Bartholomew.

Freedom of conscience and freedom of worship for those nobles with the rights of high justice, as well as for the towns of La Rochelle,

[2] H. de La Ferrière, *La Saint-Barthélemy*, Paris, 1892, p. 226.

Montauban and Nîmes, which were also exempted from being garrisoned by royal troops. All this was hastily drawn up and signed, and it was called the Treaty of La Rochelle.

Before the edict that was to ratify this astonishing agreement was published, the Spanish ambassador hurried to complain at the Louvre. 'How is it possible that you, the Most Christian rulers, having brought yourselves to do God such great services on Saint Bartholomew's day . . . can now make peace with those who are so few and who have no leaders?'

Placidly the queen-mother replied, 'There is nothing else we can do.'

The enraged Don Diego advised Philip II to throw himself upon France as soon as the Duke of Anjou should have begun his journey. The Nuncio sent a more moderate dispatch to Rome, concluding lucidly, 'The whole importance of the treaty consists in the fact that by this agreement the wretched Huguenot party is still in existence and is still tolerated in the kingdom.'

The two religions continued to confront one another, and the proportion of their strengths was scarcely changed. The massacre of Saint Bartholomew had served only to prevent war abroad and to increase the disorder at home.

CHAPTER IV

TWENTY-FIVE YEARS ON

VERY SOON the plots and civil wars began again. Charles, having recovered from his hideous intoxication, was overwhelmed by the horror of his crime. He died when he was twenty-four, carried off by consumption and bathed in a bloody sweat that, for the Protestants, was a mark of God's anger, as his father's fatal accident had been. 'Ah, my mother,' were his last words.

There were now three armed factions fighting for the kingdom. To prevent the unity of France being completely destroyed, the old queen had to send for the King of Poland. The consequences of the massacre were robbing her of all the fruits of her splendid victory.

The nation was astonished, on his return, to see Henry III so unlike the Duke of Anjou. The whimsicalities verging on extravagance, the almost feminine majesty of this last prince of the Renaissance, brilliantly-gifted degenerate, contrasted forcibly with the image the people had preserved in their minds of the victor of Moncontour. His subjects mocked, but they were unaware of another change in their former idol: the partisan who had worked for the killing of the Huguenots had discovered in himself the stuff of a king who could carry into effect his mother's precept, *Never take sides.*

The extremists foresaw the danger of the king taking the helm and rising above all factions. They opened a formidable campaign of denigration. From the outset this propaganda and his financial difficulties prevented the king from governing. One of the misfortunes that Catherine had sought to prevent on the evening of 23rd August now came about. The militant Catholics formed themselves into the powerful Catholic League, led by the Guises and financed by Philip II. At the same time, Henry of Navarre escaped, renounced Catholicism and became the head of a Calvinist republic born of the massacre. Alençon, for his part, set himself up as a rebel leader.

Henry III was obliged to give way before these conflicting

enemies; but as early as the following year, 1577, he achieved a surprising recovery and imposed upon them the 'King's Peace'.

In spite of the fact that the troubles did not abate, France obtained a short respite in the calm that lasted until 1584. Then the death of Alençon (Duke of Anjou since 1576) raised the question of the succession and the drama was resumed.

From this moment Henry of Navarre was heir to the throne—the throne upon which the League would have liked to see Henri de Guise. Navarre refused to revert to Catholicism again and Henry III refused to abolish the rights of Navarre: the League therefore insisted that Protestantism should be outlawed. A new civil war, the worst of them all, was the result of this trial of strength. It was to last no less than thirteen years.

By the end of 1587, Henry III, secretly helped by Navarre (Montaigne had been the messenger between them), had once again succeeded in restraining the extremists of both sides. It was then that Elizabeth had Mary Stuart executed and that the great war, so long expected, broke out between England and Spain.

Philip II assembled the Invincible Armada; but before sending this fleet and its cargo of inquisitors against the heretical island, he wished to neutralise France. He had lavished enormous subsidies upon Guise, and now he obliged him to make his way to Paris in spite of the king's prohibition and there provoke a riot. The Day of the Barricades gained him the capital, but not the crown, for Henry III slipped through the net and reached the banks of the Loire.

The catastrophic end of the Armada was also a catastrophe for the League. Nevertheless, when the king summoned the States-General at Blois, the embattled Protestants and the frightened Politiques left three-quarters of the seats to Guise's supporters, and Henry found that he was their prisoner.

At this critical moment the unity of France depended solely upon the spiritual strength of this prince, whom the pamphleteers named the Antichrist. Henry was most strongly Catholic: he might have made sure of his own peace and he might have eased his conscience by disinheriting the Huguenot leader. He preferred to stand fast. Guise, continually harried by Spain, then determined to take up arms. Henry forestalled him and had him assassinated, together with his brother, the Cardinal. In the dead man's pockets he found justification for his action. 'To carry on the war in France', the duke had written to Philip II, 'seven hundred thousand *livres* are needed every month.' (23rd December, 1588)

It cannot too often be repeated that in the sixteenth century the sovereign, as the highest judge and the fount of justice, had an absolute right to kill a dangerous subject. This right, exercised calmly and deliberately against a man in the pay of a foreigner at a time when the state was in peril, gave the killing of Guise the character of a judicial execution. The massacre of 1572 remains a criminal outrage, an *attentat*, for it was an improvised affair, in which the decision had been wrung from the king and the consequences left to chance.

Catherine, concerned primarily with the dynasty and with the welfare of her children, had unhappily allowed her policy to deviate since the line of Valois became doomed to extinction. She had a wild longing to secure the succession to the son of her favourite daughter, the Duchess of Lorraine, and in her hatred for Navarre she upheld the Guises.

The tragedy of Blois, engineered without her and in spite of her, killed Catherine. She died thirteen days later, abandoned like 'a dead goat'.

On hearing of the death of their hero, the Parisians rose. The Leaguers, many of whom had taken part in the massacre of Saint Bartholomew, gave themselves up to violence; at the same time the Sorbonne proclaimed that the French were now released from their duty towards the sovereign and the municipality entrusted the executive power to a council of forty members. Most of the great towns took the 'Oath of Union' against Henry III, and the Duke of Mayenne, Guise's brother, was appointed lieutenant-general. There was a reign of terror: one half of the Catholics hunted down the other half, suspected of loyalty or of moderation. The Spanish ambassador acted as the protector of the League and paid its troops. Seeing this, the Calvinist army, which had not moved since the year before, advanced as far as Saumur.

'This is the end of the kingdom,' wrote the Venetian ambassador. In fact, Henry III's dominions were reduced to three towns, Tours, Blois and Beaugency. It was far less than that which Charles VII possessed before the time of Joan of Arc.

In his distress the Valois turned to the Bourbon. To save their country the two Capetians forgot the religious barrier and the rivers of blood that had flowed between them. The treaty that they signed marked the reconciliation of the monarchy and the Reformation, and politically it wiped out the massacre of Saint Bartholomew.

On 30th April, 1589, to the applause of a delighted nation and in the presence of two armies which had fought each other for twenty-seven years, the son of Catherine de' Medici and the son of Jeanne d'Albret fell into one another's arms.

'Now I can die,' said Navarre. 'I have beheld my king! '

But it was Henry III who was to die of this reunion, and he knew it. He could no longer escape the threat of excommunication which had long hung over him. Now that the blow had fallen, the fanatics marked him down as the beast to be destroyed. The last of the Valois had given his life for France.

Three months later, when Paris was on the point of surrendering, a crack-brained monk, Jacques Clément, stabbed him mortally with a knife before the city.

Henry III was able to summon Navarre before he died, and to oblige the court to take oath to him as to the legal heir to the throne. He also earnestly begged him to become a Catholic.

Henry IV took four years to follow his advice. Five more were to pass before he could pronounce 'the remains of the civil wars buried, the parties extinguished and peace reigning throughout the whole kingdom'.

His Edict of Nantes (1598) reflected the Edict of January (1562): his realism, his tolerance and his regard for the unity of the nation were those same qualities that had earned Catherine de' Medici such hatred forty years earlier. All the ruins that had piled up during that long period, all the deaths and all the crimes did nothing in the end but prove the insanity of a sterile fanaticism. And, as everything is only a beginning all over again, it was the spirit of the massacre of Saint Bartholomew that conjured up Ravaillac, when in his turn Henry IV wished to invade the Low Countries.

EPILOGUE

THE MASSACRE of Saint Bartholomew has been the subject of furious argument for three and a half centuries. This account is scrupulously based upon the findings of modern historical criticism: it is therefore fitting at this point to sum up the conclusions of these findings.

It has been said by Pastor, 'Today no on maintains that the massacre was the last act in a plan prepared long before: similarly no one supposes that it was dictated by anything but personal and political motives; religion did not enter into it. The crime was directed, not against the Huguenots, but against the leader of an organised party who sought to impose his will upon the king in foreign policy.' [1]

On the other hand, we do not agree with the historian of the Popes when he accuses Catherine of having 'provoked the attempt against Coligny solely in order to keep control of the government'.

Having made countless efforts to preserve peace, the queen-mother decided upon the killing of Coligny because it appeared to her that a *coup d'état* was at that moment the only possible way of preventing a foreign war that she considered hopeless, a rising of the Catholic extremists and, of course, the loss of her own power. The failure of the Machiavellian plot against both the Admiral and the Guises, and her terror at seeing her favourite son pay the penalty for the failure, forced her to commit an act of desperation which, because of Charles IX's unbalanced mind and the fanaticism of the mob, assumed unforeseen and monstrous proportions.

Fate had never so thoroughly flouted human presumption. As soon as the machine was set in motion, chance, unreason and brutish passions seized control and ran it as they chose.

The massacre of Saint Bartholomew was less a political drama, less an atrocity perpetrated in the name of religion, than one of those phenomena that reveal the blind, uncontrollable forces which govern the fate of nations.

[1] Louis Pastor, *Histoire des Papes depuis la fin du Moyen Age*, vol. XIX, p. 402.

The responsibility? For a long while the odium rested upon the queen-mother alone. This was a partisan judgment, and like all partisan judgments, it went too far. We shall not be accused of favouring the Florentine if we agree with the verdict of her worst enemy, that is to say, of her son-in-law.

Passing through Blois one day, Henry IV stopped at the church of Saint-Sauveur, where Catherine's remains were temporarily resting. In a scarcely chivalrous manner he laughed, and said, 'She is just as well there.'

But when, a little later, the president of the Parliament of Rouen, Groulard, attributed all the misfortunes that had happened during the civil wars to the queen-mother, Henry IV sharply replied, 'Pray tell me, what could she have done—a poor woman with her husband dead, five children on her hands and two families in France who were thinking of encroaching upon the throne, ours and the Guises'? Was she not obliged to play some very strange roles to outwit everybody and still preserve her children, as she did? And her children reigned one after another, because of the wise conduct of that intelligent woman. I am astonished that she did not do far worse! '

The same impartiality requires one to acknowledge the loftiness of Coligny. Yet he is open to grave censure on four counts. The Admiral was wrong in posing the dilemma, foreign war or civil war; wrong in under-estimating the strength of the Catholic extremists backed by Spain; wrong in allowing himself to believe in the myth of the English alliance; and wrong in founding his bold enterprise upon an unbalanced youth.

Charles IX has been compared to Hamlet. It is true that the unfortunate young man was trying to escape from a crushing domination and to show himself worthy of his ancestors before he fell so abjectly into decline. But his case was even more tragic than that of Shakespeare's hero, for the shock of his defeat awoke the bloodthirsty madness that lay dormant in his sick mind. He may not have been responsible for provoking the massacre, but the pupil of Ronsard was responsible for many of the crimes perpetrated during those evil days.

Elizabeth of England wore mourning for the victims. Yet she precipitated their end, since Catherine's discovery of her double game had convinced the queen-mother that Coligny's war would be disastrous, and this had had a powerful influence in urging her to take her fatal step.

Philip II had long demanded the extermination of the Huguenots:

12   Panoramic view of the massacre (i)

13 Panoramic view of the massacre (ii)

14 Panoramic view of the massacre (iii)

in the end, however, he had much less to do with bringing it about than the Anglican queen.

We have seen what parts were played by Anjou, the Guises, Retz, Tavannes and Nevers. Claude Marcel's was of the first importance. Still worse was that of the mob, always the same whenever an ideology sets free its savage instincts.

An essential result of the massacre of Saint Bartholomew was that it prevented the war between France and Spain. We shall therefore never know whose estimate of the situation was correct, the queen-mother's or the Admiral's. We shall never know whether this great duel, begun fifty years before Richelieu's time, would have ended in the triumph or the destruction of France.

Seen solely from the point of view of domestic policy, the Parisian matins were unique in having been a legal ambush or trap, the treachery of a government incapable of enforcing its own authority; and for this reason the extent of their consequences deserves even greater attention.

Without looking beyond the borders of France, we see that the butcheries in the fifteenth century during the war of the Armagnacs and the Burgundians claimed infinitely more victims, as did the days of June, 1848, the Chouan rising and the Commune; for all that, they have reached the calm, impersonal regions of history. The genocides of the twentieth century make the collective murders of the sixteenth appear trivial.

And yet the massacre of Saint Bartholomew still possesses a vibrant reality, and the horror it caused then causes horror still. Many Frenchmen are completely ignorant of General Cavaignac's brutal deeds under the Second Republic, but none is unmoved by the tocsin of Saint-Germain-l'Auxerrois.

There appear to be two reasons for the persistence of this dreadful memory. The political and diplomatic background is practically forgotten: what is remembered is the appalling religious outburst and the terrifying example of fratricidal intolerance.

This is not all. The massacre of Saint Bartholomew, like the Terror of 1793, had its social character. Citizens and scholars were murdered, but the full force of fury was directed against the great nobles. Châtillon, La Rochefoucauld, La Force, Téligny and a great many others belonged to the old feudal families of France. Even Catholic lords like Biron and Cossé-Brissac only just escaped. Their enemies, on the other hand, were for the most part of foreign extraction: the Guises Teutonic; Medici, Nevers, Birague and Gondi Italian.

The misfortunes of someone one knows personally are always more moving than those of an anonymous body. The victims of 24th August were known, and their descendants are known still. The fact that these great lords, these famous captains should have gone down before a set of newcomers seemed to fly in the face of nature.

The massacre of Saint Bartholomew can only be understood in its context, in relation to its period. It bears the stamp of that humanistic and fanatical sixteenth century, heroic and savage, that century in which tolerance had the appearance of betrayal. But above all it provides a terrible proof of the folly of mankind.

APPENDIX A

PARIS IN 1572

Parts of the map of Paris drawn up by Olivier Truschet and Germain Hoyau, and at present in the library of Basle.

The Sorbonne and its immediate surroundings

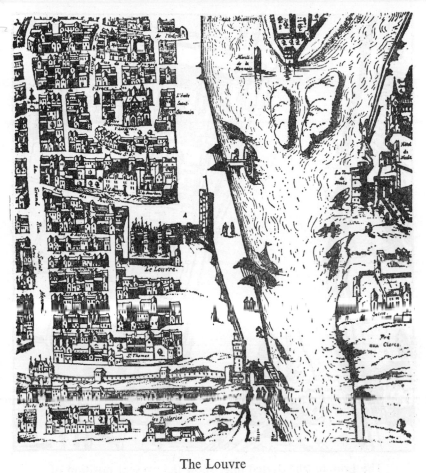

The Louvre

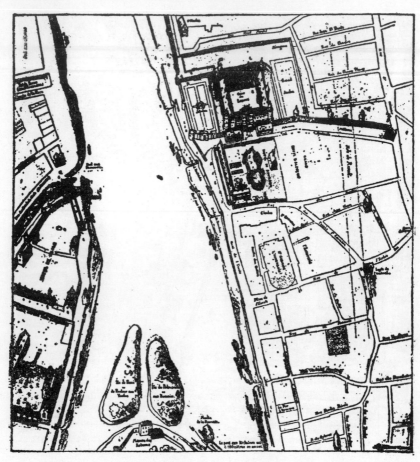

The Louvre (the dotted lines show the present position of
the Rue de Rivoli)

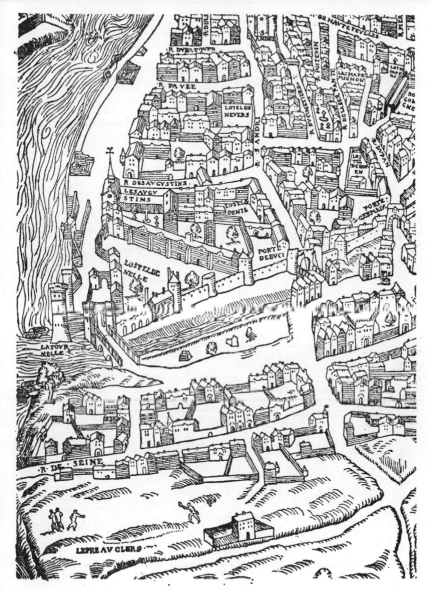

The Faubourg Saint-Germain with Le Pré-aux-Clercs
in the foreground

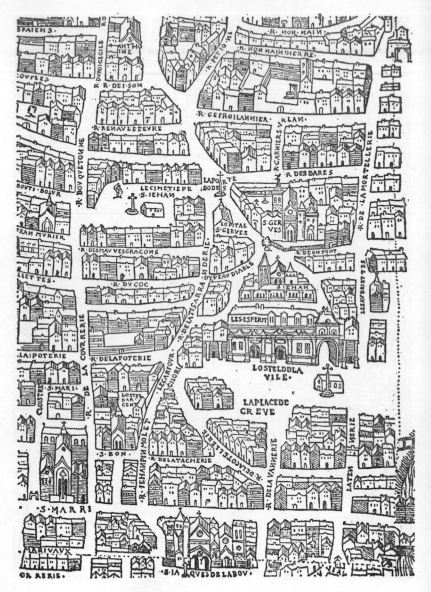

The Hôtel de Ville and its immediate surroundings

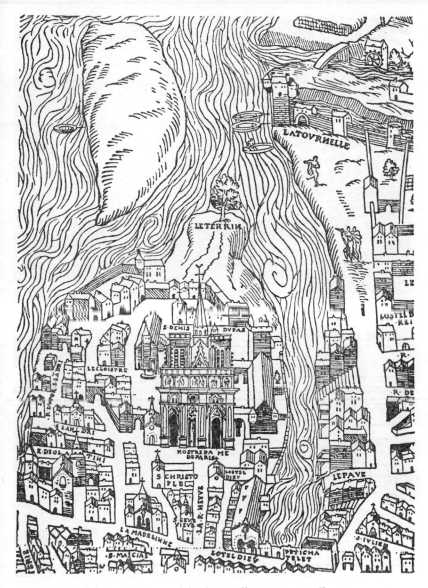

Notre-Dame and its immediate surroundings

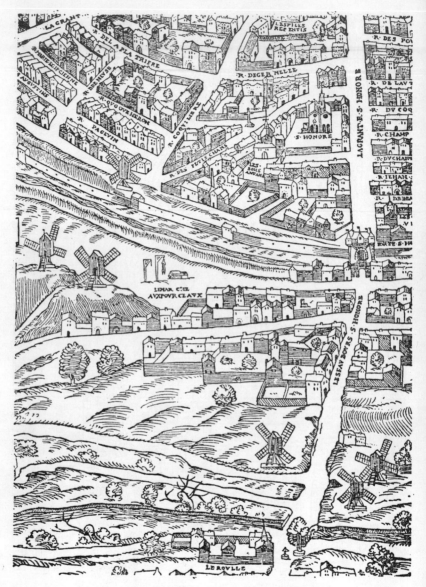

The Faubourg Saint-Honoré

A view of Paris. In the foreground a Protestant family being interrupted at prayer by a Catholic soldier

APPENDIX B

THE MASSACRE OF
SAINT BARTHOLOMEW
AS SEEN BY CONTEMPORARIES

CATHERINE DE' MEDICI AND CHARLES IX CHOSEN BY OUR LORD THE REDEEMER AS THE INSTRUMENTS OF HIS WILL.[1]

It appears to me that one should not pass over this splendid deed without examining it closely, without carefully considering the excellence of the king, the queen-mother and their counsellors in having made so noble and generous a decision, as well as having had the skill to manage it, the tact and the intelligence to disguise it, the wisdom and the discretion to keep it silent and unknown, and lastly, to the boldness and the courage to carry it out and the great happiness to bring it to a successful conclusion. For to tell the truth, if all these things are carefully considered, not only does it appear that they are worthy of eternal glory, but also it cannot be denied that, as ministers and instruments of His everlasting will, they were chosen by Our Lord the Redeemer, performing through them a deed of which it must be said that it comes from His vast and measureless power. And one is obliged to admit, also, that this wonderful act was premeditated, planned and considered many months before and not merely pitched upon by chance or hazard, nor undertaken because of the recent outrageous insolence of the Huguenots since the wounding of the Admiral, as some say and try to make others believe, it being the opinion of these people that the killing of the Admiral was a set design, but that the general execution then happened by chance, that it followed from the situation and the opportunity that was offered. This opinion may be seen to be quite false

[1] *Le Stratagème de Charles IX contre les huguenots rebelles à Dieu*, by Camille Capilupi, French version of 1579.

if one looks well into all the doings touching this matter, and particularly all the sure signs there are of the king's and the queen's thoughts and intentions, it being long since that they were made plain to certain people and at certain times.

A TRIBUTE TO CATHERINE DE' MEDICI FROM THE AMBASSADOR OF VENICE.[2]

As there are different views upon this matter of the Huguenots [3] and the Admiral's death, and as people wonder whether it was all an accident or whether it was a premeditated plan, I think it my duty to let your Serenity know what I have learned of the matter from highly-placed persons who are admitted to the secrets of this kingdom. Your Serenity is to know, therefore, that this entire business, from beginning to end, has been the work of the queen,[4] a work conceived, worked out and brought to a conclusion by her, with the help only of the Duke of Anjou, her son. The queen certainly had it in mind for a long while, since lately she herself asked Monsignor Salviati, a relation, who is Nuncio in France, to remember and bear witness of what she had secretly charged him to tell the late Pope,[5] to wit, that he would presently see the vengeance that she and the king would take upon those of the [Protestant] religion. It was with no other end in view that she worked so zealously for the marriage of her daughter with Navarre, without heeding either the King of Portugal or the other great matches that were offered her; and all this to cause the marriage to be held in Paris in the presence of the Admiral and the other leaders of the party, as she supposed the thing would happen and because there was no other way nor a better opportunity for drawing them thither.

SOME OF CHARLES IX'S REMARKS.

If it were a matter of prudently concealing within his heart some affair which ought not to be discovered, for the good of God's service and the welfare of his people, he [Charles IX] went about it with so great a prudence that there was none who, after the performance of his intentions, was not astonished by the outer coolness that concealed the ardour of his heart. In witness of this, the day after the massacre of Saint Bartholomew he answered a lord who said that it had not been expected of him with the words, 'In the same way,' said he, 'my very cap did not know of it.'

[2] Giovanni Michieli's account of the massacre, addressed to the Senate of Venice.   [3] Michieli's term for the massacre.
[4] Catherine de' Medici.   [5] Pius V, died 1st May, 1572.

(Histoire . . . de la vie, moeurs et vertus du roi très-chrétien et débonnaire Charles IX, by Arnaud Sorbin, preacher to the king.)

This slaughter took place in sight of the king, who watched it with great pleasure. A few days later, he went himself to see the gibbet at Montfaucon where Coligny's body was hanging by the feet, and as some of his train affected not to go near because the body stank, 'The smell of a dead enemy,' said he, 'is sweet and delightful.'

(Histoire de Charles IX, by Papyre Masson, historiographer to the king.)[6]

. . . Turning to the said Vaucluze, His Majesty said the following words to him, 'Tell the Comte de Carces [the king's lieutenant in Provence] that upon pain of death he is not to let it be known but to keep it secret,' by which he meant that the said Comte de Carces was not to have the Huguenots slaughtered as he had told him by La Molle [one of the king's gentlemen of the bedchamber in ordinary], for that he was determined to undertake an enterprise of high importance, and that if a slaughter were made in Provence, it might put off his own. And suddenly from behind the bolster of his bed, His Majesty took six knives as long as his arm and very sharp, for there were six of them who carried out the said undertaking at the Tuileries, that is to say, His Majesty, seconded by Monsieur de Fontaine, his chief equerry, Monsieur, his brother, seconded by Monsieur de Vins [Hubert de la Garde, sieur de Vins], and Monsieur de Guise, seconded by Monsieur de Vaux.

(Le Livre de raison d'Honoré du Teil, 1571–1586, published by J. du Teil.)

THE REPORT OF JUAN DE OLAEGUI, THE SPANISH AMBASSADOR'S SECRETARY.

That which Juan de Olaegui, secretary to the ambassador Don Diego de Çuniga, coming from the court of France with the ambassador's dispatches for Your Majesty, relates concerning the occurrences that have happened at that court.

On Thursday, 27th August, at eleven in the morning, the Admiral, having left the palace, stopped to read a letter that a Huguenot gentleman had just given him, at some fifty or sixty paces from the palace. From a neighbouring house he was hit by an arquebus shot,

---

[6] These two texts are reproduced in vol. XIII of the *Archives curieuses* of Cimber and Danjou.

which carried away one finger of his right hand and went through his arm and left hand; the ball came out near his elbow: when he felt the wound he said nothing but that they should find out who had done it.

The man who had fired the shot got out by a back door in the said house; he mounted a horse that was held ready for him; he left Paris by a gate where there was a Spanish horse awaiting him, and two leagues farther on he found another, a Turkish horse.

About four hundred mounted men, all Huguenots, set off in pursuit of the man who had wounded the Admiral, but they could not catch up with him and they came back to Paris that same day, the 22nd: that day and the next, it was widely said among the Huguenots that the Most Christian King or the Duke of Anjou were not strangers to this attempt; they further said that it had been committed by order of the dukes of Guise and Aumale, or of the Duke of Alba, and they threatened heaven and earth with unspeakable boldness and insolence.

The same day, 22nd August, the Most Christian King and his mother went to visit the Admiral, who said to the king that even if he were to lose his left arm, he would still have his right with which to avenge himself for the offence that had been done to him, and two hundred thousand men to help him; to which the king replied that although he was the ruler he had not been able to assemble fifty thousand and could not now.

After this visit, the king having returned to the palace, the Prince of Condé came to him and required him to take some measures about what had just happened; for if he did not, he was well able to revenge himself. The king satisfied him, but nevertheless as the said prince has a fiendish mind he continued threatening the king and his people.

On the said day, the king retired to his apartments early and went to bed at eight or nine o'clock. At ten he got up and summoned Marcel, the head of the citizens of Paris;[7] he bade him tell certain captains of the townsmen to hold themselves ready with their companies until they should hear the ringing of the alarm. Marcel carried out this command.

At midnight on 23rd August the king sent for the dukes of Montpensier, Guise and Aumale, together with the Bastard of Angoulême: he told each what it was that he had to do, which was that

---

[7] Olaegui seems not to know that Marcel no longer had the office of Provost of the merchants.

the Duke of Montpensier should search the apartments of the princes of Béarn [8] and Condé to see who was there, and that then the guard should kill such and such, whom he named; that the dukes of Guise and Aumale, with the Bastard,[9] should cut off the head of the Admiral and those of his suite and that they should try to take and to kill Montgomery and the Vidame of Chartres, who were staying in the Faubourg Saint-Germain, outside the gates: they took measures to this effect, but without success, for these men escaped and fled into Normandy.

On Sunday, Saint Bartholomew's day, at three o'clock in the morning, the alarm was rung: all the Parisians began killing the Huguenots of the town, breaking down the doors of the houses in which they lived and pillaging what they found within.

The said Guise, Aumale and Angoulême went to the Admiral's house, which they entered, having killed eight of the Prince of Béarn's Swiss who tried to defend it.

They went up to his room, and in the bed in which he was lying, the Duke of Guise shot him in the head with a pistol; then they took him and threw him naked out of the window into the courtyard of his house, where he received several more strokes with swords and daggers.

When they tried to throw him out of the window he said, 'Oh, Monsieur, have pity on old age', but he was not given time to say any more.

When this had been done, they went to the house of the Comte de La Rochefoucauld, and to him, his son, the captains and the gentlemen who were with him, they did the same as they had done to the Admiral.

Immediately afterwards, they went to the house of Téligny, the Admiral's son-in-law,[10] and they served him in the same way, as well as Briquemaut, the said Admiral's lieutenant, Briquemaut's sons [11] and fifteen or twenty other gentlemen, who were all thrown

---

[8] The Spanish government did not recognise Henri de Bourbon as King of Navarre.

[9] On the 28th following, the said Bastard received a gratuity of 550 livres from the king. (*Bibliothèque nationale*, fr. 7712, fol. 70.)

[10] Téligny had married Coligny's daughter on 24th March, 1571, at La Rochelle.

[11] Incorrect. On the night of the massacre Briquemaut had managed to reach the English ambassador's house disguised as a groom. After some days he was dragged from his asylum to be given up to the Parliament of Paris. Of his four sons, only one died in the massacre.

out of the windows into the streets, where the people stripped them at once.

Other Catholic gentlemen and courtiers killed a great many Huguenot gentlemen.

In the palace, Beauvais, the Prince of Béarn's tutor, was killed, as well as Captain Piles and about eighteen servants of the said prince and of the Prince of Condé, those whom they loved the best; and some others who were in the town hid themselves and escaped.

In the said Faubourg Saint-Germain, where most of the Huguenots who had come to court were lodging, a great many were killed; among others, the chancellors and certain counsellors and ministers of the said princes and the Admiral.

The Duke of Guise, the Duke of Aumale and the Bastard of Angoulême, mounted and with a good escort, went to the lodgings of Montgomery and the Vidame de Chartres, but they, having been warned by a Huguenot who had crossed the river by swimming, had had the time to mount and flee, so that they could not be caught: nevertheless, at the time of Olaegui's departure they were still being pursued.

On the said Sunday and the following Monday he saw the bodies of the Admiral, La Rochefoucauld, Téligny, Briquemaut,[12] the Marquis de Ries, Saint-George, Beauvoir, Piles and others dragged about the streets: they were afterwards put into a cart and he does not know whether they hung the Admiral up, but they threw the others into the river.

The massacre lasted until the morning of Tuesday, 27th August.

On this day, the Most Christian King, dressed in his royal robes, went to the palace and declared to the parliament that he had been obliged to make the peace that he had made with the Huguenots because his people were exhausted and ruined, but that now that God had given him victory over his enemies, he declared null and void the edict that he had given out in consequence of the said peace, and said that he desired that the edict that he had formerly published should be observed, according to which no other religion than the Catholic, Apostolic and Roman might be practised in the kingdom.

Certain princes having said to the king, concerning this massacre, that the Germans and the English would be offended, he replied that he was in no way disturbed by that, so long as he had the Catholic King's friendship.

The princes of Béarn and Condé are utterly downcast: they dare

---

[12] This obviously refers to the son.

not say a word, and an official of Villeroi, the secretary, who rode some posts with the said Olaegui as far as Bordeaux, told him that on the 27th they went to mass with the king.

The said Olaegui, at Orleans on the morning of the 27th, saw several Huguenots killed and thrown into the river: before he left Paris, which he did on the 26th in the afternoon, news had come that the same was being done at Rouen and Meaux.

On the 27th, in a town called Beaugency, this side of Orleans, there were some three hundred Huguenots being besieged, and some Catholic arquebusiers were going to execute them.

At Blois, Châtellerault, Poitiers, Bordeaux and Bayonne nothing has been done, but the Catholics are under arms there, so that no tumult may occur, this being the Most Christian King's command...

All along the road from Paris to Bayonne there had been no calling out of troops, and nothing unusual was to be seen. Now that they find that they are leaderless, the Huguenots dare not say a word about what has happened.[13]

THE ACCOUNT OF FILIPPO CAVRIANA, A MANTUAN PHYSICIAN IN THE SERVICE OF CATHERINE DE' MEDICI.

All night long there was a council at the Louvre. The guards were doubled, and so that the Admiral's suspicions should not be aroused, no one was allowed to leave without showing the king's express order. All the ladies were gathered in the queen's room, and being ignorant of what was being prepared, they were half dead with fear. In the end, when it came to the point of execution, the queen told them that traitors had determined to kill her on the coming Tuesday, her, the king and the whole court, all of which was proved by letters that she had received. At this news the ladies were struck with amazement. The king did not undress, but, laughing, he took the opinions of those who made up the council, such as Guise, Nevers, Montpensier, Tavannes, Retz, Birague and Morvillier. When Morvillier, whom they had woken up, and who had come much disturbed at having been sent for by the king at such a time, learned from His Majesty's mouth the subject of this nocturnal council, he felt his heart seized with such a terror that before the king had even asked his opinion he collapsed in his seat, incapable of uttering a single word. When he was a little better, his Majesty

[13] Published by Gachard in the *Bulletins de l'Académie royale de Belgique*, 1849, vol. XVI, 1st part.

asked him to state his views. 'Sire,' he replied, 'it is a very serious affair, and one of the highest importance, which might cause the civil war to break out again, more implacable than ever.' Then, as the king pressed him and showed him the imminent peril, he ended after much hesitation and many devious turns by concluding that if all he was told was true, the will of the king and the queen would have to be done and the Huguenots put to death. And as he spoke he could not keep back his sighs and his tears.

Without waiting any longer, the king sent for the King of Navarre and the Prince of Condé; and at this extraordinary hour they came to the king's chamber, accompanied by the men of their train. When these wished to come in—and among them were Monin and Piles—they were stopped at the door by the soldiers of the guard. Then the King of Navarre, turning towards his people with a sorrowful face, said to them, 'Adieu, my friends: God knows whether I shall see you again.'

At the same moment Guise left the palace and went to find the captain of the citizens to give him the order to arm two thousand of his men and to surround the Faubourg Saint-Germain, where more than fifteen hundred Huguenots were living, so that the massacre might take place on both banks of the river at the same time.

Nevers, Montpensier and the other lords at once armed themselves, and together with their people, some on foot, some mounted, went to the various posts that had been allotted to them, all prepared to act in concert.

The king and his brothers did not leave the Louvre.

Cossein, the Gascon commander, the German Besme, a former page to Monsieur de Guise, Hautefort, the Italians Pierre Paul Tossinghi and Petrucci, went with a numerous troop to the house of the Admiral, whom they had orders to kill. They broke down the door and went up the stairs. At the top of it they found a kind of makeshift barricade, made of chests and benches hurriedly heaped together. They thrust their way into the room, found eight or ten servants, whom they killed, and saw the Admiral, standing at the foot of his bed and dressed in a furred gown. The day was only just dawning and things could barely be made out. They asked him, 'Are you the Admiral?' He replied that he was. They rushed at him and covered him with insults. Besme grasped his sword and made to plunge it into his bosom. But he cried out, 'Ah, young soldier, have pity upon old age!' Vain words. With one stroke Besme laid him at his feet: they fired two pistols straight into his face and left him lying there lifeless. The whole house was given over to pillage. Meanwhile some of these men appeared on the balcony and said, 'He is dead.' Those below, Guise and the others, would not believe it. They asked him to be thrown out of the window, which was done. The corpse was stripped, and when it was naked pieces were cut off it.

La Rochefoucauld was killed by a Basque captain, to whom he vainly offered sixteen thousand crowns to ransom his life.[14]

Téligny escaped; he was recaptured and his throat was cut.

He and the others were dragged about the streets at the end of a rope like so many dead animals, and then thrown into the Seine, from which their bodies were taken later.

Piles, going out of the King of Navarre's room to rush from the palace, was killed by a Swiss. Before he died, he cried out 'This is the sworn peace! This is the pledged word!' His companions suffered the same fate.

All that was to be heard was the cry 'Kill! Kill!' Everything was in an uproar, and the massacre spread on all sides.

Montgomery and the Vidame de Chartres lived in the Faubourg Saint-Germain. They were woken by the din: they mounted their horses, and followed by some sixty of their people they drew up in formation in the Pré-aux-Clercs. Vins, a Provençal in the service of the Duke of Anjou, came to reconnoitre them. He asked what they wanted and what they were doing. They replied by the cry of 'Peace!' and said that they were betrayed. Vins fired his arquebus at them. Guise arriving with a large troop, the sixty Huguenots took to flight. Montgomery owed his salvation to the speed of his horse, which had wings: with the Vidame and eight or ten others he reached the forest of Montfort. All the rest were killed.

Nevers and Montpensier ran through the city with troops of infantry and horsemen to see that only the Huguenots were attacked. None was spared. Their houses were sacked to the number of about four hundred, without counting the rented rooms and the inns. Fifteen hundred persons were killed in one day, and as many in the two following days.

[14] There is no agreement as to the identity of La Rochefoucauld's assassin. For d'Aubigny, it was Raymond d'Anglerez; for Brantôme, his brother Antoine, known as Chicot. As the Chevalier François de La Barge, governor of the Vivarais in 1575, received half La Rochefoucauld's cavalry company after the massacre, he was suspected of having assassinated him by an intermediary,

Everywhere there were people who fled and others who ran after them, crying 'Kill! Kill!' There were men and women who, with the knife at their throats, were called upon to recant to save their lives, but they would not, and so lost both soul and body. There was no mercy either for age or for sex. It was in very truth a massacre. The streets were strewn with naked, mutilated corpses; the river was covered with them.

The murderers wore the sleeve of a shirt on their left arms. Their watchword was 'Glory to God and the king!'

When it was day, Monseigneur d'Anjou took horse and went through the city and the suburbs with eight hundred cavalry, a thousand foot and four pieces of artillery to beat down the houses that resisted. There was no need for them. The Huguenots, attacked without warning, thought only of flight.

There was no laughter among the shouts. The victors did not shout with joy, as victors usually do, for the spectacle before them was so heart-breaking and hideous . . .

The Louvre remained closed: everything there was in silence and terror. The king stayed in his chamber: he looked cheerful, laughed and joked. It was a long while before the court could recover and take on something of the appearance of calmness again. Today everyone is eagerly seeking to profit by the situation, soliciting either places or privileges. Up to the present nothing has been done except to give the Marquis de Villars the office of Admiral. The king is feared, and it is seen that he means to be obeyed.

It is said that Coligny, talking to his son-in-law Téligny a week ago about the prediction of an astrologer who had said that he would be hanged, made game of it and said, 'Consider whether there is any likelihood of such a thing happening—unless indeed it means that I shall be hanged in effigy, as I was some months ago.' Now the astrologer had told the truth, for his body, dragged about the streets and the object of the vilest insults, was beheaded and hanged by the feet from the gibbet of Montfaucon, there to become meat for crows.

Such was the miserable end of the man who not long before was the master of half France. Upon him there was found a medal with these words engraved, *Either a complete victory, or an assured peace, or an honourable death.* None of these wishes was to come true.

The tragedy has lasted three whole days, amid raging fury. It is only just beginning to die down. The booty has been enormous:

it is reckoned at a million and a half gold crowns. More than four hundred of the bravest gentlemen and the best captains of the party have perished. Most of them had come well provided with clothes, jewels and money, to make a good show at the wedding of the King of Navarre. The mob has enriched itself with their spoils.

The Parisians are pleased; they feel relieved and assuaged. Yesterday they hated the queen; today they proclaim her 'The mother of the kingdom and the preserver of the Christian name'.[15]

THE REPORT OF THE CHEVALIER DE GOMICOURT, THE DUKE OF ALBA'S AGENT IN PARIS.

On 22nd August, 1572, the Admiral, going from the Louvre in Paris towards his house to dine, was reading a letter, and as he passed before the house of a canon who had formerly been the tutor of the Lord of Guise, an arquebus charged with four balls was fired at him, whereby the finger next to his thumb on his right hand was shot off and his left hand shot in the palm; the ball, passing along the arm and breaking all his bones, came out two fingers above the elbow. The front door of this house was locked and the back open, where there was a Spanish horse upon which he who had wounded the Admiral fled. When the Admiral felt himself wounded, with his Huguenots he took counsel to kill the king and Messieurs his brothers and the queen, saying that this evil came about through them; he decided forthwith to go to his four hundred men who were in the Faubourg Saint-Germain, a thing that would have been easy to do at any time that he wished; but he could not do it so secretly that the king and the queen would not know: for the Admiral having sent for the King of Navarre to the place where he lay, he said these words, or words to this effect, 'My lord, I believe that you know how much I served my lord your father and my late lord your uncle, the Prince of Condé; and as I wish to continue in the same good will towards you and as I am now mortally wounded (for the balls were poisoned) I have decided to make my will before dying and to leave you the realm of France as an inheritance.' And he made known to him the means that he had prepared.

The King of Navarre, having heard all this, returned to his apartments (in the Louvre) and there, very sad and melancholy, foreseeing the great disaster to his brother the king and others, he was so much importuned by his wife that he straightway told her what the

[15] Published by A. Desjardins in *Charles IX, deux années de règne*, Douai, 1873.

said Admiral had decided; and when she understood this, after admonishing him several times not to sully his hands with the blood of the king his brother-in-law, she at once went to tell the king and the queen her mother.

Thus, on Saint Bartholomew's day, the 24th of the said month, at one in the morning, there entered into the said Admiral's house the dukes of Guise and Aumale, and the Chevalier d'Angoulême; and some of their suite entered into the aforesaid Admiral's room, which the Admiral's people defended with their swords; but they were at once defeated. Seeing this, the Admiral went back into his bed and feigned death, but he was drawn out of it by his wounded arm. As Monsieur Cousin [16] set himself to throw him out of the window he put his foot against the wall, for which reason the aforesaid Cousin said to him, 'What, you cunning fox, do you thus feign death?' With these words he threw him down into the courtyard of the house, where the Duke of Guise was waiting, to whom he said, 'There, my lord, there is the traitor who was the cause of your father's death.' The aforesaid Guise having heard this, he came to the Admiral and said these words to him, 'So there you are, you evil man: God grant, in sooth that I do not soil my hands with your blood,' and giving him a kick he went from him. Then directly some person came and shot him in the head with a pistol. This done, they began to drag him on a hurdle through the town. A gentleman cut off his head with a knife, and putting it on the end of his sword he carried it through the town crying, 'Here is the head of the evil man who did so many wrongs to the realm of France!' And as the people belonging to the parliament strove to have the body of the said Admiral back again to carry out the first sentence pronounced against him during the troubles, it was so much dismembered that none of it has been able to be recovered. If they had waited four hours before performing this, the Admiral would have done to them what the said princes have done to him, and would have killed the king and Messieurs his brothers. They at once went to La Rochefoucauld's house, where they did the same, and so to all who came into their hands; and they killed Bricquemault, the Marquis de Retz, Lespondillans,[17] Téligny, and gentlemen up to the number of LXII, they all being leaders; and these were dragged through the streets. In the same way, the Catholics pillaged all the Huguenots of the

---

[16] Cosseins, captain of the halberdiers of Charles IX's guard.

[17] Two names badly spelt by Gomicourt: they should read Ries and Pardaillan.

said town, and stripped them and threw them in the river. The king's guard also went into the city and to the houses of the Huguenots, killing them, and they did so well that within a short time they had cut more than three thousand to pieces. The chief gentlemen were thrown into the Clerks' Well, where dead animals are thrown.

At Rouen ten or twelve hundred Huguenots have been killed: at Meaux and at Orleans all have been dispatched. And, as Monsieur de Gomicourt was about to return, he asked the queen-mother for a reply to his message: she told him that she could think of no other answer than the response of Jesus Christ to Saint John's disciples; and she said, in Latin, *'Ite et nuntiate quae vidistis et audivistis; cœci vident, claudi ambulant, leprosi mundantur,'* etc., and told him that he was particularly not to forget to say to the Duke of Alba, *'Beatus qui non fuerit in me scandalisatus,'* and that she would always maintain a good and reciprocal intercourse with the Catholic King.

(Published by Gachard in the *Bulletins de l'Académie royale de Belgique*, 1842, vol. IX, part I.)

AN ACCOUNT OF COLIGNY'S MURDER, BY CAPTAIN STUDER VON WINKEL-
BACH, WHO COMMANDED THE DETACHMENT OF SWISS WHO
BROKE INTO THE ADMIRAL'S HOUSE.

Sunday, 24th August, was Saint Bartholomew's day. During the night the king said to his brother the Duke of Anjou, 'Today, I want to prove that I am king of France; for until now, I have not been king. I want to be able to count the days of my reign from this day onwards.'

At about two in the morning he called for the palace guards, of whom a hundred belonged to him, the king, fifty-six to Anjou, and fifty to Alençon, who were in the plot, to make them take the oath and to await further orders on pain of corporal punishment.

Upon this, the Duke of Anjou took all the Swiss and the archers [18] with him to lead them, at about five or six o'clock in the morning, to the Admiral's house, for the Duke of Guise had deployed his men as if for battle.

The French then rushed the gates, which were defended by eight guards, who fought them and routed them and then closed the gates again. In the uproar one of them was killed.

The Swiss attacked the gates and beat them in with their halberds.

---

[18] The *archers* had a function something between that of guards and con-
stables: they were not necessarily bowmen at this time. (Translator's note.)

The Duke of Guise called to those who were fighting in the lower part of the house to throw down their arms or they would all be run through.

When the Admiral's house was overrun, Moritz Grünenfelder of Niederuruen in the region of Glaris, was first into his room and he seized him, meaning to take him prisoner. At this Martin Koch of Freiburg, one of the Duke of Anjou's men, said to him, 'We are not ordered to do that.'

As the Admiral begged him to spare his old age, he thrust him through with the pike he was holding.

Captain Josué Studer of Saint Gall says that Moritz had found him standing up in his night-clothes and had led him to the light, saying, 'Knave, is it you?' And as it is said above, he ran the Admiral through with his halberd as he asked him to spare his old age. Presently the other also set upon him.

Guise asked if the Admiral were dead and that he should be thrown down into the street. As he struggled in his agony, he pushed his pike into his mouth. Then he was laid on the ground apart so that he could be recognised later.

(Published in *Archiv für Schweiz. Geschichte* 1879, vol. II, B. Forestié gives a French translation in his book *Un capitaine gascon, Corbeyran de Cardaillac-Sarlabour*, Paris, 1897.)

LETTER FROM FATHER JOACHIM OPSER, S.J., SUB PRIOR OF THE COLLEGE OF CLERMONT, TO THE ABBOT OF SAINT GALL, DATED 26TH AUGUST, 1572.

I do not think that I shall weary you in telling you at length of an occurrence as unexpected as it is helpful to our cause, one that not only captures the world's admiration but also raises it to the highest pitch of joy. You will hear what the captain [19] has to say upon the subject. Be happy in advance; but I beg that you will not reject or dismiss as superfluous what I write with perhaps more complacency than is fitting, for in it I state nothing that I have not derived from unimpeachable sources.

On 24th August the Admiral perished miserably, and with him the whole of the heretical part of the French nobility. (It may be said without exaggeration.) An immense slaughter! I trembled at the sight of this river filled with naked and horribly maltreated bodies. The king has so far spared only the King of Navarre; and indeed today, 26th August, at about one o'clock, the King of Navarre was

[19] Studer von Winkelbach (see above).

present at mass with King Charles, so that everybody has the highest hopes of seeing him change his religion. Condé's sons are held prisoner by the king's order, and they are in the greatest danger, for the king may make an example of these obstinate champions of heresy. Everyone agrees in praising the prudence and magnanimity of the king, who, having as it were fattened the heretics like cattle with his kindness and indulgence, has suddenly had them killed by his soldiers.

The cunning Montgomery has escaped: Monsieur de Mérue, the late Constable's third son, has been taken, together with many others. The Parisians wait anxiously to see how the king will deal with him.

All the heretical booksellers who could be found have been massacred and thrown naked into the water. Remus, who leapt from his upper storey bedroom, is still lying unclothed upon the bank, pierced with many daggers. In a word, there is nobody (not even excepting the women) who has not been either killed or wounded.

Let me tell you more about the killing of the Admiral: I have these details from the man who struck the third blow with his battle-axe, Conrad Bürg, who was at one time groom to the bursar Joachim Waldemann, at Wyl. When the Swiss under the orders of the Duke of Anjou had broken down the doors, Conrad, followed by Leonhard Grünenfelder of Glaris and Martin Koch, reached the Admiral's room, which was the third in the house. First his servant was killed. The Admiral was in an ordinary dressing-gown and at first no one chose to lay hands on him; but Martin Koch, bolder than the others, struck the wretch with his battle-axe. Conrad gave him the third blow and at last, at the seventh, he fell dead against the fireplace of his room. By order of the Duke of Guise his body was thrown out of the window, and when they had put a rope round his neck as for a criminal they dragged him to the Seine, displaying him as a sight to the people. Such was the end of this pernicious man, who not only brought so many to the edge of the abyss during his lifetime, but in dying carried a crowd of heretical nobles down with him to hell ...

(Published in vol. VIII of the *Bulletin de la Société de l'Histoire du Protestantisme français*.)

A PARISIAN CURÉ'S ACCOUNT OF THE MURDER OF COLIGNY.

On Saturday, between ten and eleven o'clock in the evening, the king having heard that the Huguenots were planning to cut his throat, kill his brothers and sack the city of Paris, the Louvre was shut up and he determined to put his enemies to death. He then sent to the *quartiniers* of Paris to warn the people to be on their guard and to arm themselves, and then on Sunday between three and four o'clock in the morning, his Grace of Guise, his Grace of Aumale and others went to the Admiral's house, where the aforesaid Admiral was wounded with a boar-spear and thrown half-dead out of the window, and the Monday afterwards, having had his head removed, and his privities cut off by the little children, he was dragged belly-up by the said little children to the number of two or three hundred along the gutters of the city of Paris, as the ancient Romans did, who dragged tyrants *ad scalas gemonias unco*, the place of the Roman cloaca; and from there they went to hang the said Admiral up by his feet at Montfaucon. And it appears that God allowed all this because of the tyranny and the ill life of the aforesaid Admiral, who alone had been the author of the civil wars and the cause of the death of a hundred thousand men and the rape of girls, women and nuns and the sacking of churches: and in short all lords should take warning from the example of this unhappy man that however much God may delay the punishment, it is all the worse for being deferred.

(*From the Journal du curé de Saint-Leu à Paris*, Bibliothèque Nationale, fr. 9913, fols. 91 vo. and 92.)

THINGS SEEN BY AN AUSTRIAN STUDENT.

Geizkofler and several of his fellow-students were lodging and boarding with the priest Blandis, in a very tall house. Blandis advised them not to show themselves outside the room, for fear of the bands who were running through the streets. Blandis himself stood before the front door in his priest's clothes and biretta: he was, moreover, highly regarded in the neighbourhood. Never an hour went by without some new band coming to ask whether there were any Huguenot birds in the house to be plucked out of their nest. Blandis replied that he sheltered none of these birds, or scholars, but only Austrians and Bavarians: in any case, was he not known? Was he capable of receiving a bad Catholic under his roof? In this way he got rid of them all. In return he took a handsome number of crowns from his lodgers by way of payment in advance, continually threatening not to keep us any more because of the perpetual danger. We had to open our wallets, which were always none too full, and pay three months' board. Three of our fellows, Frenchmen from Picardy, would not comply (perhaps they did not have the necessary sum).

Now as they dare not go outside except at the risk of their lives, since day and night the bands traversed the streets, they begged Geizkofler and his friends to lend them the travelling clothes that they had brought from Germany: dressed like this, the change of lodging would not be so perilous. So these good Picards left the priest's house: their former companions never knew where they went, but a villainous little man-servant came to tell Geizkofler that they were in quite a safe place, that they thanked him with all their heart and hoped presently to come and express their gratitude in person; and lastly they asked permission to keep the clothes, which was given to them.

The slaughter abated after the royal proclamation, though it was not yet at an end. People were arrested in their houses and taken away: Geizkofler and his comrades saw this from a window made in the roof of the house. The house was at the corner of three streets chiefly inhabited by booksellers, whose books to the value of several thousand crowns were burned. The wife of a bookbinder, who had two little children, prayed in French in her house: a band came to take her prisoner, and as she refused to leave her children, in the end they allowed her to take them by the hand. Near the Seine they met other murderers who shouted that this woman was a notorious Huguenot; and in short they threw her as well as her children into the water. However, one of the men was touched with pity and taking a boat he saved the two little ones, which excessively displeased a relative, the next heir, who in any case was killed himself because he was rich.

There were only eight or ten victims among the Germans, men who had been rash enough to venture into the suburbs too soon. Two of them were just about to cross the drawbridge of one of the outer gates when they were challenged by a guard, who asked them if they were good Catholics. 'Yes: why not?' they asked, with an awkward air. The guard replied, 'Since you are such a good Catholic (the other had given himself out to be a canon of Münster) say the *Salve Regina*.' The unhappy man could not: the guard thrust him into the moat with his halberd; and this was how he ended his days in the Faubourg Saint-Germain. His companion was a native of the bishopric of Bamberg. Round his neck he was wearing a handsome gold chain, thinking that an impressive appearance would help him to get out. The guards attacked him for all that: he and two servants defended themselves: all three were killed. The murderers learnt that they had left some fine horses in a German inn, the Iron Cross, not far from the university, and they hurried to take them away.

(*Mémoires de Luc Geizkofler*, translated by E. Fick, Geneva, 1892.)

THE OREMUS AFTER THE THANKSGIVING MASS CELEBRATED AT THE CHURCH OF SAINT-LOUIS-DES-FRANÇAIS IN ROME 'FOR THE VERY GREAT BLESSING RECEIVED FROM GOD'.

Almighty God, Who rejecteth the proud and blesseth the humble, we offer Thee the tribute of our most fervent praise, because, taking heed of Thy servants' faith, Thou hast granted them a splendid triumph over the treacherous enemies of the Catholic people; and we humbly beg Thee in Thy mercy to continue what Thou hast in Thy faithfulness begun, for the glory of Thy name, upon which we call. May this be granted, in the name of Christ.

CHRONOLOGICAL TABLE

1509 Birth of Calvin (10th July). Lefèvre of Etaples publishes his *Psautier*.

1510 Guillaume Farel comes to Paris.

1512 Lefèvre of Etaples publishes his *Commentaire des Epîtres de Saint Paul*.

1517 Luther posts his theses on the church door of Wittenberg (31st October).

1519 Birth of François, Duke of Guise (15th February).

— Birth of Gaspard de Coligny (16th February).

— Birth of Catherine de' Medici (13th April).

— Birth of Theodore Beza (14th June).

1520 A committee is formed at the Sorbonne for the examination of Luther's theses.

1521 The members of the 'committee of the faith' appointed by the Sorbonne unanimously condemn Luther's theses (15th April).

1522 The council of the archdiocese of Sens, meeting in Notre Dame in Paris, forbids the printing of anything relating to religion without leave of the Sorbonne (22nd March).

1523 Lefèvre of Etaples publishes his French translation of the Gospels (8th June).

— The monk Jean Vallières is burnt for having said that Jesus had been conceived 'like the rest of us men' (8th August).

1525 Francis I taken prisoner at Pavia (25th February).

— The wool-carder Jean Leclerc burnt for having broken an image of Our Lady (22nd July).

— Guillaume Farel attacks the mass in his *Sommaire et briefve déclaration*.

1526 Decree of the Parliament forbidding the reading or the keeping in the house of the books of the Holy Scriptures translated into French and the preaching or the teaching of Luther's doctrines (5th February).

— The bachelor of law Guillaume Joubert burnt at the Place Maubert (17th February).

1526 Francis I comes back from Spain (18th March).
— Jacques Pavane burnt in the Place de Grève for having insulted Our Lady (28th August).
1527 Luc d'Aillon, protonotary apostolic, burnt at the Place de Grève (4th March).
1528 A statue of the Virgin mutilated at the corner of the rue des Rosiers and the rue des Juifs (31st May).
— At the head of a solemn procession, Francis I sets a new statue of the Virgin in the niche in the rue des Rosiers (11th June).
— Denis de Rieux burnt at Meaux for having 'spoken ill' of the mass (3rd July).
1529 The Chevalier Louis de Berquin is burnt in the Place de Grève (17th April).
— The *Rebeine* at Lyons (25th April).
— Milles Regnault burnt in the Place de Grève for having uttered 'execrable and hateful blasphemies' against the honour of God and of the Virgin Mary (19th August).
1530 A statue of Our Lady mutilated in the rue Aubry-le-Boucher (21st May).
— Expiatory procession because of this mutilation (29th May).
— A waterman burnt for having broken a statue of Our Lady (15th December).
1531 The Sorbonne condemns a series of books 'stained with heresy' (2nd March).
— Two doctors of theology accompanied by two councillors of the parliament search the bookshops of Paris (12th July).
1532 Jean de Cahors, professor of law at the university of Toulouse, burnt for having spread Lutheran doctrines (2nd May).
1533 Meeting at Marseilles between Francis I and Clement VII (negotiations for the marriage of Henry of Orleans with the Pope's niece). An increase in the religious persecution in France results (13th October).
— At the beginning of the university term in Paris, the rector, Cop, reads a 'subversive' discourse written by Calvin (1st November).
— Etienne Lecourt, curé of Condé-sur-Sarthe, burnt at Rouen (11th December).
1534 The former monk Alexandre Canus burnt for having preached Lutheran doctrines at Lyons on Easter Day (17th June).
— An attempt at conciliation prompted by Francis I.

1534 Posting up of the *Articles* by the pastor Antoine de Marcourt (17th October).
— Seven Protestants condemned to death (17th November).
— The paralytic Barthélemy Milon burnt (13th November).
— Jean du Bourg, draper, accused of having posted up Marcourt's bills in Paris, burnt at the Halles, his hand being struck off first (14th November).
— A printer burnt (17th November).
— A weaver burnt (18th November).
— A bookseller burnt (20th November).
— A mason burnt (28th November).
— The printer Antoine Augereau burnt at the Place Maubert for having published the *Miroir de l'âme pécheresse* of Marguerite d'Angoulême (24th December).
1535 Francis I forbids all printing of books in the kingdom of France (13th January).
— He takes part in the expiatory procession in honour of the Holy Sacrament insulted by Marcourt's placards. On this occasion six heretics are burnt (21st January).
— First execution of a woman: Marie La Catelle, schoolmistress, is burnt for having made her pupils read the Gospel in French (23rd January).
— The parliament summons fugitive Lutherans to appear before it (25th January).
— Etienne de La Forge burnt for having had the Gospels printed at his own expense and for having distributed them to the poor (15th February).
— The decree concerning the prohibition of printing is suspended (26th February).
— Louis de Médicis, haberdasher, burnt at the Place Saint-Michel (same day).
— Etienne Bénard, public prosecutor, and Marin Du Val, tailor, suspected of having stuck up Marcourt's bills, burnt at the Marché des Pourceaux: the shoemaker Jean Foncin burnt at the cross-roads of the Puits-Sainte-Geneviève (5th May).
— Mathieu Ory, prior of the convent of Friars Preachers at Paris, is authorised by the king to assume the office of inquisitor of the faith throughout the realm of France (30th May).
— Francis I declines the crusade desired by Charles V and allies himself with the Protestant princes.

1536 The people of Geneva, assembled in a general council, declare that they wish 'to live according to the Gospel and the word of God' (21st May).

— Calvin reaches Geneva (first half of July).

1537 The Council of Two Hundred assents to the Confession presented by Guillaume Farel (16th January).

— At Calvin's suggestion, all the inhabitants of Geneva are required to give their individual consent to the articles of the Confession (17th April).

1538 The inquisitor Louis de Rochette and his deputy, accused of heresy, are burnt at Toulouse (10th September).

— Francis I orders the Parliament of Normandy to inflict upon the heretics 'so severe a punishment that it shall be an example to all the others' (24th December).

1540 Francis I orders proceedings against the Vaudois (31st May).

— The Pope approves the founding of the Society of Jesus (27th September).

1542 A decree of the Parliament of Paris puts all authors and printers under power of censure by the Sorbonne (1st July).

— Royal letters require all the parliaments of the kingdom to seek out and punish the heretics (30th August).

1543 The Sorbonne draws up the twenty-six Articles of Faith. The Articles drawn up by the Sorbonne are proclaimed law of the land (31st July).

1544 Calvin's *Institution chrétienne* and other books printed by Etienne Dolet are burnt before Notre Dame by order of the parliament (14th February).

— The Sorbonne publishes its first index of forbidden books (19th August).

1545 Five parliamentary councillors are sent into the provinces to seek out and punish the heretics (5th April).

— The order to exterminate all the Vaudois becomes law (13th April).

— First session of the Council of Trent (13th December).

1546 Death of Luther (18th February).

— A special section court is created in the Parliament of Normandy for the trial of heretics (17th April).

— The printer Pierre Chapot is burnt in the Place Maubert; the carpenter Nicholas Gobillon at the Porte Saint-Jacques (19th July).

— Etienne Dolet burnt in the Place Maubert (3rd August).

1546 The printer Michel Vincent burnt in the Place Maubert (19th August).

— The printer Pierre Gresteau burnt in the Place Maubert (13th September).

— The auto-da-fé of the Fourteen of Meaux (7th October).

1547 Expiatory procession ordered by Francis I in consequence of the mutilation of an image in the cemetery of the Holy Innocents (14th January).

— Death of Francis I (31st March).

— The tailor Benoît Ramasset burnt in the Place Maubert (10th September).

— The 'Burning Chamber' is set up in the Parliament of Paris (8th October).

1548 The parliamentary councillor Pierre Hotman sent to Beaugency to wipe out heresy there (5th May).

— The parliament condemns the Bible printed by Robert Estienne and put on the index by the Sorbonne (15th May).

— The parliamentary councillor Antoine Lecoq sent to Orleans to wipe out heresy there (6th June).

— Jacques Belon burnt in the forecourt of Notre Dame for having insulted the statue of the Virgin inside the cathedral (1st September).

— Marriage of Jeanne d'Albret and Antoine de Bourbon (2nd October).

— Blaise Chappière burnt in Auxerre for having been wanting in respect towards the Holy Sacrament (2nd October).

— Léonard Dupré burnt in the Place Maubert for the same reason (3rd October).

— Antoine Sebillan burnt before the Halles for the same reason (4th October).

1549 Henry II is present at the execution of the priests Florent Venet and Léonard Galimar (4th July).

— Death of Marguerite d'Angoulême (21st December).

1550 Theodore Beza is condemned to the stake *in absentia* (31st May).

— Birth of Charles IX (17th June).

— Birth of Henri de Guise (31st December).

— Henry II becomes the ally of the German Protestant princes against Charles V.

1551 Papal brief from Julius III requiring the King of France to look strictly to the maintenance of the Catholic faith (6th February).

1551 Edict of Châteaubriand regulating the persecution of heretics in forty-six articles (27th June).

— Birth of Henri, Duke of Anjou (19th September).

— The schoolmaster Claude Monier burnt in Lyons (30th October).

1552 Treaty of Chambord confirming the alliance of Henry II with the Protestant princes of Germany (15th January).

— Birth of Henri, Prince of Condé (29th December).

1553 Five students burnt in Lyons (16th May).

— Antoine Magne burnt in Paris (19th May).

— Mathieu Dimont burnt in Lyons (15th July).

— Birth of Henry of Navarre in Pau (12th or 13th December).

1554 The pedlar Guillaume d'Alençon burnt in Montpellier (7th January).

— A decree of the parliament forbids the clandestine schools known as hedge-schools (7th February).

— Birth of François, Duke of Alençon (11th March).

1555 Execution of Jérôme Casebonne in Bordeaux.

1556 Last war between Henry II and Charles V, allied to England.

1557 Jean Rebec, a cordelier, burnt in Angers (24th April).

— The Edict of Compiègne establishes a single penalty for public or private profession of heresy death (24th July).

— Battle of Saint-Quentin (10th August).

— The affair of the rue Saint-Jacques (4th September).

1558 Protestant demonstration in the Pré-aux-Clercs (13th May).

— Death of Charles V (21st September).

— Nicolas Clinet, Taurin Gravelle and Philippine Graveron, implicated in the affair of the rue Saint-Jacques, burnt in the Place Maubert (27th September).

— Nicolas Le Cène and Pierre Gabert, implicated in the same case, burnt in the Place du Pilori in the Faubourg Saint-Germain (2nd October).

1559 The Treaty of Cateau-Cambrésis puts an end to the war between France and Spain (3rd April).

— The delegates of the reformed churches meet in Paris with the pastor Morel de Collonges presiding (26th May).

— The French Protestant Church (*Eglise réformée de France*) is constituted (28th May).

1559 The Edict of Ecouen ordains the punishment or the expulsion of all Huguenots from France (2nd June).

— Speech of Anne du Bourg at the opening session of the Parliament of Paris (10th June).

— Montgomery's lance strikes Henry II (30th June).

— Geoffroy Guérin burnt in the Place Maubert (1st July).

— Henry II dies (10th July).

— Marin Marie, pedlar of religious books, burnt (2nd August).

— Marguerite Le Riche, wife of the bookseller Ricault, burnt (19th August).

— Adrien Daussy, pedlar of religious books, burnt (23rd October).

— Gilles Lecourt, student, Philippe Parmentier, shoemaker, and Marin Rousseau, goldsmith, burnt in the Place Maubert (24th October).

— The merchant Pierre Millet burnt for having sheltered Marguerite Le Riche (26th October).

— Pierre Arondeau burnt (15th November).

— Anne du Bourg, having been thrown into the flames, is hanged in the Place Saint-Jean en Grève (21st December).

1560 A meeting of Huguenot gentlemen held at Nantes decides to seize the king (1st February).

— The Edict, called that of Amboise, orders the suspension of proceedings begun because of religion (8th March).

— The failure of the attempt at Amboise (17th March).

— The Edict of Romorantin hands over the judgment of heretics to the bishops (May).

— Massacre of Protestants at Lyons (5th June).

— François Hotman publishes his *Epître au Tigre de la France* (June).

— The printer Martin L'Homme, entrusted with the diffusion of Hotman's *Epître* in Paris, is burnt.

— Before the assembly of the important men of the kingdom at Fontainebleau, Coligny calls for freedom to profess Protestantism and the grant of places of worship.

— Francis II dies at the age of eighteen (5th December).

— Opening of the States-General at Orleans (13th December).

— A decree of the Council of State puts the regency into the hands of Catherine de' Medici jointly with Antoine de Bourbon (21st December).

1560 Jeanne d'Albret, Queen of Navarre, makes public profession of Protestantism (25th December).

1561 The request of the reformed churches is presented to the States-General by Jacques Bretagne, the deputy from Burgundy (27th January).

— Catherine de' Medici dismisses the States-General (31st January).

— The court establishes itself at Fontainebleau (5th February).

— The Catholic leaders, Guise, Montmorency and Saint-André, form a triumvirate (7th April).

— Outbreak between students and Protestants in the Pré-aux-Clercs (24th April).

— Catherine de' Medici vainly asks Condé and the Protestants for protection.

— Decree of the Parliament of Dijon against 'conventicles' (19th June).

— Edict of the Council of State forbidding the meetings and the preachings of the Protestants (13th July).

— Meeting of the new States-General at Pontoise (1st August). Colloquy of Poissy, first session (9th September).

— Colloquy of Poissy, second session (16th September).

— Colloquy of Poissy, third session (13th October).

— The 'tumult of Saint-Médard' (21st December).

1562 The Edict of Saint-Germain gives the Protestants the right, for the time being, to exercise their worship outside the city walls (17th January).

— The massacre of the Protestants at Vassy marks the beginning of the wars of religion (1st March).

— The Constable de Montmorency sets fire to the pulpit and pews in a Protestant church (4th April).

— Massacre of Protestants at Sens (12th April).

— Massacre of Protestants at Aurillac (2nd September).

— The Treaty of Hampton Court delivers Le Havre up to the English (20th September).

— Rouen taken by the Duke of Guise's troops (26th October).

— Battle of Dreux (19th December).

1563 Jeanne d'Albret ordains freedom of conscience within her dominions (2nd February).

— Assassination of the Duke of Guise (18th February).

— The Peace of Amboise ends the first war of religion (12th March).

1563 Charles IX, aged fourteen, is declared of age by the Parliament of Rouen (17th August).

— Closing of the Council of Trent (4th December: see above, under the date 13th December, 1545).

1564 Treaty of Troyes between England and France (12th April).

— Death of Calvin (27th May).

— Prohibition of Protestant worship in the places visited by the king (20th June).

1565 Meeting of Bayonne (June).

1566 Cardinal Ghisieri, the Grand Inquisitor, becomes Pope under the name of Pius V (7th January).

— Mgr de La Torre communicates the *desiderata* of the new Pope to Catherine de' Medici and Charles IX (1st June).

— Beginning of the struggle of the Spanish Netherlands against Philip II.

1567 The second war of religion starts (September).

— The *'Michelade'* (massacre of the Catholics) of Nîmes (1st October).

— Condé's troops occupy Saint-Denis (2nd October).

— The Huguenots defeated before Saint-Denis (10th November).

1568 La Rochelle opens its gates to the Huguenots (11th February).

— The Peace of Longjumeau ends the second war of religion (23rd March).

— Creation of the Royal and Christian Holy League (25th July).

— Departure of the Huguenot leaders for La Rochelle: beginning of the third War of Religion (24th August).

— A royal proclamation puts an end to all rights guaranteed to the Protestants by the Peace of Longjumeau (27th September).

— Mary Stuart, who had taken refuge in England, is imprisoned.

— Death of Elizabeth of Valois, wife of Philip II, in Madrid (3rd October).

1569 Rout of the Protestants at Jarnac (14th March).

— The cloth merchant Richard, his brother and his brother-in-law, hanged for having celebrated the Lord's Supper in their house (30th June).

— The parliament sentences Coligny to death (3rd September).

— Coligny executed in effigy at the Place de Grève (13th September).

— Victory of the Catholics at Moncontour (3rd October).

1570 The Pope has the standards taken from the Protestants at Moncontour hung up in the Lateran (7th January).

1570 He sends the Duke of Anjou a hat and a sword of honour in memory of this victory (27th March).
— The abbey of Saint-Martin at Autun sacked and burnt by the Protestants (29th June).
— The Peace of Saint-Germain ends the third war of religion (8th August).
— Charles IX marries Elizabeth of Austria (27th November).
— The Protestants' houses on the Pont Notre-Dame are pillaged (15th–16th December).
1571 The Catholics begin the massacre of the Protestants in Orange on 2nd February: the killing goes on for a fortnight.
— Cardinal de Châtillon, Coligny's brother, dies, perhaps of poison (14th February).
— Coligny's second marriage (25th March).
— The Pope, Venice and Spain sign a treaty of alliance against the Turks (20th May).
— Nassau suggests that Charles IX should support the rebellion in the Low Countries.
— Coligny arrives at the château of Blois where the court is staying (12th September).
— The victory of Lepanto (7th October).
— Demolition of the cross of Gastine (19th December).
1572 The marriage contract of Marguerite de Valois and Henry of Navarre is signed (11th April).
— Franco-English alliance.
— Death of Pope Pius V ([?] 1st May).
— Nassau and a contingent of French Protestants take Mons (24th May).
— Catherine de' Medici threatens to leave France if Charles IX makes war upon Spain (30th May).
— Elizabeth of England gives Spain secret assurances.
— Coligny comes to Paris (5th June).
— Death of Jeanne d'Albret (9th June).
— Coligny upholds the plan of invading Flanders before the king's council (19th June). He fails to get his way.
— The Venetian senate sends an ambassador extraordinary to Paris to dissuade the king from declaring war on Spain (5th July).
— Henry of Navarre and the Prince of Condé arrive in Paris (7th July).
— Battle of Quiévrain (17th July).

1572 The Duke of Alba informs Catherine de' Medici that he possesses a *casus belli* and reveals Elizabeth's duplicity to her (22nd July).

— First meeting between Catherine and the Duchess of Nemours (23rd July).

— Catherine hurries back to Paris to prevent war (4th August).

— The council again rejects Coligny's request for the invasion of Flanders (9th and 10th August).

— Marriage of Marguerite de Valois and Henri de Bourbon (17th and 18th August).

— Charles IX promises Coligny to make a decision within four days (18th August).

— The Protestants are set upon and massacred as they leave church by the Catholics at Troyes (10th August).

— Attempt upon Coligny's life (22nd August).

— The provost of the merchants is sent for to the Louvre (23rd August).

— Coligny is assassinated and the massacre begins (24th August, at four o'clock in the morning).

— Declaration of the king suppressing all services, meetings and other forms of Protestant worship throughout the realm of France (28th August).

— Celebration of the massacre of Saint Bartholomew in Rome (8th September).

— Elizabeth agrees to be godmother to Charles IX's daughter (December).

GENEALOGICAL TABLES

I

THE VALOIS

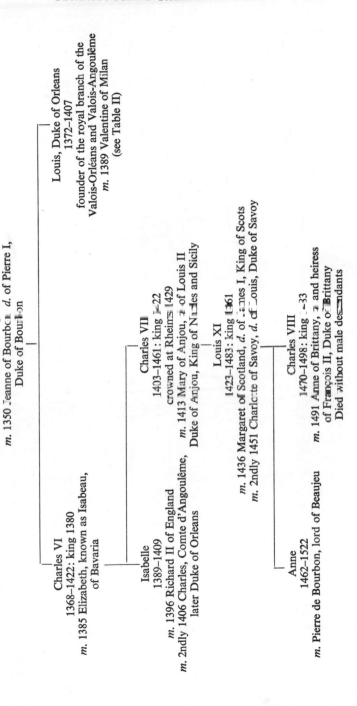

Charles V
1336–1380: king 1364
m. 1350 Jeanne of Bourbon d. of Pierre I,
Duke of Bourbon

Louis, Duke of Orleans
1372–1407
founder of the royal branch of the
Valois-Orléans and Valois-Angoulême
m. 1389 Valentine of Milan
(see Table II)

Charles VI
1368–1422: king 1380
m. 1385 Elizabeth, known as Isabeau,
of Bavaria

Isabelle
1389–1409
m. 1396 Richard II of England
m. 2ndly 1406 Charles, Comte d'Angoulême,
later Duke of Orleans

Charles VII
1403–1461: king 1422
crowned at Rheims 1429
m. 1413 Mary of Anjou, d. of Louis II
Duke of Anjou, King of Naples and Sicily

Louis XI
1423–1483: king 1461
m. 1436 Margaret of Scotland, d. of James I, King of Scots
m. 2ndly 1451 Charlotte of Savoy, d. of Louis, Duke of Savoy

Charles VIII
1470–1498: king 1483
m. 1491 Anne of Brittany, d. and heiress
of François II, Duke of Brittany
Died without male descendants

Anne
1462–1522
m. Pierre de Bourbon, lord of Beaujeu

II

THE VALOIS-ORLEANS AND THE VALOIS-ANGOULEME

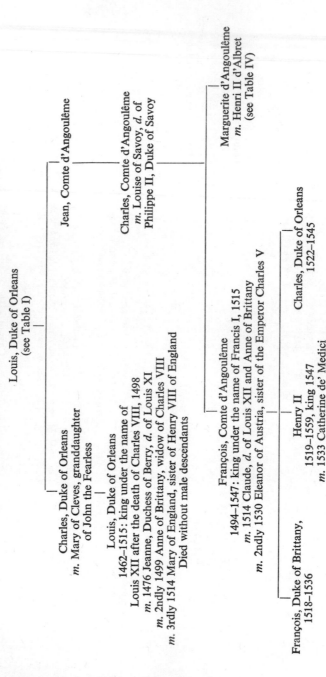

Louis, Duke of Orleans
(see Table I)

Charles, Duke of Orleans
m. Mary of Cleves, granddaughter
of John the Fearless

Louis, Duke of Orleans
1462–1515: king under the name of
Louis XII after the death of Charles VIII, 1498
m. 1476 Jeanne, Duchess of Berry, d. of Louis XI
m. 2ndly 1499 Anne of Brittany, widow of Charles VIII
m. 3rdly 1514 Mary of England, sister of Henry VIII of England
Died without male descendants

Jean, Comte d'Angoulême

Charles, Comte d'Angoulême
m. Louise of Savoy, d. of
Philippe II, Duke of Savoy

Marguerite d'Angoulême
m. Henri II d'Albret
(see Table IV)

François, Comte d'Angoulême
1494–1547: king under the name of Francis I, 1515
m. 1514 Claude, d. of Louis XII and Anne of Brittany
m. 2ndly 1530 Eleanor of Austria, sister of the Emperor Charles V

François, Duke of Brittany,
1518–1536

Henry II
1519–1559, king 1547
m. 1533 Catherine de' Medici
(for the continuation see Table III)

Charles, Duke of Orleans
1522–1545

III

THE LAST VALOIS-ANGOULEME-MEDICIS

Henry II
King of France
m. Catherine de' Medici

Francis II 1544–1560 king 1559 *m.* 1558 Mary Stuart *d.* of James V King of Scots	Elizabeth 1545–1568 *m.* 1559 Philip II King of Spain	Claude 1547–1575 *m.* 1558 Charles II Duke of Lorraine	Louis 1549–1550	Charles IX 1550–1574 king 1560 *m.* 1570 Elizabeth *d.* of Austria of the Emperor Maximilian II	Henry III 1551–1589 King of Poland 1573 King of France 1574 *m.* 1575 Louise of Lorraine Died without male descendants	Marguerite 1553–1615 *m.* 1572 Henry of Navarre (divorced 1599)	Hercule, known as François, Duke of Alençon 1554–1584

IV

THE HOUSE OF NAVARRE

Charles II, the Bad
1349–1387
|
Charles III, the Noble
1387–1425
|
Blanche
1425–1479
|
Eléonore
1479–1483
|
Catherine
1483–1517
m. Jean d'Albret
|
Henri II d'Albret
1517–1555
m. Marguerite d'Angoulême
sister of Francis I
|
Jeanne d'Albret
1555–1572
m. 1548 Antoine de Bourbon
Duke of Vendôme, a descendant in the ninth degree
from Robert, Comte de Clermont, sixth son of Saint Louis
|
Henry III of Navarre
1572–1607[1]
King of France under the name of Henry IV, 1589–1610
in default of an heir male in the House of Valois after the death
of Henry III

[1] In 1607 the kingdom of Navarre was united with France.

BIBLIOGRAPHY

SOURCES

I MANUSCRIPT SOURCES

National archives of France, Fonds Simancas. The archives now
have only photocopies of the originals, which were given back to
Spain during the last war.

Vatican archives, letters of the Nuncio Salviati, the Legate Orsini,
etc. 5 (*nuova*), VI (*vecchia*). Francia. Nuntio Salviati et altri, 1572.
Indice aff. 1, 4, lett. orig. del Nuntio alla segreteria, dal 9 giugno
1572 al 28 dicembre 1572, F. F. 14 356.

Vatican archives, 283 (*nuova*), 2071 r (*vecchia*) 4 moutii in Francia,
15/2, /3, /4, /5. Indice aff. 1–2, 492. Min. di lett. e cifre della
segreteria al Nunzio dal 9 giugno 1572 al 26 dicembre 1575, ff.
3/3–651.

Bibliothèque Nationale, Fonds Colbert. Letters and papers ex-
changed between Charles IX, Catherine de' Medici and Schomberg, for the negotiations with the Lutheran princes of Germany
before and after the massacre of St Bartholomew.

II PRINTED SOURCES

(a) Documents

Lettres de Catherine de Médicis (in the collection *Documents Inédits
de l'Histoire de France*, Paris, 1880–1919) by Hector de La
Ferrière and Gustave Baguenault de Puchesse.

*Relations des ambassadeurs vénitiens sur les affaires de France au
XVIe siècle*, collected and translated by Niccolo Tommaseo (same
collection as the former, 1838) to be completed by Eugène Alberi's
fifteen-volume publication (Florence, 1839–1863).

*Négociations de la France dans le Levant ou correspondances,
mémoires et actes diplomatiques publiés pour la première fois*,
E. Charrière (Paris, 1853–1860).

Négociations diplomatiques de la France avec la Toscane, documents collected by Giuseppe Canestrini and published by Abel Des jardins (collection *D.I.H.F.*, Paris, 1865).

Calendar of [English] *State Papers*, 1547–1580.

Calendar of State Papers, Foreign (for 1558–1579, London, 1892–1894; for 1572–1574, London, 1876).

Correspondance de Philippe II sur les affaires des Pays-Bas, edited by Louis Gachard (Brussels, 1848–1879).

Correspondance de Guillaume le Taciturne, edited by Louis Gachard (Brussels, 1847–1866).

Lettres et négociations de Claude de Mondoucet, résident de France aux Pays-Bas, 1571–1574, edited by L. Didier (Paris, 1891–1892).

Dépêches de M. de Fourquevaux, ambassadeur du roi Charles IX en Espagne de 1565 à 1572, published by the Abbé Douais (Société d'Histoire diplomatique, 1896–1904).

Correspondance diplomatique de Bertrand Salignac de la Mothe Fénelon, ambassadeur de France en Angleterre de 1568 à 1575, edited by Purton-Cooper (Paris, 1838–1840).

Registres des délibérations du bureau de l'Hôtel-de-Ville de Paris 1449–1614, Bonnardot and others (Paris, 1883). Some registers concerning the year 1572 were unfortunately destroyed in the fire of 1871.

(b) Memoirs and histories

Machiavelli, *Works*.

Mémoires de Claude Haton, contenant le récit des événements accomplis de 1553 à 1582, principalement dans la Champagne et dans la Brie, published by Félix Bourquelot (collection *D.I.H.F.*, Paris, 1857).

Jacques-Auguste de Thou, *Historiarum sui temporis* . . . (from 1543 to 1610), French edition published in London in 1734 in the translation of Le Maserier, Prévost, Desfontaines, Le Duc, Adam and Charles Lebeau.

Pierre de Bourdeilles, abbé et seigneur de Brantôme, *Oeuvres complètes, publiées pour la première fois selon le plan de l'auteur*, Prosper Mérimée and Louis Lacour (Paris, 1858–1895).

Montaigne, *Essais*.

Mémoires et lettres de Marguerite de Valois, Guessard (Paris, 1842) in the publications of the Société de l'Histoire de France.

Commentaires et lettres de Blaise de Montluc, Alphonse de Ruble (Paris, 1886–1872) in the publications of the Société de l'Histoire de France.

Théodore-Agrippa d'Aubigné. *Mémoires* (Paris, 1859).

Sommaire mémorial de Jules Gassot, secrétaire du roi (1555–1623), Pierre Champion (Paris, 1934).

Les prophéties de M. Michel Nostradamus (first edition, Lyons, 1555: the only copy known is in the Bibliothèque Nationale).

Erasme Fend, *Acta tumultuum gallicanorum, etc.*, translated and published by Henri Hauser in *Revue historique*, vols. CVIII and CIX.

Richard Verstegan, *Teatrum crudelitatum haereticorum nostri temporis*, 1592 edition republished about 1885 at Lille with the title *Théâtre des cruautés des hérétiques du XVIe siècle*.

Michel de L'Hospital, *Oeuvres* (Dufey, Paris, 1826).

La Popelinière, *L'Histoire de France enrichie des plus notables occurrences, survenues ès-provinces de l'Europe et pays voisins . . . depuis l'an 1550 jusqu'à ces temps* (La Rochelle, 1581).

Nicolas Froumenteau, *Le secret des finances de France en trois livres* (1581).

Florimond de Raemond, *Naissance, progrès et décadence de l'hérésie de ce siècle* (Paris, 1605).

Pierre Matthieu, *Histoire de France sous les règnes de François Ier, etc.* (Paris, 1631).

Simon Boulart and Nicolas des Gallars, under the direction of Theodore Beza, *Histoire ecclésiastique des églises réformées au Royaume de France* (1521–1563) (Geneva edition, 1580).

Enrico Davila, *The Historie of the Civill Warres of France*, English translation from the Italian original (Venice, 1630) by Cotterell and Aylesbury (London, 1647).

G. de Saulx de Tavannes, *Mémoires* (Paris 1829).

Renon de France, *Histoire des troubles des Pays-Bas* (1555–1591), published by Charles Piot in *Chroniques belges* (Brussels, 1886–1891).

Léon Ménard and Marquis d'Aubois, *Pièces fugitives pour servir à l'Histoire de France* (Paris, 1759).

L. Cimber and F. Danjou, *Archives curieuses de l'histoire de France, depuis Louis XI jusqu'à Louis XVIII* (Paris, 1834–1840).

Jean Buchon, *Choix de chroniques et mémoires sur l'histoire de France*, in the collection of the *Panthéon littéraire* (Paris, 1836).

Joseph Michaud and Jean Poujoulat, *Nouvelle collection des mémoires pour servir à l'histoire de France* (Paris, 1836–1839).

Sébastien Castellion, *Conseil à la France désolée. Auquel est montré la cause de la guerre présente et le remède qui pourrait être mis, et principalement être avisé si on doit forcer les consciences.* (1562.)

Jean Crespin, *Les actes des martyrs,* edited by Pierre Aubert (Geneva, 1619).

Alfred Franklin (editor), *Les Grandes scènes historiques du XVIe siècle* (Paris, 1886).

Ivan Loutchiski, *L'aristocratie féodale et les calvinistes en Frances,* in Russian, with the contemporary documents in French (*Collection des procès-verbaux des Assemblées politiques de réformés en France pendant le XVIe siècle, B.B.F.,* 1873, 22, 24n, 25 and 45). Unpublished documents concerning the history of the Reformation and the League.

Michel Félibien, *Histoire de la ville de Paris . . . revue augmentée et mise à jour par Guy Alexis Lobineau* (vol. II, Paris, 1725).

III Studies

(a) Works of a general character

J. H. Mariéjol, *La Réforme et la Ligue, l'édit de Nantes* (vol. VI of Ernest Lavisse's *Histoire de France* (Paris, 1900).

Ernest Lavisse and Alfred Rambaud, *Histoire générale,* vol. V, *Les guerres de religion (1559–1648)* (Paris, 1893–1901).

Jules Michelet, *Histoire de France* (Paris, 1876–8).

Henri Hauser, *La prépondérance espagnole 1559–1660. (Peuples et Civilisations,* vol. IX, Paris, 1933).

Augustin Fliche and Victor Martin, *Histoire de l'Eglise* (St Dizier, 1934–7).

John Viénot, *Histoire de la réforme française des origines à l'édit de Nantes* (Fischbacher, 1926).

Henri Pirenne, *Histoire de Belgique* (Brussels, 1929).

Louis Pastor, *Histoire des Papes.* (The Italian version is the most recent.)

Michel Deveze, *Les guerres de religion–France, Angleterre, Pays-Bas* (C.D.U., 1951).

Gaston Zeller, *La vie économique au XVIe siècle* (C.D.U., Paris).

Gaston Zeller, *La Méditerranée au XVIe siècle* (C.D.U., Paris).

(b) Various works

Lucien Febvre, *Les origines de la réforme et le problème général des causes de la réforme (Revue historique,* vol. CLXI, pp. 1 to 73, May).

Jean Dargaud, *Histoire de la liberté religieuse* (Paris, 1859).

Georges Weill, *Les théories sur le pouvoir royal en France pendant les guerres de Religion* (Paris, 1892).

Armand Bachet, *La diplomatie vénitienne. Les princes de l'Europe au XVIe siècle* (Paris, 1872).

Hector de la Ferrière, *Le XVIe siècle et les Valois* (Paris, 1879).

Joseph de Cruze, *Les Guise, les Valois et Philippe II* (Paris, 1886).

J. Mathorez, *Les Espagnols et la crise nationale française à la fin du XVIe siècle, un bulletin historique* (1916).

Alphonse de Ruble, *Le traité de Cateau-Cambrésis* (Paris, 1889).

Philippe Le Noir, *Histoire ecclésiastique de Bretagne* (Paris, 1851).

(c) *France and the Papacy*

Félix Rocquain, *Rome et la France pendant les guerres de religion* (Paris, 1924).

C. Hirshauer, *La politique de saint Pie V en France* (in fasc. 120, *Bibliothèque des Ecoles françaises d'Athènes et de Rome*, Paris, 1922).

Lisii Karhunen, *Grégoire XIII comme politicien et souverain* (Helsinki, 1911). In French, with a sound, copious bibliography.

Rome et Poissy, a study of the relations between the Holy See and the Church of France, in vol. XXXIX of *Mélanges d'Archéologie et d'Histoire de l'Ecole française de Rome*, for 1921, pp. 47 to 153.

(d) *The chief figures and the background of the massacre*

J.-H. Mariéjol, *Catherine de Médicis* (Paris, 1922).

Paul Van Dyke, *Catherine de Médicis* (London, 1923).

Jean Héritier, *Catherine de Médicis* (Paris, 1939).

Georges Delaborde, *La vie de l'amiral de Coligny* (Paris, 1909).

Charles Merki, *L'amiral de Coligny* (Paris, 1909).

A. W. Whitehead, *Gaspard de Coligny* (London, 1904).

Gustave Baguenault de Puchesse, *Jean de Morvillier, évêque d'Orléans, garde des sceaux de France* (Paris, 1870).

Gustave Baguenault de Puchesse, *François et Henri de Guise* (Paris, 1867).

J. Nouaillac, *Villeroy (1543–1610)* (Paris, 1909).

Jacques Caumont, *Le maréchal de La Force* (Paris, 1924).

Lucien Romier, *Les origines politiques des guerres de Religion (1547–1559)* (Paris, 1913–1914).

Lucien Romier, *La royaume de Catherine de Médicis, la France à la veille des guerres de Religion* (Paris, 1922).

Lucien Romier, *Catholiques et Huguenots à la Cour de Charles IX* (Paris, 1924).

Lucien Romier, *La Saint-Barthélemy, les événements de Rome et la préméditation du massacre, d'après les papiers du nonce Salviati* (in *Revue du XVIe siècle*, 1913, vol. I, pp. 529–560).

Pierre Champion, *Paris au temps de la renaissance* (Paris, 1935–1938).

Pierre Champion, *Catherine de Médicis présente à Charles IX son royaume* (Paris, 1937).

Pierre Champion, *Charles IX et le contrôle de l'Espagne avant et après la Saint-Barthélemy* (Paris, 1939).

Pierre Champion, *La jeunesse de Henri III* (Paris, 1941).

Pierre Champion, *La galerie des rois. Histoire de France: des origines à la mort de Henri IV* (Paris, 1934).

Pierre de Vaissière, *Récits du 'temps des troubles'* . . . *Une famille les d'Alègre* (Paris, 1914).

Pierre de Vaissière, *Récits du 'temps des troubles'* . . . *De quelques assassins* (Paris, 1912).

Erich Marcks, *Die Zusammenkunft von Bayonne, 1563–1567* (Strasbourg, 1899).

Erich Marcks, *Gaspard von Coligny* (Stuttgart, 1892).

Boutharic, *La Saint-Barthélemy d'après les archives du Vatican* (*Bibliothèque de l'Ecole des Chartes, XXIIIe année, vol. III, 5e série*, Paris, 1862, pp. 1 to 27).

Henri Bordier, *La Saint-Barthélemy et la critique moderne* (Geneva and Paris, 1879).

Abbé Lefortier, *La Saint-Barthélemy* (Paris, 1879).

H. Baumgarten, *Vor der Bartholomäusnacht* (Strasbourg, 1882).

Hector de la Ferrière, *La Saint-Barthélemy* (Paris, 1892).

Henri Hello, *La Saint-Barthélemy* (Paris, 1911).

Francis de Crue, *La cour de France et la société au XVIe siècle* (Paris, 1888).

Francis de Crue, *Le parti des politiques au lendemain de la Saint-Barthélemy, La Mole et Coconna* (Paris, 1892).

Jacques Dulaure, *Histoire physique, civile et morale de Paris* (Paris, 1825–8).

Paul Robiquet, *Histoire municipale de Paris* (Paris, 1886).

Marcel Poëte, *Une vie de cité, Paris* (Paris, 1924).

Alfred Franklin, *Paris et les Parisiens au XVIe siècle* (Paris, 1928).
Léo Mouton, *La vie municipale au XVIe siècle. Claude Marcel, Prévost des marchands (1520–1590)* (Paris, 1930).

(e) Literature

Honoré de Balzac, *Sur Catherine de Médicis* (English edition, London, 1910).
Prosper Mérimée, *Chronique du règne de Charles IX* (Paris,1847).

INDEX

Aguilon, 77, 80, 83, 87
Alava, Don Francès de, 71, 75
Alba, Duke of, 39, 40, 52; Elizabeth I and, 88–9, 96–7 and n3; his Huguenot prisoners, 107, 108, 132, 190, 210; and the Massacre, 190–1, 201; his recall, 204
Alençon, François, Duc d', 62, 70, 73, 94, 131, 217, 221; his proposed marriage to Elizabeth I, 87, 97–8, 123, 204, 213; and Henri de Bourbon, 104; and Coligny, 140; Charles IX and, 209; his death, 222
Alessandrino, Cardinal, 74, 81, 82
Amboise, Edict of, 30, 1, 41, 47 peace of, 36
Amyot, Jacques, Bishop of Damietta, 58, 128
Angoulême, Prior of, 146, 156–7
Anjou, Henry, Duke of (later Henry III), 38, 74, 77, 88, 94; his military triumphs, 43–5; a possible husband for Elizabeth I, 50–1, 52; and his brother, 52, 60, 79; his character and achievements, 59–61, 81, 110; and his sister Marguerite, 61, 128, 130, 131, 132, 133; and Coligny, 70, 71, 113, 115, 127, 140, 141, 145; and Henri de Bourbon, 104; and Mary of Cleves, 112–13, 115, 122; and the Polish crown, 114–15, 218–19; and the Massacre, 146–7, 148, 165, 169–70, 198, 209; besieges La Rochelle, 217–18; as Henry III, 221–3; his assassination, 224
Aumale, Duke of, 151, 156, 218
Ayamonte, Marquis of, 201, 202

Barnaud, *Le Reveil-Matin*, 160, 168
Barricades, Day of, 222
Béda (Bédier), Noël, 3, 7
Beggars, the, 48 and n2, 89
Berquin, Louis de, 5, 6

Birague, 42, 71, 86, 88, 117; and the Massacre, 146, 148
Biron, Baron de, 53, 213; and Coligny, 44–5; and the Massacre, 168, 177
Bordeaux, 87, 128
Bordier, Henry, 161 n9
Borgia, Fr. Francesco, 81, 82
Bourbon, Antoine de, King of Navarre, 19, 26, 29, 45; his arrest, 31, turns Catholic, 33; his death, 35
Bourbon, Cardinal of, 69, 94, 95, 150; and Marguerite's wedding, 128, 130
Bourbon, Henri de, Prince of Bearn (later Henry IV), 51, 53, 57, 75, 217; his proposed marriage to Marguerite, 45, 52, 54, 72–3, 82–3, 85–6, 105, 116–17, 126; enters Paris, 103–4; his character, 104, 110; his wedding, 129–33; and Coligny's attempted murder, 142; Charles IX and, 158; converted to Catholicism, 209–10; leader of the Calvinists, 221–22; heir to the throne, 222; becomes Henry IV, 224; on Catherine de' Medici, 226
Boyvin de Villars, 25
Brantôme, Pierre de Bourdeilles, Seigneur de, 105, 112; on Marguerite de Valois, 61, 85, 130; on Coligny, 66; and the Massacre, 130, 160
Briquemaut, 35, 71, 137, 139, 204, 205; his death, 214–15
Burning Chamber, 16

Calais, 20, 65, 97; Elizabeth I and, 30, 35, 96
Calvin, John, 17, 19, 21; his doctrine of predestination, 21–2; permits usury, 24; and bloodshed, 30; *Institutes of the Christian Religion*, 9, 11

Calvinism, 29; separates from Lutheranism, 17; the Huguenots and, 21; its geographical distribution, 22–4, 26; its fortified towns, 45; becomes republican, 213

Capilupi, Camille, *Le Stratagème de Charles IX*, 199 and n1, 238–9

Cateau-Cambrésis, Treaty of, 20, 25, 30, 37, 38n, 47, 49

Catherine de' Medici, 20; marries Henry II, 7; her position in France, 13, 29, 56–7; and the Spanish invasion, 18; becomes ruler of France, 31–2, 36–7; and the Reformation, 32–3, 52; and François de Guise's death, 35–6; her matrimonial plans, 38–9, 50; and Spain, 37–40, 51, 73–4, 75, 108–9, 119, 201–2; signs the Queen's Peace, 45; and Turkey, 47; her foreign policy, 49–50, 51; and Elizabeth I's marriage, 50, 51–2; and Louis of Nassau, 53; her character and attainments, 55–8, 65–6; and her children, 56, 58, 59, 61, 62, 79, 110, 113; and Coligny, 69–71, 72, 78, 95, 225; and the Anglo-French conversations, 80, 87; and the Queen of Navarre, 84–5; opposes intervention in the Netherlands, 90–2, 99, 100–1, 103, 105, 106–7, 108, 117–19, 121–4, 129; and the Polish elections, 114–15; plans Coligny's assassination, 126–8, 133, 138, 139–41, 143; and Marguerite's marriage, 128, 130; and the Massacre, 145–54, 158, 169, 171–3, 174; and its outcome, 177–8, 197–8, 199–200; and Philip II, 201–2, 219; and Elizabeth I, 204–6; attempts to blame the Protestants, 207; her danger from the *Politiques*, 213; triumph of her diplomacy, 219; her death, 223; her responsibility for the Massacre, 225–6

Catholic Holy League, 75, 221, 223

Catholics, the, 24; their rebirth, 17, 18–19, 21; form a triumvirate, 32; control the Court, 34; look to Spain, 35; massacred at Nîmes, 41; under Pius V, 42; sign a truce, 45; the Duke of Anjou and, 60, 79; and Henri de Guise, 62–3; defend the cross of Gastines, 77; and the invasion of Flanders, 100, 103; their supporters in Paris, 104–5; and the Valois–Navarre marriage, 129–31; and the responsibility for the Massacre, 199, 211; and Protestant conversions, 210, 211

Caumont, Geoffroy de, 162, 163, 165

Cavaigne, 71, 142, 207, 214

Cavalli, Sigismond, 5, 77, 82, 117; and Elizabeth I, 80; and Coligny's attempted murder, 152

Cavriana, Filippo, 203, 212; his account of the Massacre, 244–8

Charles V of Austria, xii, xiii, 5, 7; his crusade, 9–10; defeated by France, 15–16

Charles IX, 41, 51, 58, 104, 158, 171, 197, 204; succeeds Francis II, 31–2; and the Duke of Anjou, 44, 52, 60, 79, 115; and the Christian League, 47, 49, 54; and Coligny, 53–4, 69–70, 73, 105; his character and pursuits, 58–9, 71, 78, 81, 89; and his sister Marguerite, 61, 116–17, 130; and the cross of Gastines, 72, 77–8; and Lepanto, 73–4; his attitude to the Netherlands, 89–90, 100, 102, 105, 116–17, 119, 129; upbraided by his mother, 91, 108; renounces his policy, 108–9; and the shooting of Coligny, 139, 140–1 and n, 142, 145; orders the Massacre, 148–50, 153; his behaviour during the Massacre, 160–1 and nn, 162, 168, 169, 172, 191, 239–40; declares his responsibility, 174; his Declaration and Ordinance, 178–80; his orders to the provinces, 184, 186, 188, 189–90, 191; outside opinions of, 197, 203; praised by the Pope, 198–9; and Philip II, 201; after the Massacre, 202, 208, 213–15; and his daughter's birth, 214–15, 217; his death, 221; and the responsibility for the Massacre, 226; contemporary accounts of, 239

Charpentier, 175–6

Christian Holy League, 114, 200; creation of, 47; Philip II and, 47–8, 51

Claude, Duchess of Lorraine, 61, 105, 153

Coconnas, Annibal de, 176

Coligny, Gaspard de, 14, 15, 26, 31, 35, 43, 50, 61; and the Spanish invasion, 17, 64–6; becomes a Calvinist, 19, 25, 65; Catherine de' Medici and, 32, 36–7, 65, 69–71; leader of the Protestants, 43–5, 70, 137–8; and French intervention in the Netherlands, 52, 89, 97–100, 102, 105–7, 116–22, 140–1; returns to Court, 52–3, 63–70; his character and early life, 64–5, 66; and Charles IX, 69–70, 95, 105, 116; his growing influence, 70–1, 73; returns to Paris, 94–5; and Elizabeth I, 97–8; and the Polish royal elections, 114–15; his attempted murder, 125–8, 133, 138–41; at Marguerite's wedding, 130, 131; his murder, 155, 156–7, 180; causes of, 157; accused of the Massacre, 199, 201, 207–8, 226; his denigration, 208, 214

Coligny, Madame de (Jeanne de Laval), 34, 64

Concordat of Bologna, xii–xiii, 6 and n5

Condé, Henri, Prince de, 104, 108, 133, 217; and Marie de Clèves, 83, 116–17, 122, 132; and Coligny's shooting, 142; Charles IX and, 158; becomes a Catholic, 209

Condé, Louis, Prince de, and Protestantism, 26, 29–30, 31; Catherine de' Medici and, 34; taken prisoner, 35, 36; occupies St. Denis, 40–1; his death, 43, 66

Contarini brothers, 15, 18, 54, 73

Correro, on Catherine de' Medici, 55, 56, 57

Cossé-Brissac, Marshal de, 52, 63, 69, 71, 140

Counter-Reformation, 7, 17

Damville, 130, 140, 213

D'Aubigné, Agrippa, 31, 121; on Charles IX, 160–1 and n8

Desportes, Philippe, 111

de Thou, Jacques-Auguste, 142, 174, 191

D'Uzes, Madame de Crussol, 210

Diane de Poitiers, 12, 13, 14, 16, 19

Dreux, Battle of, 35

Du Bellay, Guillaume, 7
 Jean, 7, 9

Dubois, 161 and n11

Du Perrier, 203

Ebeling, T. W., 36 and n10

Ecouen, Edict of, 27, 30

Elizabeth I, 30, 35, 39, 44, 57, 138; her policy towards Spain, 48–9, 96; matrimonial plans for, 50–1, 52, 53, 62, 87, 97, 123, 204; Coligny and, 66, 119–20, 206; her proposed alliance with France, 74–5, 79–81, 83, 86–7, 96, 106; and Flanders, 88–9, 119–20; and Coligny's shooting, 157; her reactions to the Massacre, 204–6; visited by de Retz, 216–17; godmother to Charles IX's daughter, 217; her responsibility for the Massacre, 226

Elizabeth de Valois, Queen of Spain, 38 n1, 39, 50

Elizabeth of Austria, Queen of France, 69, 70, 107; and the Massacre, 160; birth of her daughter, 214–15

England, and an alliance with France, 74–5, 79–81, 83, 86–7, 96; and a French invasion of the Netherlands, 106, 107–8, 116, 119–20; her reactions to the Massacre, 204–6; and La Rochelle, 216, 218

Febvre, Lucien, on the placard, 8 and n7; on Protestantism and the middle classes, 23–4

Ferdinand I, Emperor, 39, 47

Ferrières, Jean de, 35, 50, 65, 141, 162

Flanders, proposed invasion of, 89, 97–100, 102, 105–6

Flushing, 89, 106

France, Louis XI and, xi; her expansion, xii; the Renaissance in, 4; anti-clericalism in, 4–5; her reaction against Lutheranism, 5–6, 11; invaded by Spain, 17–20; the Reformation and, 21; Protestantism in, 22–6, 137–8; Pius V and, 47; her attitude to Catherine de' Medici, 56; her proposed alliance

France—*cont.*
with England, 74–5, 79–81, 84, 86–7, 96; effect of the Massacre on, 211
Francis I, xii, 58; and the Concordat, xii–xiii; his humanism, 5; prisoner at Pavia, 5–6, 12n; and the papacy, 6–7; and the *placard*, 8; and Charles V's crusade, 9–10; and Protestantism, 11–12, 16; his death, 12, 13
Francis II (as dauphin), marries Mary Queen of Scots, 14, 18; (as King) succeeds Henry II, 28–9; his death, 31
Frangipani, 198
Frederick of Saxony, Elector, 3, 4
Fumée, Antoine, 27

Gallican Councils, 5
Gallicans, 21
Gastines, Philippe de, cross of, 72, 77
Genlis, Comte de, 99, 102, 106, 107
Germany, 15; and the Reformation, 6, 21; her reaction to the Massacre, 203
Gomicourt, Chevalier de, 128–9; his account of Coligny's murder, 248–50
Goudimel, Claude, 183
Goulard, *L'Estat de la France*, 160, 209
Granvelle, Cardinal, 90, 99, 107, 202
Guise, Charles, Archbishop of Rheims, 13, 30, 61, 62; his power, 14; and Henry II, 16; Charles IX and, 78; and the shooting of Coligny, 125; and the aftermath of the Massacre, 198–9; his assassination, 222
Guise, Francis, Duke of, 13, 14, 15, 125; his military triumphs, 18, 35; massacres Huguenots, 34; his death, 35
Guise, Henri, Duke of, 61–2, 70 n3; the Catholics and, 62; his assassination, 126, 143 n4, 223–3; and the Massacre, 154, 155, 156–7, 163, 170, 172, 202, 217
Guises, the, their increasing power, 14–15; and the Spanish invasion, 19; Francis II and, 28–9; Condé and, 30; and Protestantism, 30, 31; Catherine de' Medici and, 32, 36;

invited to Court, 78, 81; return to Paris, 94, 104; and the shooting of Coligny, 125–6, 127, 129, 139, 145; and the Massacre, 144, 172

Hampton Court, Treaty of, 35, 65
Henry II, marries Catherine de' Medici, 7; succeeds Francis I, 12–13; his character, 15, 16, 19, 58; and the Protestants, 16–17, 19, 25, 27–8; and the Reformation, 19; accepts Spain's terms, 19–20; his death, 28
Héritier, Jean, 20; 65–6, 150, 155 n13, 161 n12 (*Catherine de Médicis*)
Hotman, François, 11; *Le Tigre*, 30; *Franco-Gallia*, 213
Huguenots, 11, 21, 53; massacred at Wassy, 33–4; attack the Court, 40–1; rise in revolt, 43; Catherine de' Medici and, 52; attacked in Paris, 77; in Flushing, 90; Charles IX and, 104; slaughtered at Quiévrain, 107, 108; plans for their destruction, 125–8, 146–8; and the Valois–Navarre marriage, 129, 131; effect of the shooting of Coligny on, 139, 141–2, 145, 147–8; Charles IX orders their massacre, 150; list of proposed victims, 150–1; Massacre of, 158ff; their fate in the provinces, 182–9; estimates of those killed, 191–3; their subsequent fortune, 210, 212; become republican, 213; Treaty of La Rochelle and, 219–20

Inquisition, 17, 48
Italy, 7, 15, 51; and Catholicism, 21; the Inquisition in, 48

Jarnac, Battle of, 43, 66
Jeanne d'Albret, Queen of Navarre, 14, 22, 38, 43, 45, 75, 92; returns to Court, 52–3, 75–6, 81–3, 84–5; and Marguerite's marriage to her son, 72, 82–3, 84–6; and Catherine de' Medici, 84–5; her death, 95–6; the head of Protestantism, 137

King's killer, 70 and n3, 129

L'Aubespine, 13, 16
La Force family, 162, 165, 176, 177

Lagebaston, 189
La Noue, 71, 90, 191, 213–14, 218
La Renaudie, Sieur de, 30–1
La Rochefoucauld, Comte François II de, 83, 137; and Charles IX, 104, 153–4; his assassination, 164, 246 n14
La Rochelle, 48, 181, 213; the Protestant stronghold, 42, 45, 52–3, 71, 181; Strozzi and, 212; asks help of Elizabeth, 216–17; siege of, 217–18
    Treaty of, 219–20
La Vigerie, 165, 176, 177
Le Charron, 144, 151, 169
Le Havre, 106; surrendered by Coligny, 35, 37, 65, 206
L'Hospital, Michel de, 31, 39, 42, 43, 71, 188, 202
Lepanto, 73–5
Lévis-Mirepoix, Duke of, *Les Guerres de Religion*, 25, 29
Lignerolles, 79
Longjumeau, Peace of, 42
Longueville, Duke of, 88, 91, 92, 106, 130
Luther, Martin, xiii, 3–4
Lutheranism, 21; separates from Calvinism, 17; and the Massacre, 203

Madelin, Louis, 7, 13
Mandelot, Monsieur de, 182–4, 198
Marcel, Claud, 77; and the Massacre, 144, 151–2, 162
Marguerite d'Angoulême, 5, 6
Marguerite de Valois, her proposed marriage to Henri de Bourbon, 44, 52, 72–3, 82–3, 85–6, 104, 105, 116–17, 126, 155 n13; her character, 61; and Henri de Guise, 61; her wedding, 129–33; and the Massacre, 149 n2, 152 and n9, 158 and n4, 159–60, 210
Mary of Cleves, Marquise de l'Isle, 83, 209; Anjou and, 112–13, 115
Mary Stuart, Queen of Scots, 14, 80; marries the Dauphin, 14, 18; flies to England, 49, 74; her execution, 222
Matignon, Monsieur de, 185, 186
Maurevert (king's killer), 70, 129; and the shooting of Coligny, 138–9

Maximilian, Emperor, 203
Medici, Cosimo, Duke of Tuscany, 51, 77, 106
Melanchthon, Philip, 7, 8, 9
Méré, Poltrot de, 35–6, 125
Michelade, the, 41
Michieli, Giovanni, 103, 117, 130; and Catherine de' Medici, 108–9, 124, 127; on Protestantism in France, 137–8; describes the Massacre, 168, 176–7, 239
Middlemore, 97–8
Moncontour, Battle of, 44, 66
Mondoucet, 89, 108, 191
Monluc, 115, 218
Montgomery, Gabriel, Comte de, 17, 28, 162 and n1, 163
Montmorency, Anne, Duc de, 10, 13, 19, 64; his advancement, 14; and Charles V, 15; Henry II and, 19; and Protestantism, 26, 27; Catherine de' Medici and, 32, 39; his death, 42
Montmorency, Duc de (son of above), 53, 60, 71, 100, 113, 217, 218; his mission to England, 96, 105; and the Massacre, 125–6, 132, 170, 172
Montpensier, Duke of, 69 and n2, 140, 148; and the Massacre, 165, 185, 186–8, 198
Morvillier, 121, 148, 149
Moulins, Enactments of, 40

Nantes, Edict of, 224
Nassau, Count Louis of, 42, 83, 204; asks help of Charles IX, 51–2; at La Rochelle, 53; and the Netherlands revolt, 90–2; in Paris, 99
Nemours, Duchess of, 127, 129, 172, 207
Nevers, Duke of, 60, 110, 112, 140; and the Massacre, 146, 148, 150, 163–4, 211
Nompar, Jacques, 176, 177

Odet de Châtillon, Cardinal, 14, 23, 50
Opser, Fr. Joachim, on Coligny's murder, 251–2
Orsini, Cardinal, 200
Ottoman Empire, its westward advance, 46–7; the Christian League and, 47; defeated at Lepanto, 73;

Ottoman Empire—*cont.*
France's treaty with, 123; Poland and, 218–19

Pacification, Edict of, 73, 170, 204, 205
Papacy, the, 21; and Luther, 3; Francis I and, 6–7; and the Massacre, 198–9
Pardaillan, Monsieur de, 147, 159
Paré, Ambroise, 139, 156, 210
Paris, 77; defends the cross of Gastines, 77; a political centre, 92–3, 94; receives Henri de Bourbon, 103–4; and Marguerite's marriage, 129–30, 131; its reaction to Coligny's shooting, 142–3; its hatred of the Huguenots, 144, 166; its pre-Massacre state, 144, 146–7, 151; its mob fury, 157; number of victims in, 191–2
University of, and Luther, 3–4; and the Reformation, 23
Parlement de Paris, and Luther, 4 and n; persecutes Protestants, 16–17; admits heresy, 24–5, 27; defies Charles IX, 72; and the Massacre, 174–5; degrades Coligny, 208
Pastor, Louis, on the Massacre, 225 and n.
Philip II, 16, 28, 33, 57; invades France, 17–18; and Catholicism, 21, 48; his marriage, 38n; Catherine de' Medici and, 38–40, 201–2; leader of the Christian League, 47; his prestige, 47–8; Elizabeth I and, 48–9, 51, 74; and Lepanto, 73; and a French invasion of Flanders, 100, 106, 107, 109, 119; and the shooting of Coligny, 127; rejoices at the Massacre, 200–1; defeat of his Armada, 222
Piles, Monsieur de, 137, 139, 148, 159
Placard, the affair of, 8–9
Poissy, Colloquy of, 33
Poland, 113–14; her royal election, 114–15, 123, 218–19
Politiques, the, 63, 100, 212, 213, 219
Popes—Clement VII, 7, 57; Gregory XIII, 99, 198–9, 199–200, 217–18; Leo X, 3, 57; Paul III, 7, 8–9; Paul IV, 16, 21; Pius IV, 46; Pius V, 42, 46–7, 72, 82, 146

Pré-aux-Clercs, affair of, 19
Protestantism, Francis I and, 5, 6–7, 16; its geographical distribution, 22–4; the middle classes and, 23–4; among the nobility, 25–6; its structure in France, 137–8; becomes republican, 212
Protestants, and the *placard*, 8–9; persecution of, 11–12, 16–17, 18, 27, 34, 42; Henry II and, 16–17, demonstrations by, 19; Catherine de' Medici and, 33–4, 41, 42; take up arms, 34–5, 40–1; defeated at Jarnac, 43–4; effect of persecution on, 47; Anjou and, 60; and Jeanne D'Albret's death, 95–6; in Paris, 104–5; and the defeat at Quiévrain, 107; in Poland, 113; and the Valois–Navarre marriage, 129, 132; and the shooting of Coligny, 141–2; Charles IX forbids their services, 178; their treatment in the provinces, 182–90; and the responsibility for the Massacre, 199, 207
Provinces, the Massacre in, 182–90
Provincial governors, their treatment of the Huguenots, 182–9
Pyrenees, Treaty of, 20

Quiévrain, Battle of, 106, 107–8, 127

Ramus, Pierre, 175
Reformation, the, xiii, 3 and n4; Germany and, 6; diverges from the Renaissance, 9–10; Henry II and, 19, 20; its European progress, 21ff; and the middle classes, 23–4; Philip II and, 48; in Poland, 113
Renaissance, the, xiii; and French thought, 4; Francis I and, 5; divorced from the Reformation, 9–10; Henry II and, 15
Renty, Battle of, 15
Retz, Jérôme de Gondi, Comte de, 42, 77, 106, 116, 117, 118, 121, 140; and the Massacre, 146, 148, 149, 203, 211 n3; visits Elizabeth, 216
Romier, Lucien, 20, 125
Romorantin, Edict of, 21
Ronsard, Pierre de, 44 and n3, 58, 111
Rosny, Baron de (Sully), 165, 210

Rötze, Hans, on the Massacre in Lyons, 182, 183

Saint-André, 13, 19, 32, 35
Saint Bartholomew's Day, Massacre of, 34, 36; international background to, 46; its supernumeraries, 63; Elizabeth I and, 96; Catherine de' Medici and, 109, 145ff; planning of, 144, 145; events leading up to, 144–8; list of proposed victims, 150–1; plans for its execution, 151–2; its beginning, 154–5, 156; the events in the Louvre, 158–60; Charles IX's reactions to, 160–1; its rapid spread, 164–8; its methodical character, 166; its religious impulse, 168; subsequent hysteria, 170; its renewal, 175; in the provinces, 181–90; estimates of its victims, 191–3; outside reactions to, 197–206; papal rejoicing at, 198–9; considerations of the responsibility for, 211–12, 225–8; contemporary views of, 238–55
Saint Germain, Treaty of, 45, 47, 71–2, 219–20
Saint-Germain l'Auxerrois, Church of, 154 and n12, 162, 217
Saint-Gouard, 201, 219
Saint Lawrence, Battle of, 17, 64
Saint-Quentin, Battle of, 17, 64
Salviati, Cardinal, 81, 99, 116, 217; and the Massacre, 171, 198, 202; and Charles IX's Declaration, 179
Savoy, Duke of, 17–18, 64
Sens, Council of, 5
Smith, Sir Thomas, 35, 74–5, 79, 82
Sorbonne, the, xi, 5; and Lutheranism, 3, 8; its Index, 11; and the king's authority, 223
Spain, xii; invades France, 17; her terms, 19–20; and Catholicism, 21; Catherine de' Medici and, 38–40, 42, 51, 73–4, 75, 108–9, 119, 201–2; suppresses Protestantism, 48; Elizabeth I and, 48–9, 96; and Lepanto, 73–5; and the Franco-English alliance, 80, 87; and French intervention in the Netherlands, 91–2

Spanish Netherlands, the Reformation in, 21; revolt in, 40, 48; possible French intervention in, 51–2, 89 92, 97–100, 102, 105–7, 116–22, 121–4, 129, 140–1
Strozzi, Pietro, 105; at Bordeaux, 80; and La Rochelle, 181 n5, 212

Tavannes, Gaspard de, 43, 90–1, 100, 121, 141; and the Massacre, 146, 148, 150 n5, 155 n13, 163, 164
Téligny, 45, 71, 89, 104, 107, 142, 153; and Coligny, 144, 145; his death, 164
Tessé, Marshal de, 161 and n9
Throckmorton, Sir Nicholas, 29, 30
Toledo, Don Fadrigue de, 106, 107, 109
Trent, Council of, 17
Troyes, Treaty of, xi, 37

Vaucelles, Truce of, 15
Vaucluse, Comte de, *Mémoires*, 160
Venice, 46, 54, 77; and Lepanto, 73–4; and the Franco-English alliance, 80; and the invasion of Flanders, 103, 108
Viénot, John, 3n, 33, 162 n3
Voltaire, *Henriade*, 161 and n9

Walsingham, Sir Francis, 86, 97, 106, 108; and the invasion of the Netherlands, 120; and the Massacre, 204–5, 206; on Charles IX, 215
Wassy, 33–4
William the Silent, Prince of Orange, 42, 43, 103, 107, 202; and the Massacre, 203–4
Winkelbach, Captain Studer von, his account of Coligny's murder, 250–1
Worcester, Earl of, 217
Worms, Colloquy of, 17, 21

Zuniga, Don Diego de, 87, 90, 99 106, 130, 217; and Catherine de' Medici, 92, 107, 117–18; and the shooting of Coligny, 139, 143 n3; on the Massacre, 200–1